Prevention and School Transitions

The *Prevention in Human Services* series:

- *Helping People to Help Themselves: Self-Help and Prevention*, edited by Leonard D. Borman, Leslie Borck, Robert E. Hess, and Frank L. Pasquale
- *Early Intervention Programs for Infants*, edited by Howard A. Moss, Robert E. Hess, and Carolyn Swift
- *R Television: Enhancing the Preventive Impact of TV*, edited by Joyce Sprafkin, Carolyn Swift, and Robert E. Hess
- *Innovations in Prevention*, edited by Robert E. Hess and Jared A. Hermalin
- *Strategies for Needs Assessment in Prevention*, edited by Alex Zautra, Kenneth Bachrach, and Robert E. Hess
- *Aging and Prevention: New Approaches for Preventing Health and Mental Health Problems in Older Adults*, edited by Sharon Simson, Laura B. Wilson, Jared A. Hermalin, and Robert E. Hess
- *Studies in Empowerment: Steps Toward Understanding and Action*, edited by Julian Rappaport, Carolyn Swift, and Robert E. Hess
- *Prevention: The Michigan Experience*, edited by Betty Tableman and Robert E. Hess
- *Beyond the Individual: Environmental Approaches and Prevention*, edited by Abraham Wandersman and Robert E. Hess
- *The Ecology of Prevention: Illustrating Mental Health Consultation*, edited by James G. Kelly and Robert E. Hess
- *Prevention and Health: Directions for Policy and Practice*, edited by Alfred H. Katz, Jared A. Hermalin, and Robert E. Hess
- *Prevention: Toward a Multidisciplinary Approach*, edited by Leonard A. Jason, Robert E. Hess, Robert D. Felner, and John N. Moritsugu
- *A Guide to Conducting Prevention Research in the Community: First Steps*, by James G. Kelly with the collaboration of Nancy Dassoff, Ira Levin, Janice Schreckengost, Stephen P. Stelzner and B. Eileen Altman
- *The National Mental Health Association: Eighty Years of Involvement in the Field of Prevention*, edited by Robert E. Hess and Jean Delong
- *Protecting the Children: Strategies for Optimizing Emotional and Behavioral Development*, edited by Raymond P. Lorion
- *Prevention in Community Mental Health Centers*, edited by Robert E. Hess and John Morgan
- *Career Stress in Changing Times*, edited by James Campbell Quick, Robert E. Hess, Jared Hermalin, and Jonathan D. Quick
- *Ethical Implications of Primary Prevention*, edited by Gloria B. Levin, Edison J. Trickett, and Robert E. Hess
- *Religion and Prevention in Mental Health: Conceptual and Empirical Foundations*, edited by Kenneth I. Pargament, Kenneth I. Maton, and Robert E. Hess
- *Religion and Prevention in Mental Health: Community Intervention*, edited by Kenneth I. Maton, Kenneth I. Pargament, and Robert E. Hess
- *Religion and Prevention in Mental Health: Research, Vision, and Action*, edited by Kenneth I. Pargament, Kenneth I. Maton, and Robert E. Hess
- *Prevention and School Transitions*, edited by Leonard A. Jason, Karen E. Danner, and Karen S. Kurasaki

Prevention and School Transitions

Leonard A. Jason
Karen E. Danner
Karen S. Kurasaki
Editors

The Haworth Press, Inc.
New York · London · Norwood (Australia)

Prevention and School Transitions has also been published as *Prevention in Human Services,* Volume 10, Number 2 1993.

© 1993 by The Haworth Press, Inc. All rights reserved. No part of this work may be reproduced or utilized in any form or by any means, electronic or mechanical, including photocopying, microfilm and recording, or by any information storage and retrieval system, without permission in writing from the publisher. Printed in the United States of America.

The development, preparation, and publication of this work has been undertaken with great care. However, the publisher, employees, editors, and agents of The Haworth Press and all imprints of The Haworth Press, Inc., including The Haworth Medical Press and Pharmaceutical Products Press, are not responsible for any errors contained herein or for consequences that may ensue from use of materials or information contained in this work. Opinions expressed by the author(s) are not necessarily those of The Haworth Press, Inc.

The Haworth Press, Inc., 10 Alice Street, Binghamton, NY 13904-1580 USA

Library of Congress Cataloging-in-Publication Data

Prevention and school transitions / Leonard A. Jason, Karen E. Danner, Karen S. Kurasaki, editors.
    p. cm.
    "Has also been published as Prevention in human services, volume 10, number 2 1993"–CIP t.p. verso.
    Includes bibliographical references.
    ISBN 1-56024-576-X
    1. Transfer students–United States. 2. Student adjustment–Social aspects–United States. 3. School children–United States–Psychology. 4. School children–United States–Social conditions. I. Jason, Leonard A. II. Danner, Karen E. III. Kurasaki, Karen S.
LB3064.2.P74 1993
371.2'914'0973–dc20   93-33337
                                                                                                CIP

INDEXING & ABSTRACTING

Contributions to this publication are selectively indexed or abstracted in print, electronic, online, or CD-ROM version(s) of the reference tools and information services listed below. This list is current as of the copyright date of this publication. See the end of this section for additional notes.

- *Abstracts of Research in Pastoral Care & Counseling*, Loyola College, 7135 Minstrel Way, Suite 101, Columbia, MD 21045
- *Child Development Abstracts & Bibliography*, University of Kansas, 2 Bailey Hall, Lawrence, KS 66045
- *Excerpta Medica/Electronic Publishing Division*, Elsevier Science Publishers, 655 Avenue of the Americas, New York, NY 10010
- *Inventory of Marriage and Family Literature (online and hard copy)*, National Council on Family Relations, 3989 Central Avenue NE, Suite 550, Minneapolis, MN 55421
- *Mental Health Abstracts (online through DIALOG)*, IFI/Plenum Data Company, 3202 Kirkwood Highway, Wilmington, DE 19808
- *Psychological Abstracts (PsycINFO)*, American Psychological Association, P. O. Box 91600, Washington, DC 20090-1600
- *Referativnyi Zhurnal (Abstracts Journal of the Institute of Scientific Information of the Republic of Russia)*, The Institute of Scientific Information, Baltijskaja ul., 14, Moscow, A-219, Republic of Russia
- *Social Planning/Policy & Development Abstracts (SOPODA)*, Sociological Abstracts, Inc., P. O. Box 22206, San Diego, CA 92192-0206
- *Social Work Research & Abstracts*, National Association of Social Workers, 750 First Street NW, 8th Floor, Washington, DC 20002
- *Sociological Abstracts (SA)*, Sociological Abstracts, Inc., P. O. Box 22206, San Diego, CA 92192-0206
- *SOMED (social medicine) Database*, Institute fur Dokumentation, P. O. Box 20 10 12, D-4800 Bielefeld 1, Germany

(continued)

SPECIAL BIBLIOGRAPHIC NOTES

related to indexing, abstracting, and library access services

☐ indexing/abstracting services in this list will also cover material in the "separate" that is co-published simultaneously with Haworth's special thematic journal issue or DocuSerial. Indexing/abstracting usually covers material at the article/chapter level.

☐ monographic co-editions are intended for either non-subscribers or libraries which intend to purchase a second copy for their circulating collections.

☐ monographic co-editions are reported to all jobbers/wholesalers/approval plans. The source journal is listed as the "series" to assist the prevention of duplicate purchasing in the same manner utilized for books-in-series.

☐ to facilitate user/access services all indexing/abstracting services are encouraged to utilize the co-indexing entry note indicated at the bottom of the first page of each article/chapter/contribution.

☐ this is intended to assist a library user of any reference tool (whether print, electronic, online, or CD-ROM) to locate the monographic version if the library has purchased this version but not a subscription to the source journal.

☐ individual articles/chapters in any Haworth publication are also available through the Haworth Document Delivery Services (HDDS).

Prevention and School Transitions

CONTENTS

Introduction   1
    Karen E. Danner
    Leonard A. Jason
    Karen S. Kurasaki

**The Nature of "Schooling" in School Transitions:
A Critical Re-Examination**   7
    Jennifer Alvidrez
    Rhona S. Weinstein

The Nature of School Transitions	9
Setting Factors in School Transitions	9
Relationships Between School and Child Characteristics: Implications for Transitions	16
An Environmental Approach to Transition Intervention	18
Conclusion	22

**A Comprehensive, Preventive, Parent-Based
Intervention for High-Risk Transfer Students**   27
    Leonard A. Jason
    Joseph H. Johnson
    Karen E. Danner
    Stephanie Taylor
    Karen S. Kurasaki

Method	29
Results	34
Discussion	35

Entry into Middle School: Student Factors Predicting Adaptation to an Ecological Transition   **39**
    Carolyn Pisano Leonard
    Maurice J. Elias

  Method   44
  Results   47
  Discussion   52

Negotiating the Transition to Junior High School: The Contributions of Coping Strategies and Perceptions of the School Environment   **59**
    David L. Causey
    Eric F. Dubow

  Method   64
  Results   67
  Discussion   74

Trajectory Analysis of the Transition to Junior High School: Implications for Prevention and Policy   **83**
    Barton J. Hirsch
    David L. DuBois
    Ann B. Brownell

  Identification of Contrasting Self-Esteem Trajectories   86
  Implications for Prevention and Policy   90
  Conclusion   99

Restructuring the Ecology of the School as an Approach to Prevention During School Transitions: Longitudinal Follow-Ups and Extensions of the School Transitional Environment Project (STEP)   **103**
    Robert D. Felner
    Stephen Brand
    Angela M. Adan
    Peter F. Mulhall
    Nancy Flowers
    Barbara Sartain
    David L. DuBois

  School Transitions: Guiding Frameworks   110

The School Transition Environmental Project	111
Five-Year Longitudinal Follow-Up of STEP	116
STEP Replications	121
Method	122
Results	125
Discussion	129

Identifying High-Risk Students During School Transition — 137
Olga Reyes
Don Hedeker

Method	141
Results	144
Discussion	147

Alternative Schools: A School Transition for Adolescent Mothers — 151
G. Anne Bogat
Belle Liang
Robert A. Caldwell
William Davidson II
Martha Bristor
Marian Phillips
Mary Suurmeyer

Introduction	152
Method	156
Results	158
Discussion	163

Easing Postpartum School Transitions Through Parent Mentoring Programs — 169
Jean E. Rhodes

Postpartum Transitions	171
Mentoring	172
Program Description	173
Self-Management Strategy	175
Conclusion	176

Transition Tasks and Resources: An Ecological Approach to Life After High School 179
Charles Barone
Edison J. Trickett
Kathleen D. Schmid
Peter E. Leone

Ecological Considerations in Adolescent Transitions	181
Outcome Studies	183
Methods	185
Results	188
Discussion	195

 ALL HAWORTH BOOKS & JOURNALS ARE PRINTED ON CERTIFIED ACID-FREE PAPER

ABOUT THE EDITORS

Leonard A. Jason, PhD, is Professor of Psychology at DePaul University in Chicago. He has published over 200 articles and chapters on various topics, including preventive school-based interventions, substance abuse prevention, media interventions, program evaluation, smoking cessation, and behavioral assessment.

Karen E. Danner is Project Director for the School Transitions Project at DePaul University where she is completing her BA in psychology. She has worked as Research Coordinator and as a tutor on the Transitions Project for the past three years. Her research interests center around child, adolescent, and family mental health issues.

Karen S. Kurasaki, MA, is a doctoral candidate in clinical and community psychology at DePaul University. Her research interests are in primary prevention in the schools and ethnic identification among Japanese-Americans.

Introduction

All children change schools during their educational careers. Many school transfers are considered routine, such as transferring from middle to high school. Other children experience unscheduled school transfers, which are due to situations not considered as part of the usual educational experience (Jason, Betts et al., 1992). For example, children sometimes have to change schools because their parents move due to a job change. Some parents place their children into a new school because they are seeking a better setting for their children's education. Other students transfer to schools with specialized programs that address their specific needs, such as schools for pregnant teenagers. Whatever the reason for the transfer, at least some of these children are at risk for academic difficulties (Lacey & Blane, 1979; Jason, Filippelli, Danner, & Bennett, 1992) as well as emotional and social problems (Holland, Kaplan, & Davis, 1974; Turner & McClatchey, 1978).

A key question involves how to identify those transfer students who will experience difficulties in their new schools (Bensen, Haycraft, Steyaert, & Weigel, 1979; Brockman & Reeves, 1987; Schaller, 1970). A number of studies indicate that children from lower socioeconomic status groups, who have experienced multiple life stressors, and have lower academic abilities are especially at risk for failure (Burke & Weir, 1978; Jason, Weine et al., 1992). In addition, a variety of other stressors including changes in the curriculum,

---

[Haworth co-indexing entry note]: "Introduction." Danner, Karen E., Leonard A. Jason and Karen S. Kurasaki. Co-published simultaneously in *Prevention in Human Services* (The Haworth Press, Inc.) Vol. 10, No. 2, 1993, pp. 1-6; and: *Prevention and School Transitions* (ed: Leonard A. Jason, Karen E. Danner, and Karen S. Kurasaki) The Haworth Press, Inc., 1993, pp. 1-6. Multiple copies of this article/chapter may be purchased from The Haworth Document Delivery Center. Call 1-800-3-HAWORTH (1-800-342-9678) between 9:00 - 5:00 (EST) and ask for DOCUMENT DELIVERY CENTER.

© 1993 by The Haworth Press, Inc. All rights reserved.

new standards for acceptance by peer groups and teachers, gang activity and crime within neighborhoods can pose additional hurdles for some children during school transitions.

An example of the multitude of difficult situations that can confront some children is illustrated in the following case study. John, a ten year old boy, lived in a low-income neighborhood in an innercity. Shortly after his parents separated, John's mother obtained a new job and moved the family closer to her new work place. John was now confronted with the challenge of adapting to his new setting. The new school had higher academic standards, and John soon found himself having difficulty understanding lessons in reading and math. Along with the problems in academic areas, John was confronted with learning the norms and social rules required to be accepted among his peer groups in the neighborhood and in the school. In addition, a gang member began exerting pressure on John to join the local gang.

John also had to adapt to the role changes occurring within his family structure. With the absence of his father, John was assigned a much larger responsibility within the household; he was now required to babysit and care for his younger siblings. John was also receiving less attention from his mother, whose time was now consumed with adapting to her new job. Obviously, the combination of several changes in John's life put him at high-risk for experiencing academic and social difficulties after the transition into the new school.

Many school systems have recognized the difficulties some transfer children experience and have established orientation programs to assist in the transition (Cornille, Bayer, & Smyth, 1983; Donohue & Gullotta, 1981; Jason & Bogat, 1983). These programs help the transfer students feel more comfortable and accepted in their new schools. However, even with the provision of orientation programs, many transfer students continue to be at risk for later school difficulties (Jason, Weine et al., 1992). The case history of John, mentioned above, provides a glimpse of the hurdles some transfer children encounter when entering their new neighborhoods and schools. Preventive programs for these types of high risk children will need to take into account the broad range of personal and environmental stressors confronting these children.

The purpose of this volume is to assemble a collection of studies from many of the leading ecological and systems-oriented theorists in the area of school transitions. The authors carefully describe the stressors, personal resources available, and coping strategies among different groups of children and adolescents undergoing school transitions. Several of the articles describe prevention-based programs that are aimed at off-setting the potentially negative consequences of school transitions.

In the first article, Alvidrez and Weinstein provide a comprehensive review of conceptual issues related to school transitions. In general, they propose that the environmental characteristics for school children are ill-matched to students' developmental and individual needs. They suggest that school reform is necessary in order to make school settings more compatible with students' needs.

In the next study, Jason, Johnson, Danner, Taylor, and Kurasaki address the issue of unscheduled school transitions. Specifically, coping is examined in high-risk elementary students transferring into third, fourth, and fifth grades. Those children who received high levels of parent and para-professional tutoring were most successful in coping with the social and academic demands of their new school, enabling many of the vulnerable children to move out of the high-risk category.

Several articles specifically address issues related to the middle and junior high school transitions. Leonard and Elias examine the potential factors that predict adjustment outcome of students transferring from elementary to middle school. Their findings support the importance of self-evaluation and self-concept as mitigators of future stress. In the next paper, Causey and Dubow examine the impact of different coping styles and perceptions of the school environment on adjustment to junior high school. They conclude that certain types of coping strategies, as well as favorable perceptions of the environment, are related to better adjustments seen in the first semester of the new school. Hirsch, DuBois, and Brownell examine the methodological concerns of conducting longitudinal trajectory analyses with school transition research. They illustrate the use of cluster analytic techniques to complement traditional analysis of variance in their investigation of self-esteem changes during the elementary to junior high school transition.

Several papers focused on the transition to high school. Felner, Brand, Adan, Mulhall, Flowers, Sartain, and DuBois examine a five year follow-up of a preventive program to help students transferring into high school. The intervention included restructuring the school to reduce the risks experienced by students. Adolescents provided the intervention, had reduced dropout rates, and increased school performance and attendance. Also addressing issues related to high school success, Reyes and Hedeker presented three ecological components that were determined to be critical to the success of their drop-out prevention program. In particular, they propose that extending homeroom teachers' involvement with students beyond academic concerns, reorganizing the school environment so as to minimize class changes, and establishing a communication system between parents and teachers are critical to reducing school dropout.

In efforts to help pregnant teenagers complete their education, two papers focus on school transitions in alternative schools. Bogat, Liang, Caldwell, Davidson, Bristor, Phillips, and Suurmeyer examine the effects of the alternative school experience–a transition period away from regular high school–on such academic areas as grade point average, attendance rate, and matriculation. Despite mixed findings, their investigation supports a positive relationship between grade point average and attendance at the alternative educational setting. Similarly, Rhodes focuses on assisting postpartum mothers in their transition back into the regular high school. Rhodes suggests that mentoring programs can help prevent academic and social problems associated with adolescent pregnancy and parenthood.

The last paper by Barone, Trickett, Schmid, and Leone examines both the risk factors presented and the resources used during the transition to life after leaving high school. They suggest giving special attention to the impact of social network changes when planning future interventions. Barone and colleagues also propose strengthening formal and informal resources to mitigate the adjustment challenges.

The authors of this diverse set of papers in this volume provide an overview of some of the difficulties and challenges faced by students experiencing school transfers. Many of these ecologically-oriented papers attempt to: (a) understand the complicated set of relationships between different components of school systems, (b) appreciate how schools create and use new resources, (c) clarify how school and family environments shape adaptation, and (d) assess the changing demands for children's adaptive capacities over time (Kelly, 1968; Kelly et al., 1988). This volume can provide parents, school personnel, mental health professionals, and educational and psychological researchers new ways of thinking about preventive interventions for children confronted with the challenges of succeeding in new school settings.

Karen E. Danner
Leonard A. Jason
Karen S. Kurasaki

REFERENCES

Bensen, G. P., Haycraft, J. R., Steyaert, J. P., & Weigel, D. J. (1979). Mobility in sixth graders as related to achievement, adjustment, and socioeconomic status. *Psychology in the Schools, 16,* 444-447.

Brockman, M. A., & Reeves, A. W. (1967). Relationship between transiency and test achievement. *Alberta Journal of Educational Research, 13,* 319-330.

Burke, R. J., & Weir, T. (1978). Sex differences in adolescent life stress, social support, and well being. *Journal of Psychology, 98,* 277-288.

Cornille, T. A., Bayer, A. E., & Smyth, C. K. (1983). Schools and newcomers: A national survey of innovative programs. *Personnel and Guidance Journal, 62,* 229-236.

Donohue, K. C., & Gullotta, T. P. (1981, November-December). FIT: What corporations can do to ease relocation stress. *Mobility, 2,* 53-57.

Holland, J. V., Kaplan, D. M., & Davis, S. D. (1974). Interschool transfers: A mental health challenge. *Journal of School Health, 44,* 74-79.

Jason, L. A., Betts, D., Johnson, J. H., Weine, A. M., Neuson, L., Filippelli, L., & Lardon, C. (1992). Developing, implementing and evaluating a preventive intervention for high risk transfer children. In T. R. Kratochwill (Ed.), *Advances in school psychology* (pp. 45-77). Hillsdale, NJ: Lawrence Erlbaum.

Jason, L. A., & Bogat, G. A. (1983). Evaluating a preventive orientation program. *Journal of Social Service Research, 7,* 39-49.

Jason, L. A., Filippelli, L., Danner, K. E., & Bennett, P. (1992). Identifying high risk children transferring into elementary schools. *Education, 113*(2), 325-330.

Jason, L. A., Weine, A. M., Johnson, J. H., Warren-Sohlberg, L., Filippelli, L. A., Turner E. Y., & Lardon, C. (1992). *Helping readjustment.* San Francisco: Jossey-Bass.

Kelly, J. G. (1968) Towards an ecological conception of preventive interventions. In J. W. Carter (Ed.), *Research contributions from psychology to community mental health*, (pp. 76-97). New York: Behavioral.

Kelly, J. C., Dassoff, N., Levin, I., Steltzner, S. P., & Altman, B. E. (1988). *A guide to conducting prevention research in the community: First steps.* New York: The Haworth Press, Inc.

Lacey, C., & Blane, D. (1979). Geographic mobility and school attainment: The confounding variables. *Education Research, 21*, 200-206.

Schaller, J. (1976). Geographic mobility as a variable in ex-post facto research. *British Journal of Educational Psychology, 46*, 341-343.

Turner, I., & McClatchey, L. (1978). Mobility, school attainment, and adjustment. *Association of Educational Psychologists Journal, 4*, 45-50.

The Nature of "Schooling" in School Transitions: A Critical Re-Examination

Jennifer Alvidrez
Rhona S. Weinstein
University of California, Berkeley

SUMMARY. Despite an ecological framework, much of the work on school transitions has focused on the characteristics of children that are associated with poor school adjustment. This paper addresses three levels of complexities about schooling–generic changes in assumptions, roles, and social supports that accompany grade transitions, differential demands and opportunities that create different lives within the same school or classroom, and temporal/societal pressures that alter the fabric of schooling. We highlight the complex match or mismatch between different school conditions and particular characteristics of children that determine the ultimate quality of the transition outcome. Finally, we urge greater attention toward environmental intervention, that is, school reforms that enhance the capacity of settings to better meet the developmental needs of children and the diversity of the school population.

The term transition denotes "a passage from one state, stage, subject, or place to another" (Webster's Dictionary). Developmen-

---

[Haworth co-indexing entry note]: "The Nature of "Schooling" in School Transitions: A Critical Re-Examination." Alvidrez, Jennifer, and Rhona S. Weinstein. Co-published simultaneously in *Prevention in Human Services* (The Haworth Press, Inc.) Vol. 10, No. 2, 1993, pp. 7-26; and: *Prevention and School Transitions* (ed: Leonard A. Jason, Karen E. Danner, and Karen S. Kurasaki) The Haworth Press, Inc., 1993, pp. 7-26. Multiple copies of this article/chapter may be purchased from The Haworth Document Delivery Center. Call 1-800-3-HAWORTH (1-800-342-9678) between 9:00 - 5:00 (EST) and ask for DOCUMENT DELIVERY CENTER.

tal theorists have sought to understand how children, individuals, and families change along the life course (Cowan, 1991). Transitions and how successfully individuals adapt to the accompanying changes in their psychosocial environment play a critical role in the development of psychopathology (Dohrenwend & Dohrenwend, 1974). For this reason, there is heightened interest in normative and non-normative transitions as providing important opportunities for primary prevention (Felner, Felner, & Primavera, 1983).

Much of the work on school transitions draws upon an ecological framework. As Bronfenbrenner (1979) argues, transitions are "a joint function of biological changes and altered environmental circumstances" and are thus "both a consequence and an instigator of developmental processes" (p. 27). In the study of school transitions, poor school adjustment is viewed to result from a mismatch between the skills, resources, and experience of the child and the structure and demands of the new school setting (Felner, Primavera, & Cauce, 1981; Hansen, 1986; Stewart & Healy, 1984; Hoier, McConnell & Pallay, 1987).

Ironically, despite the adoption of an ecological model, the research has focused exclusively on the characteristics and behaviors of children that are associated with poor school adjustment, that is, what factors place children at risk during transitions (Crockett, Peterson, Graber, Schulenberg, & Ebata, 1989; Spillman & Lutz, 1985). Far fewer studies have addressed how the characteristics of the school setting can influence the transition process (Blyth, Simmons, & Carlton-Ford, 1983; Hirsch & Rapkin, 1987; Jason, Weine, Johnson, Warren-Sohlberg, Filippelli, Turner, & Lardon, 1992; Midgley, Feldlaufer & Eccles, 1989). Still fewer have proposed interventions to make the school environment more accommodating to the special needs of children in transition (Felner, Ginter, & Primavera, 1982).

Even when the setting is considered as a factor in the transition process, researchers have largely ignored the reality that children are making transitions into different school environments. Children at risk for making poor transitions, in particular, marginal-income and ethnic minority students, are also more likely than their more advantaged peers to be in inferior learning environments that pose additional stresses (Alexander & Entwistle, 1988; Felner, Primavera, & Cauce, 1981; Stewart & Healy, 1984).

This paper explores salient dimensions of schooling that together create both generic and differential demands facing children in their transitions up the school career ladder. We highlight the complex interaction between different school conditions and the particular characteristics of children–matches and mismatches that set the stage for the quality of the transition and its outcome. We also underscore that despite attendance at the same school or membership in the same classroom, children experience differential treatment and thus are not making transitions into the same or equitable school environments (Weinstein, 1993). Finally, we suggest possible avenues for environmental intervention.

THE NATURE OF SCHOOL TRANSITIONS

In the course of a school career, children face a host of transitions that vary in intensity and scope. A child's initial entry into school as a kindergarten student is followed by a second transition into the more academically focused first grade. Later transitions include changes in physical environment, class structure, teaching practices, and peer interaction upon entry into both junior high and high school. Most importantly, *all* children start over *each* year with new teachers and new peers in a different classroom environment. These milestones in schooling signal expected individual accomplishments in attitude and skill development.

Some children also experience unexpected and non-normative transitions, such as in school transfers due to relocation or school closure (Jason et al., 1992). Whether normative or non-normative, school transitions are associated with increased psychological distress, lowered self-esteem, and a decline in academic performance (Blyth et al., 1983; Crockett et al., 1989; Felner et al., 1981; Hirsch & Rapkin, 1987).

SETTING FACTORS IN SCHOOL TRANSITIONS

Any look at the setting characteristics or the context of school transitions must examine (a) the generic changes in schooling format which confront children at entry and at different levels, (b) the differential experiences which arise out of variations between and within schools and classrooms, and (c) the historical and societal forces which shape the schooling situation. Felner, Farber, and Primavera (1983) suggest that life transitions are best understood as a process involving many changes rather than a single, discrete event. They highlight three kinds of tasks which individuals must master in their adaptation to life transitions: (1) reordering of assumptive worlds (Parkes, 1971), (2) shifts in role definition and role behavior (Pearlin, Meneghan, Lieberman, & Mullen, 1981), and (3) reconstruction of social networks and social supports. We apply this task model toward our review of critical schooling factors, and describe the transition setting in terms of its implications for children's belief systems, role behaviors, and social relationships.

Generic Transitions to School and Between Grades

The kindergarten and first grade transitions. There are predictable discontinuities between the family and the early school-like situations that children must master in order to "learn how to 'go to school' and how to 'do school work'" (Dreeben, 1968; Good, 1986, p. 87; Hess, Dickson, Price, & Leong, 1979). Across these early transitions, children must change their underlying assumptions about self and others. They must forge an academic self and recognize that some, but not all, parts of themselves are important in schooling. They take on new roles as classroom worker (following rules and routines) and as learner (mastering new and unknown tasks against criteria of excellence) in ways that serve the group rather than the individual. Finally, they must learn to accept others' views and treatment of them and to find social support from transitory adults, who engage in normative and comparative judgments about performance, and from peers, who compete for the same scarce rewards. Children cannot avoid these challenges since attendance in school is mandated and their efforts are largely made in public.

Despite these regularities, the discrete transitions, from preschool to kindergarten to first grade, may vary a great deal, depending upon the relative emphases of work versus play and cooperation versus competition in teacher and school philosophy (Good, 1986).

Nevertheless, in early schooling, children often have more opportunities to engage in self-initiated and cooperative activities that reflect more parts of the self than later in schooling when the academic mission takes over.

Between elementary and high school. The transition into middle or junior high school places students in new relationships to subject matter, teachers, peers, and to the school as a whole. Student self-definitions undergo change as they shift from being the oldest to the youngest again, in relation to their peers, and as they choose or are assigned to different levels of learning opportunities (tracks) from advanced to remedial. They learn to change classes on time, coordinate preparation for multiple homework assignments and tests, and participate in school-wide extracurricular activities–a complexity of actions that presses for a system of tight control, accountability, and discipline. They are pushed into developing relationships with multiple teachers (who are now subject-matter specialists) and a larger peer group across different classes. Life outside the classroom becomes as salient as life within.

How many of these changes are in place for which age group of students varies enormously across school districts, with much diversity in grade-level organization and in degree of subject departmentalization (Ward, 1986). Although the predominant target groups include sixth, seventh, and eighth graders, many in-between schools include fifth graders or ninth graders in different combinations (Lounsbury, Marani, & Compton, 1980). As Ward (1986) notes, these differing arrangements respond to many competing needs–to keep schools open, to aid desegregation, to provide subject-specialization earlier, to reduce the variation in developmental and social level between students, and more recently, to better meet the needs of these adolescents. Further, a variety of subject area and teacher assignments are made–for example, students might change teachers each period or stay with the same teacher for several periods, and they may be taught by a single teacher or by a team of instructors. Patterns that involve the least change serve to cushion the transition from self-contained classrooms to fully departmentalized programs.

The high school transition. High school confronts students with a fully departmentalized and differentiated (tracked) academic program. Track placement defines a student's identity as well as his or her opportunities after high school. Accountability (in the frequent testing of performance and in the press for adherence to rules and regulations) drives student action. Peer groups influences can push students towards academic achievement and school-level involvement or pull them away. Coping with such an organizational structure forces students to learn to function in a bureaucracy, relate to authority, utilize the formal and informal networks to solve problems, and develop coherence across activities and within the self (Cusick, 1986).

Differential Conditions in Schooling

State level. Among many differences, states vary in the curricular frameworks they provide to guide education, in the textbooks they adopt, and in the requirements they set for mandated courses and high school completion (Cusick, 1986). When children transfer schools across state lines, they can face large discrepancies in exposure to material or repetition of material already learned. By simply changing schools and curricular expectations, students can become a high or a low achiever relative to the student body of comparison, with concomitant shifts in self-views, role opportunities, and relationships with teachers and peers.

District and school level. Not all schools are created equal. After controlling for student characteristics, school conditions contribute to differential student outcomes, including absenteeism, dropout, achievement, college attendance, and later employment patterns (Rumberger, 1987; Rutter, 1983). One area in which school inequity is readily apparent is the level of resources. Because schools are financed through property taxes, poor neighborhoods generally have poor schools. Even if the district as a whole is not poor, the allocations to schools with high concentrations of disadvantaged students are generally lower than those in more affluent neighborhoods (National Board of Inquiry, 1985). Unlike wealthier schools, poor schools are often lacking in a range of services and resources, from the most basic needs, such as textbooks and lab equipment, to services for at-risk children, including preschool and reading programs, guidance counseling and parent involvement programs. A lack of funding also results in greater class size, a higher proportion of inexperienced or unqualified teachers, a more limited curriculum, and fewer extra-curricular activities (Taylor & Piche, 1990). A study using 1980 Census data by Card and Krueger (1990) illustrates the relationship between school resources and later outcomes. After controlling for family background and regional differences of one million men born between 1920 and 1949, the authors found that school quality, measured by student-teacher ratios, year length, and teacher salary, was positively related to job earnings in adulthood.

Though often related, school quality is not solely a function of available resources. Both the size of the school and ratio of opportunities to individuals play a role in how involved students are in developing mastery across a wide variety of areas (Barker & Gump, 1964; Wicker, 1968). The climate of a school is another important factor, and one in which schools vary dramatically. Some schools have a strong academic focus and high expectations for all students, devote the bulk of class time to academic material, and have higher levels of interaction between teachers and principals, conditions that are associated with consistently high student achievement (Good & Weinstein, 1986; Rutter, 1983). In contrast, other schools, often those with large minority populations, are characterized by demoralization and apathy, and with low investment in the school on the part of the students, teachers, and administrators. In an example from *Barriers to Excellence* (Board of Inquiry, 1985), when one teacher from such a school in Massachusetts tried to get more textbooks for her class, she was told to have her students share the books because half of them would drop out anyway.

Classroom level. The climate in different classrooms in the same school may differ drastically as well. The motivational goals that teachers hold influence how children think and act. For example, task-mastery goals which focus on the intrinsic and personal meaning of the activity rather than on comparative performance (ego goals) influence student self-perceptions, effort and willingness to take on challenging tasks (Ames, 1992; Maehr & Midgley, 1991). Teachers' sense of efficacy is reflected in their behavior and in student achievement (Ashton & Webb, 1986). Teacher effectiveness and enthusiasm varies from classroom to classroom, and the effect of a single teacher on children may be quite important. For example, Pedersen, Faucher, and Eaton (1978) followed the students of one first grade teacher and found that they were more likely to stay in school and have higher status jobs after graduation than students who had other teachers.

More systematic differences result from academic tracking or homogeneously-grouped classrooms. Ethnic minority and low SES children are more likely than white or middle class children to be labeled as low achievers and placed in low academic tracks (Oakes, 1987), or misclassified as learning disabled and placed in special education classes (National Board of Inquiry, 1985). Children in such classes are provided with fewer opportunities to challenge themselves, express their creativity, and engage in tasks requiring higher-order thinking skills (Rutter, 1983). The focus of low-track classes tends to be on basic skills to be learned through repetitive drill-and-practice activities (Finley, 1984; Slavin, 1988). Furthermore, teachers in these classes are often less experienced or qualified, and there is less teacher interaction and rapport with students than in high-track classrooms. In essence, low-track students are not expected to perform at grade level and are placed in a setting which virtually guarantees that they never will (Levin, 1987). Not surprisingly, low-track placement is associated with low self-esteem and motivation, poor peer relations, misconduct, and school dropout (Oakes, 1987; Rumberger, 1987).

Within classrooms. Children may also experience differential learning environments in the same classroom. Within-classroom ability grouping in reading and other subjects often begins as early as kindergarten, and the labels that accompany such group assignments often stay with children throughout their schooling (Goodlad, 1984; Weinstein, 1976). With or without explicit ability grouping, the expectations of teachers can be transmitted to students through differential treatment. In classrooms where teachers differentiate the treatment of high and low achievers, students who experience high teacher expectations generally receive more approval and explicit feedback, less criticism, and are provided with more challenging and stimulating material (Brophy, 1983). Low expectation students tend to be called on less often, experience less friendly interaction with the teacher, and are often not expected to do high quality or even correct work (Brophy, 1983). In an example from an inner-city kindergarten classroom observed by Rist (1970), the teacher seated some of her lowest expectation students so that they were not even facing the blackboard. Low teacher expectations may not only result in restricted learning opportunities but may also lead to low motivation and negative self-expectations of ability in students (Weinstein, Marshall, Sharp, & Botkin, 1987).

Historical and Societal Context

It is critically important to underscore the dynamic and changing context in which children make transitions in schooling. Nothing about institutional life stands still across time–neither the qualities children bring to school, nor the defining features of family or community support of schooling itself. These changes can be felt from one school year to the next.

Three major revolutions in public education still reverberating today (compulsory schooling at the turn of the century, the 1954 desegregation decision, and the 1975 Education for All Handicapped Children's Act) have broadened the diversity of the school population and changed its distribution within schools and classrooms (Sarason & Klaber, 1985). Today, more children than ever before are reared in poverty, have inadequate access to health and child care, live in single-parent families, and suffer from abuse and violence (Vanderpool & Richmond, 1990)–all factors which are primary indicators of risk for school failure (Fox, 1990). Given the continuing influx of immigrant populations, urban schools in particular are becoming more heterogeneous in nature with regard to language and to culture. These shifts in diversity and in accompanying supports for children place severe stress on schools to provide more services to develop and sustain children's readiness to learn.

As pressures mount to broaden the mission of schooling, severe budgetary problems erode basic support services–particularly the programs and personnel important to ensuring that children make successful transitions at each level of schooling. Other pressures also serve to narrow the focus of schooling and heighten its accountability. During a decade of severe criticism and scrutiny (e.g., National Commission on Excellence in Education, 1983), the threat of international competition feeds discontent with schooling outcomes and underscores a preoccupation with student performance on standardized tests, to the exclusion of the development of the whole child. These historical and societal cross-currents are among the forces that shape the daily and yearly challenges experienced as school sites grapple with their mission, client population, and resources.

RELATIONSHIPS BETWEEN SCHOOL AND CHILD CHARACTERISTICS: IMPLICATIONS FOR TRANSITIONS

Given this description of generic, differential, and temporal school factors that serve to define the schooling environment into which children are making a transition, it is important to look at how the qualities of children interact with the qualities of settings in ways that promote or undermine successful transitions. We will briefly touch upon four aspects of child differences (developmental level, gender, personality, and culture) where research has suggested a mismatch between the child's needs and the school setting's demands or opportunities.

Developmental Stage

Eccles and Midgley (1989) point to a stage-environment fit problem in the transition that children make to junior high school–a transition in which young adolescents show a downward shift in motivational orientation and perceived competence, which are two potential precursors to school failure. They argue that there is a developmental mismatch between young adolescent needs for a more personalized, student-managed, and task-focused environment and the reality of middle-level schooling which heightens teacher control and discipline, raises standards of comparative performance, and provides fewer opportunities for student initiation and warm teacher-student relationships. This analysis of mismatch is echoed in the paper by McCaslin and Good (1992) which points to a misalliance between school goals to produce self-motivated, active learners and current classroom management practices that press for obedience.

Personality and Individual Difference Factors

Kelly's (1979) study of how high school structure influences student socialization contrasts the match of fluid versus static environments with the exploratory style of adolescents. He provides evidence that high explorers cope better and are perceived in more favorable ways in fluid high schools where change is the norm rather than in static schools where change is the exception. Singer and colleagues (1989) highlight the relationship between school district policies on special education and whether children's different learning styles (or disabilities) will be labeled. Most importantly, school districts differ in the criteria they use to identify groups of handicapped students and in the functional level of the students so labeled. These differences suggest that students are over- or under-identified as disabled across districts and thus have differential social and educational experiences as a regular or special education labeled student–a mismatch of concern, given the negative consequences of labeling and segregated or pull-out instruction.

Gender

Research has documented the ways in which school environments provide different learning opportunities for boys and girls– through sex-stereotyped textbooks, through the underrepresentation of women in administration, and through differential teacher-student interaction, with higher frequencies of interactions accorded males at all educational levels (Sadker, Sadker & Klein, 1991). These observed differential environments are hypothesized to contribute to documented gender gaps in attributions for performance (girls are more likely than boys to attribute failure to lack of ability) and in intellectual abilities, particularly quantitative and spatial abilities. Girls may also be discouraged from entering these scientific fields by teachers and counselors.

Class and Culture

There is substantial evidence that racial and ethnic minority, low socioeconomic class, and limited English speaking students experience lower teacher expectations and less challenging educational programs, than do majority and middle class students (Alexander & Entwistle, 1988; Baron, Tom, & Cooper, 1985; Oakes, 1987). Many studies as well have pointed out the poignant mismatch between home and school environments for children who come from different cultural backgrounds. Au and Mason (1981) provide data showing minority children as less familiar with bidding rather than waiting for a turn in classroom interaction. The culture of Latino students promotes more cooperative learning styles in contrast to the individualistic and competitive ideals of schooling (Garcia, 1992). Hansen (1986) suggests that "children are relatively advantaged in classrooms that are similar to their families in rules of interaction, and relatively disadvantaged in classrooms that are dissimilar" (p. 656).

AN ENVIRONMENTAL APPROACH TO TRANSITION INTERVENTION

Barriers Within School Environments

The transition literature has identified two primary reasons why children have difficulty making school transitions: (1) they lack necessary skills, knowledge, or ability to adapt to the new school setting, or (2) their ability to perform in the new setting is disrupted by the change. The first reason, deficit, is the basis for programs such as Head Start that attempt to help at-risk students "catch up" to their peers socially or academically so they do not enter school at a disadvantage (Lazar & Darlington, 1982; McClellan & Trupin, 1989). The second reason, disruption, has been the focus of programs addressing the problems associated with changing schools as a part of both normative and non-normative transitions. Such programs include those that offer special services to new or transfer students to ease the transition and help them become integrated into the new school (Jason, 1980; Jason et al., 1992; Matus & Reid, 1983), and those that change the structure of the setting to better serve the needs of the population in transition (Felner, Ginter, & Primavera, 1982; Reyes & Jason, 1991).

From our examination of school settings, it is clear that there is a third factor in transition difficulty: barriers exist in the school environment that may prevent children from developing or using skills needed to adjust to and succeed in that environment. These environmental barriers pose special risks for certain groups of children–triggering a person-environment fit problem. As noted earlier, Eccles and Midgley (1989) argue that the observed decline in motivation among adolescents has less to do with developmental stage than with the mismatch of need to opportunities provided by most middle-school settings. They urge developmentally appropriate middle-school reform centered on the encouragement of student initiative and personal teacher-student relationships.

This same problem holds for disadvantaged, ethnic minority, and immigrant youngsters. Given societal changes buffeting schools, each year, the diversity of children who attend school increases exponentially. Our common practices in addressing such diversity are to sort and select students for differential learning opportunities–targeted at remediating difficulties but most often, exacerbating failure. At each transition, prior labels and prior experience further narrow the pathways and available supports ahead. These children are often treated as if they are not as smart or able as their classmates. They are placed in low-ability classrooms where they learn that they are not supposed to learn. They attend run-down schools where students are as likely to carry guns and beepers as schoolbooks. Even if efforts are successful in building competencies or facilitating adjustment to new school settings, children faced with such environmental obstacles are still not likely to do well in school. This might be one reason why the beneficial effects of many early education programs fade after a couple of years (Gray, Ramsey, & Klaus, 1983; Slavin & Madden, 1989).

In situations where environmental barriers are the cause of poor transitions, efforts to remove the barriers are more appropriate than those that address deficits of the child. When applying the transactional model, if characteristics such as gender, ethnicity, SES, or low achievement are the reasons that a child does not "fit" into an educational setting, the goal is not to find an alternate setting in which the child does "fit," such as a low-ability track classroom, but to create a setting which accommodates children with a diversity of characteristics. Designing schooling which is responsive to diversity enables the differences between individuals to be viewed as strengths and as resources valued within the school environment (Trickett & Birman, 1989).

Interventions Addressing the Reform of School Environments

Several interventions have attempted to remove the barriers to success in school for all children, but particularly for those that are likely to be denied access to a quality education in existing educational settings. At the early elementary level, one such effort is the Success for All program for inner-city preschool and elementary school children (Slavin, Madden, Karweit, Livermon, & Dolan, 1990). With coordinated programs involving intensive reading training and tutoring, frequent assessment of student progress, and parental support services, the Success for All program attempts to bring all children up to grade level by the third grade. After one year of participating in a pilot program in a Baltimore school, children scored better on measures of reading ability and language skills than control children. In addition, grade retention and special education referrals and assignments decreased.

Similar programs have been developed by Levin (1987) and Comer (1988). Levin's Accelerated Schools aims to bring disadvantaged children up to grade level by the end of sixth grade so they will be less likely to drop out of high school in the future (Levin, 1987). Program components include an extended day during which children receive tutoring from community volunteers and are exposed to an accelerated pace of teaching that reflect the high expectations that teachers hold for the students. Comer and colleagues at the Yale University Child Study Center began a project in 1968 in two inner-city schools in New Haven that were ranked the lowest in student achievement in the city. The project aimed to create a climate in which children were encouraged to learn rather than alienated from learning. A governance and management team composed of parents, teachers, the principal, and a mental health worker developed a clear set of objectives for the school that would address the specific needs of the student population, such as a transfer orientation program and social skills training. The role of parents was further expanded by social activities and job opportunities within the school. As the result of these changes, parents, students, teachers, and the principal became more invested in the success of the school. By 1980, behavior problems and truancy had declined and student achievement was above the national average. This program has now been implemented in over 50 schools nationwide.

Other programs have targeted specific facets of school practices which limit student success: for example, cooperative learning, in which mixed-ability students work in groups on tasks where every member of the group must master the material. Students are therefore encouraged to teach and learn from one another rather than compete. Studies of cooperative learning have found that this technique can enhance achievement of students in several subject areas (Slavin, 1988). Ames (1992) and Maehr and Midgley (1991) have developed teaching and policy strategies for the classroom and the school which highlight task-mastery motivational goals–goals which promote student motivation rather than competitive comparison, a mindset particularly important for adolescents at the transition to middle school.

Weinstein and colleagues (1991) report efforts to diminish the effects of teacher expectations and differential treatment for students making the transition into high school. The program was a collaborative effort between the research team, teachers, and administrators in a California high school to develop ways of increasing awareness of expectancy effects and treatment of low-track students. Implemented practices included team teaching, heterogeneous grouping, higher-level curricula, parent involvement efforts, and the fostering of schoolwide participation by low-track students. Students participating in the project as compared to a comparison group had better grades and fewer disciplinary referrals after one year and a lower dropout rate at the two year follow-up, although the achievement changes were not maintained for a second year. However, project teachers changed perceptions about lower-track students. Through their efforts, they educated their fellow teachers and brought about changes in the tracking policies of the school. As a result, attitudinal and systemic changes in the school opened the door for the creation of a better environment for students in the future.

CONCLUSION

Children considered to be at risk during school transitions are also more likely to attend schools which are developmentally or culturally inappropriate, gender-biased, impoverished, demoralized or reflective of low expectations. Thus, outcomes considered to be indicative of poor school adjustment, such as low academic achievement and school dropout, may, in fact, be more indicative of an inadequate learning environment. Many interventions focus on deficits in the child when deficits in the environment may be the more serious problem. As we have illustrated, it is possible to remove the barriers to quality educational experience for children. We urge that more efforts be made to develop programs of this nature. By considering *all* of the factors which can lead to difficulty in school transition–characteristics of the child, features of the environment, and the interaction between the two–we can better choose the most appropriate focus of an intervention to foster better school adjustment for all children, which, in turn, will help more children make successful transitions into adulthood.

REFERENCES

Alexander, K. L., & Entwistle, D. R. (1988). Achievement in the first two years of school: Patterns and processes. *Monographs of the Society for Research in Child Development, 53*, 1-157.

Ames, C. (1992). Classrooms: Goals, structures, and student motivation. *Journal of Educational Psychology, 84*, 261-271.

Ashton, P. T., & Webb, R. B. (1986). *Making a difference: Teachers' sense of efficacy and student achievement.* White Plains, NY: Longman.

Au, K. H., & Mason, J. M. (1981). Social organizational factors in learning to read: The balance of rights hypothesis. *Reading Research Quarterly, 17*, 115-152.

Barker, R. G., & Gump, P. V. (1964). *Big school, small school: High school size and student behavior.* Stanford, CA: Stanford University Press.

Baron, R. M., Tom, D. Y. H., & Cooper, H. M. (1985). Social class, race, and teacher expectations. In J. B. Dusek (Ed.), *Teacher expectancies* (pp. 251-270). Hillsdale NJ: Erlbaum.

Blyth, D. A., Simmons, R. G., & Carlton-Ford, S. (1983). Adjustment of early adolescents to school transitions. *Journal of Early Adolescence, 3*, 105-120.

Bronfenbrenner, U. (1979). *The ecology of human development.* Cambridge, MA: Harvard University Press.

Brophy, J. E. (1983). Research on the self-fulfilling prophecy and teacher expectations. *Journal of Educational Psychology, 75*, 631-661.
Card, D., & Krueger, A. (1990). *Does school quality matter? Returns to education and the characteristics of public schools in the United States.* National Bureau of Economic Research Working Paper Series, no. 3358.
Comer, J. (1988). Educating poor minority children. *Scientific American, 259*, 42-48.
Cowan, P. A. (1991). Individual and family life transitions: A proposal for a new definition. In P .A. Cowan and E. M. Hetherington (Eds.), *Advances in family research Volume II: Family transitions.* Hillsdale, NJ: Erlbaum.
Crockett, L. J., Peterson, A. C., Graber, J. A., Schulenberg, J. E., & Ebata, A. (1989). School transitions and adjustment during early adolescence. *Journal of Early Adolescence, 9*, 181-210.
Cusick, P. A. (1986). Public secondary schools in the United States. In T. M. Tomlinson and H. J. Walberg (Eds.), *Academic work and educational excellence* (pp. 137-152). Berkeley, CA: McCutchan.
Dohrenwend, B. S., & Dohrenwend, B. P. (1974). Overview and prospects for research on stressful life events. In B. S. Dohrenwend & B. P. Dohrenwend (Eds.). *Stressful life events: Their nature and their effects.* New York: Wiley.
Dreeben, R. (1968). *On what is learned in school.* Reading, MA: Addison-Wesley.
Eccles, J. S., & Midgley, C. (1989). Stage-environment fit: Developmentally appropriate classrooms for young adolescents. In C. Ames and R. Ames (Eds.), *Research on motivation in education: Volume 3. Goals and Cognitions* (pp. 139-186). New York: Academic Press.
Felner, R. D., Farber, S. S., & Primavera, J. (1983). Transitions and stressful life events: A model for primary prevention. In R. D. Felner, L. A. Jason, J. N. Moritsugu, & S. S. Farber (Eds.), *Preventive psychology: Theory, research, and practice* (pp. 199-215). New York: Pergamon.
Felner, R., Ginter, M., & Primavera, J. (1982). Primary prevention during school transitions: Social support and environmental structure. *American Journal of Community Psychology, 10*, 277-290.
Felner, R., Primavera, J., & Cauce, A. M. (1981). The impact of school transitions: A focus for preventive efforts. *American Journal of Community Psychology, 9*, 449-459.
Finley, M. K. (1984). Teachers and tracking in a comprehensive high school. *Sociology of Education, 57*, 233-243.
Fox, B. J. (1990). Antecedents of illiteracy. *Social Policy Report, VI*, 1-13.
Garcia, E. E. (1992). "Hispanic" children: Theoretical, empirical, and related policy issues. *Educational Psychology Review, 4*, 69-93.
Good, T. L. (1986). What is learned in elementary schools. In T. M. Tomlinson and H. J. Walberg (Eds.), *Academic work and educational excellence* (pp. 87-114). Berkeley, CA: McCutchan.
Good, T. L., & Weinstein, R. S. (1986). Schools make a difference: Evidence, criticisms, and new directions. *American Psychologist, 41*, 1090-1097.

Goodlad, J. I. (1984). *A place called school*. New York: McGraw-Hill.
Gray, S. W., Ramsey, B. K., & Klaus, R. A. (1983). The early training project. In Consortium for Longitudinal Studies (Eds.) *As the twig is bent: Lasting effects of preschool programs* (pp. 33-70). Hillsdale NJ: Erlbaum.
Hansen, D. (1986). Family-school articulations: The effects of interaction rule mismatch. *American Educational Research Journal, 23*, 643-659.
Hess, R., Dickson, W. P., Price, G. G., & Leong, D. J. (1979). Some contrasts between mothers and preschool teachers in interaction with four-year-old children. *American Educational Research Journal, 16*, 307-316.
Hirsch, B. J., & Rapkin, B. D. (1987). The transition to junior high school: A longitudinal study of self-esteem, psychological symptomatology, school life, and social support. *Child Development, 58*, 1235-1243.
Hoier, T., McConnell, S., & Pallay, A. (1987). Observational assessment for planning and evaluating educational transitions. *Behavioral Assessment, 9*, 5-19.
Jason, L. A. (1980). Prevention in the schools: Behavioral approaches. In R. H. Price, R. F. Ketterer, B. C. Bader, & J. Monahan (Eds.), *Prevention in mental health: Research, policy, and practice*, (Vol.1, pp. 109-134). Beverly Hills, CA: Sage.
Jason, L. A., Weine, A. M., Johnson, J. H., Warren-Sohlberg, L., Filippelli, L. A., Turner, E. Y., & Lardon, C. (1992). *Helping transfer students: Strategies for educational and social adjustment*. San Francisco: Jossey-Bass.
Kelly, J. G. (1979). *Adolescent boys in high school: A psychological study of coping and adaptation*. Hillsdale, NJ: Erlbaum.
Lazar, I., & Darlington, R. (1982). Lasting effects of early education: A report from the consortium for longitudinal studies. *Monographs of the Society for Research in Child Development, 47*. Chicago: University of Chicago Press for the Society for Research in Child Development.
Levin, H. M. (1987). Accelerated schools for disadvantaged students. *Educational Leadership, 44*, 19-21.
Lounsbury, J. H., Marani, J. V., & Compton, M. F. ((1980). *The middle school in profile: A day in seventh grade*. Fairborn, Ohio: Middle School Association.
Maehr, M. L., & Midgley, C. (1991). Enhancing student motivation: A schoolwide approach. *Educational Psychologist, 26*, 399-427.
Matus, A., & Reid, M. (1983). Helping parents deal with children's educational transitions. *Social Work in Education*, 89-96.
McClellan, J., & Trupin, E. (1989). Prevention of psychiatric disorders in children. *Hospital and Community Psychiatry, 40*, 630-636.
McCaslin, M., & Good, T. L. (1992). Compliant cognition: The misalliance of management and instructional goals in current school reform. *Educational Researcher, 21*, 4-17.
McConnell, S. R., Strain, S. S., Kerr, M. M., Stagg, V., Lenkner, D. A., & Lambert, D. L. (1984). An empirical definition of elementary school adjustment. *Behavior Modification, 8*, 643-695.
Midgley, C., Feldlaufer, H., & Eccles, J. S. (1989). Change in teacher efficacy and

student self- and task-related beliefs in mathematics during the transition to junior high school. *Journal of Educational Psychology, 81*, 247-258.

National Board of Inquiry. (1985). *Barriers to excellence: Our children at risk.* Boston: National Coalition of Advocates for Students.

National Commission on Excellence in Education. (1983). *A nation at risk.* Washington, DC: U.S. Department of Education.

Oakes, J. (1987). Tracking in secondary schools: A contextual perspective. *Educational Psychologist, 22*, 129-153.

Parkes, C. M. (1971). Psycho-social transactions: A field for study. *Social Science and Medicine, 5*, 101-115.

Pearlin, L. I., Meneghan, E. G., Lieberman, M. A., & Mullen, J. T. (1981). The stress process. *Journal of Health and Social Behavior, 22*, 337-356.

Pedersen, E., Faucher, T. A., & Eaton, W. W. (1978). A new perspective on the effects of first-grade teachers on children's subsequent adult status. *Harvard Educational Review, 48*, 1-31.

Reyes, O., & Jason, L. A. (1991). An evaluation of a high school drop out program. *Journal of Community Psychology, 19*, 221-230.

Rist, R. C. (1970). Student social class and teacher expectations: The self-fulfilling prophecy in ghetto education. *Harvard Educational Review, 40*, 411-451.

Rumberger, R. W. (1987). High school dropouts: A review of issues and evidence. *Review of Educational Research, 57*, 101-121.

Rutter, M. (1983). School effects on pupil progress: Research findings and policy implications. *Child Development, 54*, 129.

Sadker, M., Sadker, D., & Klein, S. (1991). The issue of gender in elementary and secondary education. *Review of Research in Education, 17*, 269-334.

Sarason, S. B. & Klaber, M. (1985). The school as a social situation. *Annual Review of Psychology, 36*, 115-140.

Singer, J. D., Palfrey, J. S., Butler, J. A., & Walker, D. K. (1989). Variation in special education classification across school districts: How does where you live affect what you are labeled? *American Educational Research Journal, 26*, 261-281.

Slavin, R. E. (1988). Synthesis of research on grouping in elementary and secondary schools. *Educational Leadership, 46*, 67-77.

Slavin, R. E., & Madden, N. A. (1989). What works for students at risk: A research synthesis. *Educational Leadership, 46*, 4-13.

Slavin, R. E., Madden, N. A., Karweit, N. L., Livermon, B. J., & Dolan, L. (1990). Success for all: First year outcomes of a comprehensive plan for reforming urban education. *American Educational Research Journal, 27*, 255-278.

Spillman, C. V., & Lutz, J. P. (1985). Criteria for successful experiences in kindergarten. *Contemporary Education, 56*, 109-113.

Stewart, A. J., & Healy, J. M. (1984). Adaptation to life changes in adolescence. In P. Karoly & J. J. Steffan (Eds.), *Advances in Child Behavioral Analysis and Therapy: Vol. 3. Adolescent behavior disorders: Foundations and contemporary concerns* (pp. 39-60). Lexington, MA: Lexington Books.

Taylor, W., & Piche, D. (1990). *A report on shortchanging children: The impact of fiscal inequality on the education of students at risk*. Washington DC: General Printing Office.

Trickett, E. J. & Birman, D. (1989). Taking ecology seriously: A community development approach to individually based preventive intervention in schools. In L. A. Bond & B. E. Compas (Eds.), *Primary prevention and promotion in the schools* (pp. 361-390). Newbury Park, CA: Sage.

Vanderpool, N. A. & Richmond, J. B. (1990). Child health in the United States: Prospects for the 1990's. *Annual Review of Public Health, 11*, 185-205.

Ward, B. A. (1986). Between elementary and high school. In T. M. Tomlinson & H. J. Walberg (Eds.), *Academic work and educational excellence* (pp. 115-136). Berkeley, CA: McCutchan.

Weinstein, R. S. (1976). Reading group membership in first grade: Teacher behaviors and pupil experience over time. *Journal of Educational Psychology, 68*, 103-116.

Weinstein, R. S. (1993). Children's knowledge of differential treatment in school: Implications for motivation. In T. M. Tomlinson (Ed.), *Hard work and High Expectations: Motivating students to learn*. National Society for the Study of Education Series. Berkeley, CA: McCutchan.

Weinstein, R. S., Soule, C. R., Collins, F., Cone, J., Mehlhorn, M., & Simontacchi, K. (1991). Expectations and high school change: Teacher-researcher collaboration to prevent school failure. *American Journal of Community Psychology, 19*, 333-363.

Weinstein, R. S., Marshall, H. H., Sharp, L., & Botkin, M. (1987). Pygmalion and the student: Age and classroom differences in children's awareness of teacher expectations. *Child Development, 58*, 1079-1093.

Wicker, A. W. (1968). Undermanning, performance, and students subjective experiences in behavior settings of large and small high schools. *Journal of Personality and Social Psychology, 10*, 255-261.

A Comprehensive, Preventive, Parent-Based Intervention for High-Risk Transfer Students

Leonard A. Jason
Joseph H. Johnson
Karen E. Danner
Stephanie Taylor
Karen S. Kurasaki

DePaul University

SUMMARY. High-risk students transferring into the 3rd, 4th, and 5th grades were placed in one of three conditions: no tutoring (control), school tutoring (child component), or school and home tutoring (parent component). High-risk children were identified as having low SES, academic lags, and multiple life stressors. High and low intensity levels of parent involvement in tutoring high-risk school transfer children were examined to determine the effects on chil-

---

Leonard A. Jason, Joseph H. Johnson, Karen E. Danner, Stephanie Taylor, and Karen S. Kurasaki wish to thank the many principals and teachers who have supported this preventive intervention. Funding for this project was provided by the National Institute of Mental Health, Grant number MH40851. Address correspondence to Leonard A. Jason, PhD, Department of Psychology, DePaul University, 2219 North Kenmore Avenue, Chicago, IL 60614.

[Haworth co-indexing entry note]: "A Comprehensive, Preventive, Parent-Based Intervention for High-Risk Transfer Students." Jason, Leonard A. et al. Co-published simultaneously in *Prevention in Human Services* (The Haworth Press, Inc.) Vol. 10, No. 2, 1993, pp. 27-37; and: *Prevention and School Transitions* (ed: Leonard A. Jason, Karen E. Danner, and Karen S. Kurasaki) The Haworth Press, Inc., 1993, pp. 27-37. Multiple copies of this article/chapter may be purchased from The Haworth Document Delivery Center. Call 1-800-3-HAWORTH (1-800-342-9678) between 9:00 - 5:00 (EST) and ask for DOCUMENT DELIVERY CENTER.

© 1993 by The Haworth Press, Inc. All rights reserved.

dren's adjustment throughout the school year. At the end of the year, the percent of children who moved from the poor to good coping category was examined. Fifty percent of the children in the high intensity parent component versus 30% of the children in the low intensity, had moved from the poor coping category to the average or good category by the end of the school year. These results suggest that more comprehensive and intensive tutoring helps high-risk transfer children to better cope with the social and academic demands of a new school.

Many researchers have found that transferring from one school to another can be the source of much stress and tension. Stewart, Sokol, Healy, Chester, and Weinstock-Savory (1982), for example, found that upon entering a new school, children often feel sad, abandoned, and helpless. Frequent movers have fewer well-developed peer ties (Douvan & Adelson, 1966) and describe themselves as more insecure, inconsistent, complaining and critical (Shaw, 1979) when compared to less-frequent movers. Changes in sleeping and eating patterns, and increases in negative statements and activity levels have been observed even in preschoolers who transfer to a new school (Tiffany, 1984). Parents of elementary age children rank school mobility as the fourth most significant childhood problem from a list of 35 life events (Coddington, 1972 a, b).

Children from lower socioeconomic status backgrounds are at higher risk for difficulties following a school transition, whereas those from upper to middle class backgrounds are more likely to profit from the varied experiences involved in changing schools (Glidewell, Kantor, Smith, & Stringer, 1965). Morris, Pestaner, and Nelson (1967) also found that downwardly mobile families are less equipped to help children deal with the pressures and demands of transferring into a school. In addition to low SES, life stressors and previously repeated academic failures might negatively affect children's abilities to cope with school transitions (Jason, Betts et al., 1992).

Preventive intervention programs involving parents have been implemented in schools to help students improve academic and social competencies. For example, to increase the quantity and quality of homework, parents have been effectively trained in contingency management (Goldberg, Merbaum, Even, Getz, & Safir,

1981). Other programs have focused on parents signing home-notes that attest to homework activity (Froelich, Blitzer, & Greenberg, 1967). Parents of high-risk children from lower SES backgrounds have been found to be competent tutors (Chandler, Argyris, Barnes, Goodman, & Snow, 1983; Shuck, Ulsh, & Platt, 1983).

As mentioned previously, some children transferring into new schools are at-risk for school difficulties, and several intervention programs have been directed at these children. Jason et al. (1989) designed a project in which high-risk transfer children were provided an orientation program and twice weekly tutoring by paraprofessionals. The orientation combined basic school information with a discussion of students' feelings associated with the transfer experience. Findings from this program indicated significantly higher scores on standardized achievement tests for tutored students versus control students. Most of the parents indicated an interest in being provided training to tutor their children.

The second year of the project introduced a parent tutoring component that was combined with a school orientation and weekly paraprofessional tutoring (Jason, Kurasaki, Neuson, & Garcia, in press). Findings indicated that those children provided with additional parent tutoring evidenced better academic grades and adjustment by the end of the school year.

In the research discussed above, we also found that involving parents in the preventive school-based intervention had been effective in enhancing coping among high-risk transfer children. In the present study, we again examined parent involvement with some parents having high levels of involvement and some parents less involvement. School tutors were also examined as having high and low levels of involvement. We predicted that children who received the highest levels of parent and tutor involvement would evidence better adjustment throughout the school year than children who received less parent and tutor involvement.

METHOD

Participants

Thirty-one urban, parochial, elementary schools with diverse ethnic populations were selected for this study. Twenty of the schools were randomly assigned to either control or child component tutoring conditions during the first year of the project. During the third year of the project, additional schools were added in order to have enough schools for two separate interventions. The original group of schools were divided into either a parent or child component. Parent permission for testing was obtained for approximately 98% of the sample.

Three criteria were used to identify children as high-risk. They were from a lower socioeconomic background (Hollingshead, 1975), evidenced a lag in at least one area of a standardized achievement test (Jastak & Wilkinson, 1984), and experienced two or more life stress events based on parent reports (Sandler, 1980; Sandler & Block, 1979). During the 1988-89 school year, 174 of the 400 transfer children were identified as being high-risk: The control component consisted of 57 high-risk children, the child component consisted of 58 high-risk children, and the parent component consisted of 59 high-risk children. The final sample with complete pre-post sociometric and grade point average data for the analysis conducted in this study involved 51 children in the control, 48 in the child, and 48 in the parent component. Children that transferred to another school during the year and children without complete pre-post data were deleted from analyses.

Forty percent of the high-risk children were entering the third grade, 30% were entering fourth, and 30% were entering the fifth grade. The ethnic backgrounds were African-American (41%), Hispanic (49%), White (8%), and Biracial and Asian-American (2%). Fifty-two percent were male and 48% were female.

Procedure

Timetable. All transfer children entering third, fourth, and fifth grade were administered a standardized achievement test and a confidential sociometric interview at the beginning and end of the academic year. During the pretesting stage, parents of all transfer children were phone interviewed regarding household information, family history, parental socioeconomic status (SES), and stressful events that may have occurred in the child's life. Tutoring for child and parent components began in October and continued until the end of the school year.

Orientation Program. A one hour orientation program occurred at all experimental schools following pre-point testing. Children were placed in groups of 15 to 20 and provided a review of school rules, personnel information, and clubs by a sixth grade peer leader. The students were encouraged to ask questions about the school and activities. In addition, the project personnel guided discussion and activities that facilitated comfortable sharing of feelings regarding the transfer. All transfer students were provided a same sex non-transfer buddy who participated in the orientation program. During the orientation session, the pairs discussed school rules, feelings about the transfer, and ways in which they could become friends.

Child Component Tutoring. Paraprofessionals conducted individual tutoring sessions for approximately 40-60 minutes twice per week. Tutors integrated classroom materials into a personalized curriculum to accommodate the various skill levels of all children. The Model-Lead-Test method, a Direct Instruction technique developed by Rosenshine and Berliner (1978), was implemented to cover four main academic areas: spelling, reading, math and phonics. Each area of tutoring was monitored weekly to assess the child's academic improvements. Several minutes per session were also allocated to discuss any personal issues or problems the student may have been experiencing.

Weekly reading assessments (measuring accuracy, rate, and comprehension) and spelling assessments (test scores for the second tutoring session of the week) were recorded by the tutor. For the first three tutoring sessions of the year, the scores for reading accuracy, rate and comprehension were averaged and subtracted from the average of the last three tutoring sessions. Similarly, spelling assessment scores from the first three weeks of tutoring were averaged and subtracted from the average scores of the last three weeks of tutoring. These scores were used to determine the child's overall improvement (or decline) in that subject area and were included in evaluating the level of tutoring intensity (Weine, Kurasaki, Jason, Danner, & Johnson, in press).

Parent Component Tutoring. Children in the parent component received the same tutoring program at school as child component children. In addition, these students received tutoring in the home by parents or primary caregivers ("parents" will be used to refer to both parents and primary caregivers) that agreed to participate in the program. Throughout the school year, project members maintained contact with the parents to provide support and continually encourage a healthy parent-child interaction towards academic development.

To maintain consistency between school-tutoring and home-tutoring sessions, parents were instructed in the Model-Lead-Test method during a one-hour training session (Jason, Weine et al., 1992). Explicit to the home-tutoring program was the use of SRA cards (Parker & Scannel, 1982), which consist of a short story followed by exercises testing reading comprehension, vocabulary, and word structure. The child was responsible for completing cards with their parents during the home tutoring session and returning them to the school tutors to be scored on a one-hundred point scale. The number of cards completed and returned determined the number of parent-tutoring sessions held. The number of sessions held and the average score of all the SRA cards returned were used to evaluate the appropriate level of parent tutoring intensity.

Materials

Parent Questionnaire. Pretesting interviews were conducted over the phone between project members and a parent or guardian of the child. Interviewees were informed that inquiries–regarding parents' occupation, education, age and race, household information, family relationships and history, and child behavior–would be strictly confidential and honesty was necessary to maximize their child's benefit from the program. The family's SES was classified according to Hollingshead's Four Factor Index of Social Status (Hollingshead, 1975). Lower income families included those with scores within the lower 33% of the range.

Grade Reports. Report cards were collected at the end of the academic year from the school. Based on a 4-point scale, letter grades were converted to numerical scores (A = 4.0, B = 3.0, C = 2.0, D = 1.0, and F = 0). Grades in math, reading, and spelling were used to evaluate intervention effects on classroom performance.

Sociometric Interview. All children were administered a sociometric interview in which they were asked to nominate the three classroom peers that they liked most and three classroom peers they liked least. The raw nominations for these categories were tallied, standardized, and transformed into social preference and social impact scores. These scores were standardized by grade level, so that equivalent selection procedures were employed, and used to identify children's social status (Coie, Dodge, & Coppotelli, 1982).

Ratings

Achievement Ratings. Based on cluster analysis, high-risk students were categorized into three achievement groups based on first quarter grade-point-average (GPA) for reading and math: the high achievement group earned a GPA of 3.0 or above; the average group earned a GPA of 2.0 to 2.9; and the low achievement group earned a GPA of 1.9 or below.

Social Status. Social status of the child was determined using the classroom peer nomination interview developed by Coie and his colleagues. Social status scores identify children in one of five groups (listed from least to most social): rejected, neglected, controversial, average and popular (Coie, Dodge, & Coppotelli, 1982). "Unclassified" is a sixth sub-group considered as average in this analysis.

Coping. High-risk children were grouped into one of three "coping" categories. Determined by combining their achievement rating and social status, the criteria for categorization is as follows: **Good copers** were students within the high achievement group and were popular or average in social status, or were within the average achievement group and were popular in social status. **Average copers** included average achievement children who were average or controversial in social status. High achievers who were controversial in social status, and low achievers who were popular in social status were also considered average copers. **Poor copers** were students within low achievement groups who were average or controversial in social status. Children who were classified as rejected or neglected by peer nominations were considered as poor copers regardless of achievement level (Jason, Weine et al., 1992). At pre-point testing, 13 children were classified as good copers, 47 as average copers, and 71 children were classified as poor copers.

Intensity of Tutoring. High- and low-intensity levels of tutoring were established for both the parent and child components. High-intensity tutoring resulted in a final sum of greater than, or equal to, 2 on the variables described below. If the child attended more than 36 school-tutoring sessions, she or he received a score of 1. If the number of SRA cards returned from home-tutoring sessions was greater than 15, the child received a score of 1. An average score of more than 93% on all SRA cards resulted in a score of 1. As indicated in the Child Component Tutoring section, reading and spelling performance was included to determine intensity. The difference of the averages of the first three and last three assessment scores indicated overall performance (improvement or decline) for the year. If the improvement in reading performance was greater than or equal to 16, the child received a score of 1. If the child's change in spelling performance for the year was greater than or equal to 4, then the child received a score of 1. If the above qualifiers were not achieved, the child received a score of 0 for that variable.

Parent component variables included the number of school-tutored sessions, reading performance and spelling performance, number of SRA cards returned, and the average percent of correct answers on all SRA cards. Child component variables included the number of school-tutored sessions, reading performance, and spelling performance. Approximately one-half of the children in the parent component received final scores placing them in the high intensity condition, and one-half received scores placing them in the low intensity condition. As with the parent component, approximately one-half of the children in the child component were in the high intensity and about one-half were in the low intensity condition. A few of the participants were not included in this analysis because complete in-process data were not available.

RESULTS

At the beginning of the school year, there were no significant gender, ethnic, or SES differences between children in the three components (parent, child, or control). In addition, there were no significant differences between components in children's grades before the school transfer.

We examined the children who were able to move from the

poor-cooping category at pretesting to the average or good coping category by the end of the year. The percentage of children who moved out of the poor coping category for the controls was 21%. Among children provided high intensity child tutoring, 33% of the poor copers moved out of this category; for children in the low intensity child group, 27% moved out of this category. For children in the high and low intensity parent tutoring, 50% and 30% respectively, moved out of the high risk group. Of interest, all of the children in the parent group who received the highest possible score on the 5-point intensity condition had moved out of this high-risk condition by the end of the intervention.

DISCUSSION

The high-intensity tutoring in the parent intervention was the most effective in helping high-risk transfer children move out of the poor coping group. In the absence of intervention, most children in the poor coping groups remained in the high-risk group at the end of the year. Frequent tutoring with a friendly and helpful tutor and a committed parent may have helped students to view school work more positively; this positive attitude and behavior may then generalize to the class. The additional attention and focused tutoring seems to have helped many of the most at-risk transfer children cope better over the course of the year at the new school.

It is interesting that high and low intensity child tutoring had somewhat similar effects, which were somewhat higher than the control condition. It is possible that child-tutoring alone is just not a potent enough intervention to help the majority of children change risk status over time. The low intensity parent condition was about as effective as either of the child tutoring conditions. However, children of parents who were more actively involved in the tutoring program, had a higher likelihood of moving out of the high-risk category over the course of the year.

More of the children in the poor coping category with high-intensity parent tutoring succeeded in moving into the average or good coping category compared to those children without tutoring. This supports our hypothesis that the greater the efforts towards comprehensive and intensive tutoring, the greater the development of the children's coping skills in the academic environment.

There are several factors that affect the intensity and support parents give to their children. Economic struggles sometimes force the parents into work schedules that minimize their amount of time at home. Families with several children sometimes find it difficult to allocate time to support each child's individual needs. It is clear there are legitimate reasons for some parents not having the time to more comprehensively and intensively work with their children on tutoring in the home.

The findings of the present study will need to be replicated with further samples before definite conclusions can be made. However, it is our opinion that program intensity can make a difference in helping children improve their risk status. Within the school-and-home tutoring component, there were parents who worked consistently and patiently to improve their children's abilities, while others had less time, skills or motivation to be as effective in this role. Children whose parents were able to establish routine, comprehensive home-tutoring sessions received the greatest benefits from the program.

REFERENCES

Chandler, J., Argyris, D., Barnes, W. S., Goodman, I. F., & Snow, C. E. (1983). *Parents as teachers: observations of low income parents and children in a homework-like task* (Report No. SP 022 704). Cambridge, MA: Harvard University, Graduate School of Education. (ERIC Document Reproduction Services No. ED 231 812).

Coddington, R. D. (1972 a). The significance of life events as etiologic factors in the disease of children-I. A survey of professional workers. *Journal of Psychosomatic Research, 16*, 17-18.

Coddington, R. D. (1972 b). The significance of life events as etiologic factors in the disease of children II. A study of a normal population. *Journal of Psychosomatic Research, 16*, 205-213.

Coie, J. D., Dodge, K. A., & Coppotelli, H. (1982). Dimensions and types of social status: A cross-age perspective. *Developmental Psychology, 18*, 557-570.

Douvan, E., & Adelson, J. (1966). *The adolescent experience.* New York: John Wiley & Sons.

Froelich, M., Blitzer, F. K., & Greenberg, J. W. (1967). Success for disadvantaged children. *The Reading Teacher, 21*, 29-30.

Glidewell, J. C., Kantor, M. B., Smith, L. M., & Stringer, L. A. (1965). Social structure and socialization in the elementary school classroom. *A report of a* workgroup to the committee on social structure and socialization of the Social Science Research Council. Clayton, MO: The St. Louis Health Department.

Goldberg, J., Merbaum, M., Even, T., Getz, P., & Safir, M. P. (1981). Training mothers in contingency management of school-related behavior. *The Journal of General Psychology, 104*, 3-12.

Hollingshead, A. B. (1975). *Four Factor Index of Social Status.* Unpublished manuscript, Yale University, Department of Sociology, New Haven.

Jason, L. A., Betts, D., Johnson, J. H., Smith, S., Krueckeberg, S., & Cradock, M. (1989). An evaluation of an orientation plus tutoring school-based prevention program. *Professional School Psychology, 4*, 273-284.

Jason, L. A., Betts, D., Johnson, J. H., Weine, A. M., Neuson, L., Filippelli, L., & Lardon, C. (1992). Developing, implementing, and evaluating a preventive intervention for high risk transfer children. In T. R. Kratochwill (Ed.), *Advances in School Psychology* (pp. 45-77). Hillsdale, NJ: Lawrence Erlbaum.

Jason, L. A., Kurasaki, K. S., Neuson, L., & Garcia, C. (in press). Training parents in a preventive intervention for transfer children. *The Journal of Primary Prevention.*

Jason, L. A., Weine, A. M., Johnson J. H., Warren-Sohlberg, L., Filippelli, L. A., Turner, E. Y., Lardon, C. (1992). *Helping transfer students: Strategies for educational and school readjustment.* San Francisco: Jossey-Bass.

Jastak, S., & Wilkinson, G. S. (1984). *Wide Range Achievement Test-Revised.* Wilmington, DE: Jastak Associates.

Morris, J., Pestaner, M., & Nelson, A. (1967). Mobility and achievement. *The Journal of Experimental Education, 35*, 74-79.

Parker, D. H., & Scannell, G. (1982). *SRA Reading Laboratory.* Chicago: Science Research Associates, Inc.

Rosenshine, B. V., & Berliner, D. C. (1978). Academic engaged time. *British Journal of Teacher Education, 4*, 3-16.

Sandler, I. N. (1980). Social support resources, stress and maladjustment of poor children. *American Journal of Community Psychology, 8*, 41-52.

Sandler, I. N., & Block, M. (1979). Life stress and maladaptation of children. *American Journal of Community Psychology, 7*, 425-440.

Shuck, A., Ulsh, F., & Platt, J. S. (1983). Parents encourage pupils (PEP): an inner city parent involvement reading project. *Reading Teacher, 36*, 524-528.

Shaw, J. A. (1979). Adolescents in the mobile military community. In S.C. Fienstein & P.L. Giovacchini (Eds). *Adolescent psychiatry. Development and clinical studies, Vol III* (pp. 191-198). Chicago: University of Chicago Press.

Stewart, A. J., Sokol, M., Healy, Jr., J. M., Chester, N. I., & Weinstock-Savory, D. (1982). Adaption to life changes in children and adults: Cross sectional studies. *Journal of Personality and Social Psychology, 43*, 1270-1281.

Tiffany, F. (1984). Separation stress of young children transferring to new schools. *Developmental Psychology, 20*, 786-792.

Weine, A. M., Kurasaki, K., Jason, L. A., Danner, K. E., & Johnson, J. H. (1992). An evaluation of preventive tutoring programs for transfer students. *Child Study Journal.*

Entry into Middle School: Student Factors Predicting Adaptation to an Ecological Transition

Carolyn Pisano Leonard

Head Start, Montgomery County Maryland

Maurice J. Elias

Rutgers University

SUMMARY. The transition to middle school has not been a frequent topic of empirical research. This article presents six guideposts for conceptualizing this transition. These guideposts focus upon the transaction between attributes of students and multiple levels of their ecological environment. How these operate to influence students' adaptation to middle school is discussed and data which focus on the child portion of this transaction are presented. Predictive relationships between measures of pre-transition adjustment and adaptation following middle school entry are examined, with a special focus on

---

The authors would like to thank their spouses and children for their patience and support during the many years of work that have gone into this project. Correspondence should be addressed to either author, in care of Maurice J. Elias, Department of Psychology, Rutgers University, Livingston Campus, New Brunswick, NJ 08903.

[Haworth co-indexing entry note]: "Entry into Middle School: Student Factors Predicting Adaptation to an Ecological Transition." Leonard, Carolyn Pisano, and Maurice J. Elias. Co-published simultaneously in *Prevention in Human Services* (The Haworth Press, Inc.) Vol. 10, No. 2, 1993, pp. 39-57; and: *Prevention and School Transitions* (ed: Leonard A. Jason, Karen E. Danner, and Karen S. Kurasaki) The Haworth Press, Inc., 1993, pp. 39-57. Multiple copies of this article/chapter may be purchased from The Haworth Document Delivery Center. Call 1-800-3-HAWORTH (1-800-342-9678) between 9:00 - 5:00 (EST) and ask for DOCUMENT DELIVERY CENTER.

© 1993 by The Haworth Press, Inc. All rights reserved.

social-cognitive problem solving skills. Other indices included self-concept, peer relations, academic performance, school behavior, and students' self-reported ability to cope with typical stressors of middle school. Significant findings, as well as implications for research and intervention, are discussed in terms of an ecological model.

In 1990, approximately 3.2 million youngsters made the expected transition from elementary to middle or junior high school in the public school system (U.S. Department of Education, 1992). For most, this represents a major alteration in many of the school-based characteristics influencing a child's development (Elias, Gara, & Ubriaco, 1985; Felner, Farber, & Primavera, 1983; Petersen & Hamburg, 1986). Patterns of interpersonal interaction change as the student shifts from one teacher and a constant set of classmates, to multiple teachers and a fluctuating and expanded peer group. This change in peer group offers more exposure to negative role models and a diffusion of emotional and social support (Elias et al., 1985). Infrequent movement within the relatively small physical environment of the elementary school is replaced by frequent migration within a larger, more diverse, and less familiar structure. Changing personnel and no single source of accountability are among the new patterns of authority the student finds in middle school. Organizational routines are different and a new set of rules and regulations in both the social and academic realms is in force. Greater individual responsibility for academic work accompanies greater academic pressure. Both teacher and parental expectations take on a more serious tone as past views of the student as a child are replaced with visions of a young adult. For the transitioning student, the entire social system is in a state of flux, as all incoming students are simultaneously attempting to adapt to this more complex setting.

The transition to middle school has not been a frequent topic of empirical research. What has been published research on the shift to middle, junior, or high school substantiates the notion that this type of change is a significant and influencing event in children's lives. Normatively, these transitions are associated with a decline in indices of child well-being and adjustment, including self-concept, grades, and participation in extra-curricular activities. Increases have been found in perceptions of anonymity, victimization, and absenteeism (Blyth, Simmons, & Bush, 1978; Blyth, Simmons, & Carlton-Ford, 1983; Felner, Ginter, & Primavera, 1982; Felner, Primavera, & Cauce, 1981; Finger & Silverman, 1966; Schulenberg, Asp, & Petersen, 1984; Simmons, Blyth, Van Cleave, & Bush, 1979; Ward, Mergendoller, Tikunoff, Rounds, Dadey, & Mitman, 1982). The long-term effect of these negative consequences (Pumphrey & Ward, 1976; Toepfer & Marani, 1980) is underscored by Blyth et al.'s (1983) longitudinal study which found that children did not rebound through tenth grade.

How the transition to middle school is conceptualized has important implications for both research and intervention. Applying existing theoretical frameworks is a useful start. From these, we derive six critical guideposts for conceptualizing the transition to middle school for research purposes. These are outlined below, along with brief justifications. The first two, that the *transition to middle school involves adjustment to a variety of changes in context and role* and that *these changes require adaptive efforts and the accomplishment of specific tasks in order that a child make a healthy adjustment to middle school,* already have been discussed.

The third is that *one's reaction to these changes and the stress associated with them reflect and are mediated by (a) the students' current level of adaptive functioning, (b) the student's evaluation of the event, and (c) the personal and environmental resources she or he can draw upon or generate during the transition.* The period of preadolescence is marked by a conjunction of rapid physiological, social, cognitive, and psychological changes. Pubescence brings dramatic changes in body configuration and a propensity toward major swings in energy level, mood, and appetite (Dorman & Lipsitz, 1984; Hamburg, 1974). Socially, there is a new ambivalence toward parents and a seeking of peer companionship as the preadolescent grapples with changing loyalties and the conflicting feelings of dependence and independence (Lipsitz, 1980; Gilligan, 1987). Expected behaviors now entail more responsibility and the youngster is expected to negotiate interpersonal interactions and resolve interpersonal problems with less adult intervention.

Lazarus and Folkman (1984) emphasize that preadolescents' response to school change also is dependent upon their cognitive appraisal of the implication of these events on their future well-being. This, in turn, is influenced by children's developing sense of identity (Erikson, 1963) and its incumbent issues of autonomy, achievement, and intimacy. Cognitively, students are just beginning to move from concrete to formal operations and to reflect upon their own thinking. This is often accompanied by critical self-evaluation and heightened self-consciousness that detract from, rather than promote, accurate or consistent appraisals (Petersen & Hamburg, 1986; Thornburg, 1981). Dohrenwend's (1978) model underscores that environmental resources such as material and social support make significant contributions to managing the stress of critical life events such as school transitions. The ability of a student to muster helpful outside resources may be influenced by personal qualities and skills, as well as the availability and means of accessing such resources.

In sum, what Moos (1984) terms the "personal system," comprising cognitive, biological, psychological, and social characteristics or qualities is undergoing a series of simultaneous transformations. There is a confluence of contextual and intraindividual change for the preadolescent entering middle school, taxing both behavioral and cognitive competencies. How a youngster traverses this life stage increasingly is seen to play a large role in subsequent adolescent and adult adjustment (Carnegie Council on Adolescent Development, 1989; DuBois, Felner, Brand, Adan, & Evans, 1992; Kendall, Lerner, & Craighead, 1984).

Perhaps the most neglected area of inquiry is reflected in the fourth guidepost: *certain cognitive skills and processes play an integral role in the process of adaptation, encouraging or discouraging adaptive, coping behaviors.* Elias and his associates (Elias et al., 1985; Elias, Gara, Ubriaco, Rothbaum, Clabby, & Schuyler, 1986) demonstrated that (a) new middle schoolers face a variety of stressors sufficiently potent to derail a meaningful number of students and generate formal and informal referrals to special services and (b) a set of social problem solving skills plays an important mediating role in coping with these stressors. This is consistent with research demonstrating that cognitive skills oriented to resolving social or interpersonal problems play a role in understanding adaptive processes and adjustment (Elias & Clabby, 1992; Shure & Spivack, 1982; Weissberg, Jackson, & Shiver, 1993).

Fifth, *aspects of the new context as well as one's psychological qualities and situational circumstances are together responsible for how well the student adjusts during the transition process.* In Felner's life transition model (Felner et al., 1983), experienced level of stress is much less of a concern than the tasks that must be accomplished cognitively and/or behaviorally to adapt to the new life circumstances. Concerning the transition to middle school, these include learning the rules and organizational patterns of the new school, adjusting to different adult behaviors and expectations, and adjusting to altered membership and status within one's peer group. Because of the emphasis on active task mastery in this model, coping skills and problem-solving abilities are emphasized in determining the outcome of adaptive processes.

Finally, *the process of the transition is itself a powerful influence on human development, effectively altering the child's position in all levels of her or his ecological environment and causing inevitable disequilibration in interpersonal interaction and relationships.* Bronfenbrenner (1979) defines an ecological transition as occurring when a change in role and/or setting alters one's position in her or his ecological environment. This is precisely one of the effects of the transition to middle school. However, his ecological framework is not limited to person-environment relations within the person's immediate settings (e.g., home, school, or office), but also takes into account the larger social contexts in which the person's immediate settings are embedded, and the transactions between them. These define a person's ecological environment. Obviously, middle school transition yields a change in one of the child's immediate settings (or the microsystem). The child leaves one school having one set of features, participants, activities, and roles and enters another one having a different set. This shift in context leads to a change in the interrelations between immediate settings (or the mesosystem). Home-school and peer group-school relationships are altered as a function of different participants and expected behaviors. For example, the more formal and bureaucratic atmosphere of the middle school often encourages less parent involvement and necessitates that student groups negotiate with committees rather than with individuals. Finally, to the extent that cultural institutions discriminate between the two levels of schools and their participants, the child's macrosystem will also be influenced. An example would be the unspoken assumption that middle school teachers are smarter and have a more difficult job than elementary school teachers and therefore should receive a higher salary.

The present study. Taken together, the six guideposts suggest that, as a function of the change from elementary to middle school, the child's position in all levels of her/his ecological environment is altered. Coping with this ecological transition must be understood in terms of the embedded and interrelated functioning of all elements of children's personal and environmental systems. The present study focused on the child portion of the transaction, specifically, on an examination of the relationships between measures of pre-transition adjustment and adaptation following the entry into middle school. Indices of self-concept, peer relations, academic performance, and social and task behavior in elementary school were chosen, with a special focus on social-cognitive problem solving skills. The focus at this relatively early stage of empirical inquiry was on which variables operate as critical predictors of a child's experience of the transition and their relative contributions in explaining outcome. Outcome was viewed as "transitional adaptation" and was based on academic achievement, school behavior, and self-reported ability to cope with typical stressors of middle school.

METHOD

Participants

The data for this study were collected as part of the Improving Social Awareness–Social Problem Solving Project, a longitudinal, preventive action research program (Elias & Clabby, 1992). Participants came from a primarily blue collar, multi-ethnic community of 15,000 in central New Jersey. The school district involved conforms to a modal pattern in the Northeast: several elementary schools feeding into one middle school. At sixth grade, students enter middle school where they remain through grade eight. One hundred fifteen fifth graders (61 boys and 54 girls) from three elementary schools from whom parental permission was obtained (98% of the possible sample) participated. Fifth graders in this school system are 10 to 11 years old and sixth graders are 11 to 12 years old. Academically, the majority of the sample ranged from average to about one year above grade level on standard academic tests.

Measures

Group Social Problem Solving Assessment. The GSPSA is a written measure of social problem solving (SPS) skills. The child is presented two common problem situations, being excluded by peers and being subjected to peer pressure, and asked to record three ways each problem could be solved. The child is also asked to generate potential consequences of a nonprosocial solution, and plans to help a prosocial solution work. Finally, the child is asked how the problem could be solved, given two different types of obstacles. GSPSA vignettes are scored for number of alternatives, number of consequences, proportion of negative consequences listed for the nonprosocial solution, number of planning steps listed, and in response to obstacles, expectancy for outcome, number of proactive alternatives and amount of planning described (Elias, 1982). Based upon principal component factor analyses of item responses, three scores were used: Specificity of Planning (based upon consequences and planning), The Obstacle Scale (based upon a child's responses to solution obstacles), and Inappropriate Positive Consequences (based upon the proportion of negative to total consequences listed for a nonprosocial solution). GSPSA scores have discriminated behaviorally and emotionally disturbed middle school students from other subgroups in their school and are not correlated with academic abilities (Elias, Rothbaum, & Gara, 1986). Interrater agreement exceeded 85% across all variables.

Piers-Harris Self-Concept Scale. The Piers-Harris Self-Concept Scale (Piers, 1969) is a self-report instrument designed for children aged 8 through 18 years. When administered as a group assessment, it requires approximately a third grade reading knowledge. The original form includes 80 items covering six factors. For the present study, students responded to a modified version of 44 items, adjusted to cover the same factors, but eliminating cross-loading items. Factor structure and internal consistency analyses indicated that creating a single composite score using all 44 items was appropriate by conventional standards. This score has been found to be both highly reliable (alpha = .86) and stable, with r = .73 over a 6 month period (Elias, Beier, & Gara, 1989).

Peer Opinion Survey. The Peer Survey is a version of the standard nomination type assessment of sociometric status within a designated group. It was derived from the Peer Attribution Inventory (PAI) developed by Elias, Larcen, Zlotlow, and Chinsky (1978). The PAI has a stable factorial structure and a test-retest reliability of r > .70 over six months. Eight questions were chosen to conform to Peery's (1979) procedure to allow combinations of positive and negative ratings to calculate a social impact score and a social preference score. To standardize scores across elementary school settings, Z scores were computed.

Survey of Adaptation Tasks–Middle School (SAT–MS) Measure. The Survey of Adaptation Tasks–Middle School (SAT–MS) Measure is a paper and pencil, self-report assessment of the stress encountered at the transition to middle school. Developed by Elias, Ubriaco, Reese, Gara, Rothbaum, and Haviland (1992), it consists of a list of 28 commonly occurring situations in middle school identified through a series of systematic assessments of students, school personnel, and parents as taxing coping abilities and potentially leading to distress or upset. Stressors range from dealing with aspects of the new environment, to acclimating to new academic routines, adjusting to new peer relationships, and being exposed and pressured to do things one does not want to do. Students are asked to rate each item according to the intensity of the problem for them since entering middle school. To determine the main dimensions tapped by the items of this measure, a principal components factor analysis with varimax rotation was performed (Elias et al., 1992). Three factors, accounting for nearly 80% of the variance were found: Substance Abuse, Verbal Peer Pressure and Exclusion, and Coping with School Conflicts. The SAT–MS Measure has an internal consistency coefficient greater that .90 across different samples. The three factor scores are each highly reliable (alpha = .93, .83, .85 respectively).

The Activity, Mood Learning (AML) Teacher Rating of School Behavior. Originally designed by Cowen and his colleagues (Cowen, Trost, Lorion, Dorr, Izzo, & Isaacson, 1975), this measure asked teachers to rate their students' school behavior on a four point scale. A high score indicates that a student copes well with all or most of the behavioral demands at school and is generally well-adjusted. For the present study, only the overall rating was used. Cross teacher agreement exceeds 90%.

Academic Achievement. The students' permanent school records were used. Grades in academic subjects were used to compute a grade point average (GPA) based upon a four point scale (top = 4 points, bottom = 1 point).

Procedure

Data were gathered over a twelve month period. In the fall and spring of fifth grade, about a six month time interval, students completed the Piers-Harris Self-Concept Scale, the GSPSA, and the Peer Opinion Survey. Measures were identical with the exception of the vignettes in the GSPSA. Teacher ratings of school behavior and grade point averages for the corresponding marking periods were also gathered at these times. Data were collected again following the students' transition into middle school. Approximately four weeks into sixth grade, students responded to the SAT–MS Measure to assess their adaptation to the new school. Teacher ratings of school behavior and grade point averages were also gathered in the fall of sixth grade, soon after the students completed the written measure.

RESULTS

The primary method of analysis for the study was multiple regression. Stepwise regression was chosen because the goal was to discover which variables of a particular variable set, each considered as having equal potential as a predictor, were the best predictors of transitional outcome. To reduce the variable set to those that were most meaningful, initial correlations were computed to check for multicollinearity or lack of convergence with other indices. By so doing, the Obstacle Scale was dropped from further analyses and the use of total scores for most independent variables was confirmed. Therefore, the main analytic model involved seven independent variables (overall scores for self-concept, sociometric preference, sociometric impact, school behavior, and GPA, and two distinct social-cognitive problem solving skills, SPS Specificity of Planning and SPS Inappropriate Positive Consequences) regressed stepwise on each dependent variable.

In addressing the primary study question of which student factors best predict transitional adaptation, results will be organized by dependent variable. As described above, for purposes of this study, transitional adaptation was based upon academic achievement (GPA), school behavior (teacher ratings), and self-reported difficulty coping with stressors. Findings are reported first for predictor variables measured in Spring of fifth grade.

As can be seen in Table 1, sixth grade GPA was significantly predicted by fifth grade GPA and the social-cognitive problem solving skill Specificity of Planning. The remaining variables were not significant. (Note that only adjusted R squared values are reported throughout.) When teachers' ratings of school social and task behavior was the criterion variable, significant predictors were fifth

TABLE 1

Stepwise Regression Results for Sixth Grade GPA

Predictor Variables	Significance Level	R^2 For Each Step
1. GPA 5	.001	.513
2. SPS Specificity of Planning	.037	.535
3. SPS Inappropriate Positive Consequences	n.s.[a]	
4. Sociometric Impact	n.s.	
5. Sociometric Preference	n.s.	
6. Teacher-Rated School Behavior	n.s.	
7. Self-Concept	n.s.	

F = 44.21, p < .001
n = 76

[a] n.s. = not significant

grade GPA, sociometric preference, and sociometric impact respectively. See Table 2 for a summary of the regression results.

Students' self-reported coping difficulty was significantly predicted by self-concept and an expectation of positive consequences following an antisocial solution (termed SPS Inappropriate Positive Consequences). (See Table 3.) In an effort to explain what predicts different aspects of the stress students encountered in acclimating to middle school, regressions were also run on the three subscales of the SAT–MS Measure: Verbal Peer Pressure and Exclusion, Coping With School Conflicts, and Substance Abuse. SPS Inappropriate Positive Consequences significantly predicted both Coping With School conflicts and Substance Abuse. In fact, it was the single best predictor for each subscale. Self-concept was the best predictor for Peer Pressure and Exclusion. None of the other variables contributed significantly. Self-concept followed SPS Inappropriate Positive Consequences in making a significant contribution to explaining the variance for Coping With School Conflicts. No other variables were significant. Following SPS Inappropriate Positive

TABLE 2

Stepwise Regression Results for Teacher Rated School Behavior

Predictor Variables	Significance Level	R^2 For Each Step
1. GPA 5	.001	.281
2. Sociometric Preference	.000	.349
3. Sociometric Impact	.016	.390
4. SPS Specificity of Planning	n.s.[a]	
5. Self-Concept	n.s.	
6. Teacher-Rated School Behavior	n.s.	
7. SPS Inappropriate Positive Consequences	n.s.	

F = 17.47, p < .001
n = 78

[a] n.s. = not significant

TABLE 3

Stepwise Regression Results for Coping With Stressors

Predictor Variables	Significance Level	R^2 For Each Step
1. Self-Concept	.001	.181
2. SPS Inappropriate Positive Consequences	.010	.249
3. Sociometric Impact	n.s.[a]	
4. Teacher-Rated School Behavior	n.s.	
5. GPA 5	n.s.	
6. Sociometric Preference	n.s.	
7. SPS Specificity of Planning	n.s.	

$F = 12.25$, $p < .001$
$n = 69$

[a] n.s. = not significant

Consequences, GPA was the only other significant contributor for Substance Abuse. (See Table 4.)

In sum, predictors of student adaptation to middle school vary according to the outcome specified. To predict academic achievement, clearly, the best choice is prior academic achievement. It is notable however, that the SPS skill concerning consequences and planning (SPS Specificity of Planning) provides a significant increase in the variance accounted for. Neither teacher ratings of school behavior, self-concept, nor sociometric status takes precedence. To predict teacher ratings of students' social and task behavior, again, prior academic achievement is most significant. Both sociometric preference and status were significant predictors as well, and SPS Specificity of Planning narrowly missed significance. Interestingly, prior teacher rating played no predictive role. Students' difficulty coping with stressors was not predicted by academic achievement. Rather, how students felt about themselves, as well as their social-cognitive problem solving skills were the significant predictors. Neither teacher's nor peer's ratings played a predictive

TABLE 4

Stepwise Regression Results for SAT--MS Subscales

Stepwise Regression Results for Coping With School Conflicts[a]

Predictor Variables	Significance Level	R^2 For Each Step
1. SPS Inappropriate Positive Consequences	.002	.115
2. Self-Concept	.010	.183

Stepwise Regression Results for Substance Abuse[b]

Predictor Variables	Significance Level	R^2 For Each Step
1. SPS Inappropriate Positive Consequences	.018	.076
2. GPA 5	.045	.116

Stepwise Regression Results for Peer Pressure and Exclusion[c]

Predictor Variables	Significance Level	R^2 For Each Step
1. Self-Concept	.002	.120

Note: The following variables were included in all regressions but did not contribute significant increments of variance in any of them: sociometric impact, sociometric preference, teacher-rated school behavior, and SPS specificity of planning

[a] $F = 9.08$, $p < .0003$; $n = 73$
[b] $F = 5.71$, $p < .005$; $n = 73$
[c] $F = 10.72$, $p < .002$; $n = 72$

role. SPS Inappropriate Positive Consequences was the primary predictor for the subscales Coping With School Conflicts and Substance Abuse, linking students who reported positive consequences resulting from nonprosocial solutions, with using cigarettes, alcohol, and drugs, and with experiencing school conflicts and problems with authority relationships.

Results of regressions using Fall scores instead of Spring scores to predict sixth grade outcome were compromised due to reductions in N's. However, Pearson product-moment correlations computed on difference scores for each variable (based upon change from fall to spring of fifth grade), demonstrated a high degree of stability. Further, regressions using the Fall scores were quite similar to those of Spring in most cases, indicating a significant degree of stability.

As an additional method of analysis, directionality of change over the course of the pre-transition year was examined as a predictor of the composite variable, transitional adaptation. Using the difference scores, students were divided into three equal groups: students who increased in adjustment over the course of the year, those who stayed the same, and those whose functioning declined, for each independent variable. Students were grouped into high, medium, and low, based on scores on the dependent variable, transitional adaptation for sixth grade. Chi square tests were computed for each of the seven independent variables. Significant findings were found indicating that students who showed improved teacher ratings over the course of fifth grade ($p < .03$) and students whose sociometric impact decreased over the course of fifth grade ($p < .02$) were most likely to have positive transitional adaptation. This supplemented the regression findings, suggesting that children who showed a greater pattern of conformity to adult standards and a corresponding decrease in peer salience turn out to be better prepared for the more academically serious and demanding world of middle school.

DISCUSSION

In examining what child factors predict the quality of adaptation to the transition to middle school, the present study found a variability of predictors. What predicts middle school adaptation depends upon the criterion used. This finding in itself is not surprising. What is notable however, is that social-cognitive problem solving skills appear to play a role at this critical juncture in children's development. It is particularly interesting that GPA, a widely acknowledged measure of ability and success is related to aspects of a child's ability to solve interpersonal problems (which might include, for example, asking for help from a difficult-to-approach teacher or resisting peer pressure to cheat). That teacher-rated school behavior, self-concept, or sociometric status (all assumed to be important contributing factors) did not emerge as significant in predicting sixth grade GPA further emphasizes the significance of social problem solving skills.

The second particularly notable finding concerns the predictors of students' overall problems coping with stressors. This was the only outcome not predicted by fifth grade GPA. Thus, the quality of a student's academic achievement does not foretell whether she or he will report difficulty coping with the stressors of middle school. Students' sociometric status was not found to be a useful predictor either. Instead, self-concept and the social-cognitive problem solving skill concerning inappropriate expectancies of positive consequences for antisocial solutions were the significant predictors. This supports intuitive assumptions that a student's self-evaluation and self-concept mitigate future stress. It is among the first empirical demonstrations that social-cognitive problem solving abilities may do the same.

It is fitting that SPS Inappropriate Positive Consequences remained a significant predictor of SAT–MS subscales Substance Abuse and Coping With School Conflicts. Sixth graders who have difficulty in conflict situations and with the use of controlled substances (alcohol, drug, and cigarettes) are those who as fifth graders expected positive outcomes from antisocial solutions to interpersonal problems. Indeed, they may be students who expect positive outcomes from using controlled substances or engaging in school conflicts. It is interesting to note that neither sociometric preference nor impact emerged as a significant predictor of students' difficulty coping with stressors, given the importance of peer relations at this age. A possible explanation is that sociometric status is likely to be only partially related to friendship patterns, and it is interpersonal skills rather than status that aid children in managing typical stressors (Cauce, 1986; Heller & Swindle, 1983).

Considering these findings in the context of the six guideposts presented earlier serves as a reminder that children's skills still serve as the central point even in ecological models. If students' appraisals of risky actions is positive and if they lack the social-cognitive problem solving skills to think through the many adaptational tasks they face, poorer adjustment is likely. Further, the extent to which they are not able to orient themselves to adult standards over the course of their pre-transition year suggests that they might not be as equipped to adapt to middle school as peers who come to be viewed in increasingly positive terms by teachers, part of which is probably linked to a reduction in peer attention.

Several limitations of the present study should be noted. To advance research in this field, a priority would be to discover if the predictors found in this study are reliable across samples and settings. Measurement issues need to be addressed, including expanding the assessment of school behavior and including some in vivo assessment of social problem solving skills to complement the GSPSA. With reference to data analysis, the findings of this study aid the development of a hierarchical multiple regression model, suggesting variables that can serve as building blocks of a more comprehensive ecological model.

Perhaps the most important implication of these findings for research and intervention from an ecological model is that studies of environmental factors must conceptualize how they link to children's social cognitive and appraisal skills, and that environmental interventions, if they are to achieve ultimate success, must also show how the processes they set in motion will be related to child factors. Among the important contextual features to study are school size, class size, degree of academic emphasis in school, organizational structure, degree of parental involvement in school, opportunity for student involvement in school or class decision making, and teacher accessibility. It is further suggested that environmental/contextual features not be limited to the school. Examples of other aspects of students' contexts include parents' level of education, home-based patterns of child management, and community's socioeconomic status. Additional child factors to investigate might include perceived level of social support, number of simultaneous stressful life events, or daily hassles. Discovery of how these variables operate alone or in concert would make significant contributions to the field and serve theory well.

Frequency analyses from the present study corroborated other data indicating that about one quarter of middle school children have poor transitions, based upon measures of achievement, school behavior, and coping with stressors. That one in four children will have significant problems compels action, particularly given the possible deleterious sequelae of the disequilibration begun by poor adaptation. Present findings provide at least some justification for programming to teach and/or improve students' social problem solving skills by advancing students' abilities to determine appropriate consequences of alternative solutions and to plan how to carry out chosen solutions. The incorporation of strategies to strengthen self-concept is also suggested. Specific programs and intervention procedures already have been developed and await implementation opportunities (Elias, 1993). Without question, teacher training, programming, and/or curriculum adaptations to accomplish these recommendations must be preceded by policy statements and school system commitments to legitimize the importance of personal and social objectives, alongside the more traditional academic areas. Middle schools are indeed "turning points" for millions of children who, without significant intervention, may find themselves adrift on a path toward disaffection and alienation from learning, work, and productive citizenship (Carnegie Council on Adolescent Development, 1989).

REFERENCES

Blyth, D., Simmons, R., & Bush, D. (1978). The transition into early adolescence: A longitudinal comparison of youth in two educational contexts. *Sociology of Education, 51*, 149-162.

Blyth, D., Simmons, R., & Carlton-Ford, S. (1983). The adjustment of early adolescents to school transitions. *Journal of Early Adolescence, 3*, 105-120.

Bronfenbrenner, U. (1979). *The ecology of human development: Experiments by nature and design.* Cambridge: Harvard University Press.

Carnegie Council on Adolescent Development. (1989). *Turning points: Preparing American youth for the 21st century.* New York: Author.

Cauce, A.M. (1986). Social networks and social competence: Exploring the effects of early adolescent friendships. *American Journal of Community Psychology, 14*, 607-628.

Cowen, E., Trost, M., Lorion, R., Dorr, D., Izzo, L., Isaacson, R. (1975). *New ways in school mental health: Early detection and prevention of school maladaptation.* New York: Human Sciences Press.

Dohrenwend, B.S. (1978). Social stress and community psychology. *American Journal of Community Psychology, 6*, 1-14.

Dorman, G., & Lipsitz, J. (1984). Early adolescent development. In G. Dorman (Ed.), *Middle grades assessment program* (pp. 3-8). Carrboro, NC: Center for Early Adolescence.

DuBois, D., Felner, R., Brand, S., Adan, A., & Evans, E. (1992). A prospective study of life stress, social support, and adaptation in early adolescence. *Child Development, 63,* 542-557.

Elias, M.J. (1982). *Scoring manual for the Group Social Problem Solving Assessment.* New Brunswick, NJ: Rutgers University.

Elias, M.J. (Ed.) (1993). *Social decision making and life skills development: Guidelines for middle school educators.* Gaithersburg, MD: Aspen.

Elias, M.J., Beier, J., & Gara, M. (1989). Children's responses to interpersonal obstacles as a predictor of social competence. *Journal of Youth and Adolescence, 18,* 451-465.

Elias, M.J., & Clabby, J. (1992). *Building social problem solving skills: Guidelines from a school-based program.* San Francisco: Jossey-Bass.

Elias, M.J., Gara, M., & Ubriaco, M. (1985). Sources of stress and coping in children's transition to middle school: An empirical analysis. *Journal of Clinical Child Psychology, 14,* 112-118.

Elias, M.J., Gara, M., Ubriaco, M., Rothbaum, P., Clabby, J., & Schuyler, T. (1986). Impact of a prevention social problem solving intervention on children's coping with middle school stressors. *American Journal of Community Psychology, 14,* 259-275.

Elias, M.J., Larcen, S., Zlotlow, S., & Chinsky, J. (1978, August). *An innovative measure of children's cognitive responses in problematic interpersonal situations.* Paper presented at the meeting of the American Psychological Association, Toronto, Canada.

Elias, M.J., Rothbaum, P., Gara, M. (1986). Social-cognitive problem solving in children: Assessing the knowledge and application of skills. *Journal of Applied Developmental Psychology, 7,* 77-94.

Elias, M.J., Ubriaco, M., Reese, A., Gara, M., Rothbaum, P., & Haviland, M. (1992). A measure of adaptation to problematic academic and interpersonal tasks of middle school. *Journal of School Psychology, 30,* 41-57.

Erikson, E.H. (1963). *Childhood and society* (2nd Ed.). New York: Norton.

Felner, R., Farber, S., & Primavera, J. (1983). Transitions and stressful life events: A model for primary prevention. In R. Felner, L. Jason, J. Moritsugu, & S. Farber (Eds.), *Preventive Psychology: Theory, research and practice* (pp. 199-215). New York: Pergamon Press.

Felner, R., Ginter, M., & Primavera, J. (1982). Primary prevention during school transitions: Social support and environmental structure. *American Journal of Community Psychology, 10,* 277-290.

Felner, R., Primavera, J., & Cauce, A. (1981). The impact of school transitions: A focus for preventive efforts. *American Journal of Community Psychology, 9,* 449-459.

Finger, J., & Silverman, M. (1966). Changes in academic performance in the junior high school. *Personnel and Guidance Journal, 45,* 157-164.

Gilligan, C. (1987). Adolescent development reconsidered. In C. Irwin, Jr. (Ed.), *Adolescent social behavior and health: New directions for child development* (No. 37, pp. 63-92). San Francisco: Jossey-Bass.

Hamburg, B.A. (1974). Early adolescence: A specific and stressful stage of the life cycle. In Coelho, G., Hamburg, D., Adams, J. (Eds.), *Coping and adaptation* (pp. 101-124). New York: Basic Books.

Heller, K., & Swindle, R. (1983). Social networks, perceived social support, and coping with stress. In R. Felner, L. Jason, J. Moritsugu, & S. Farber (Eds.), *Preventive psychology: Theory, research, and practice*, (pp. 87-103). New York: Pergamon Press.

Kendall, P., Lerner, R., & Craighead, W. (1984). Human development and intervention in childhood psychopathology. *Child Development, 55*, 71-82.

Lazarus, R., & Folkman, S. (1984). *Stress, appraisal, and coping.* New York: Springer.

Lipsitz, J. (1980). The age group. In M. Johnson (Ed.), *Toward adolescence: The middle school years. Seventy-ninth yearbook of the National Society of the Study of Education* (pp. 7-31). Chicago: University of Chicago Press.

Moos, R.H. (1984). Context and coping: Towards a unifying conceptual framework. *American Journal of Community Psychology, 12*, 5-36.

Peery, J.C. (1979). Popular, amiable, isolated, rejected: A reconceptualization of sociometric status in preschool children. *Child Development, 50*, 1231-1234.

Petersen, A., & Hamburg, B. (1986). Adolescence: A developmental approach to problems and psychopathology. *Behavior Therapy, 17*, 480-499.

Piers, E. (1969). *The Piers-Harris Children's Self-Concept Scale.* Nashville, TN: Counselor Recordings and Tests.

Pumphrey, P., & Ward, J. (1976). Adjustment from primary to secondary school. *Educational Research, 19*, 25-34.

Shure, M., & Spivack, G. (1982). Interpersonal problem-solving in young children: A cognitive approach to prevention. *American Journal of Community Psychology, 10*, 341-356.

Simmons, R.G., Blyth, D., Van Cleave, E., & Bush, D. (1979). Entry in early adolescence: The impact of school structure, puberty, and early dating on self-esteem. *American Sociological Review, 44*, 948-967.

Thornburg, H.D. (1981). Developmental characteristics of middle schoolers and middle school organization. *Contemporary Education, 52*, 134-138.

Toepfer, C., & Marani, J. (1980). School based research. In M. Johnson (Ed.), *Toward adolescence: The middle school years. Seventy-ninth yearbook of the National Society for the Study of Education* (pp. 269-281). Chicago: Univ. of Chicago Press.

U.S. Department of Education (1992). *Report of the Education Information Branch.* Office of Education Research and Improvement: Washington, D.C.

Ward, B., Mergendoller, J., Tikunoff, W., Rounds, T., Dadey, G., & Mitman, A. (1982). *Junior high school transition study, Volume VII: Executive Summary.* San Francisco, CA: Far West Laboratory for Educational Research. (ERIC Document Reproduction Service No. ED 230 505).

Weissberg, R.P., Jackson, A.S., & Shriver, T. (1993). Promoting positive social development and health practices in young urban adolescents. In M.J. Elias (Ed.), *Social decision making and life skills development: Guidelines for middle school educators* (pp. 45-78). Gaithersburg, MD: Aspen.

Negotiating the Transition to Junior High School: The Contributions of Coping Strategies and Perceptions of the School Environment

David L. Causey
Eric F. Dubow

Bowling Green State University

SUMMARY. Investigated are the contributions of seventh graders' coping strategies and their perceptions of the school environment to predicting changes in their adaptation during the transition to junior high school. The students completed measures three weeks into the new school year and again three months later. Resource variables included students' use of approach and avoidance coping strategies in response to a specific transition-related stressor, and their perceptions of their new school environment. Criterion variables included students' ratings of how effectively they coped with the specific stressor, and their general adaptation to the transition. Zero-order and cross-lag correlations generally showed that the use of approach

---

This article is based on a dissertation by David L. Causey submitted in partial fulfillment of the requirements for the doctoral degree, Bowling Green State University, 1992. Please send any correspondences to Eric F. Dubow, Department of Psychology, Bowling Green State University, Bowling Green, OH 43403.

[Haworth co-indexing entry note]: "Negotiating the Transition to Junior High School: The Contributions of Coping Strategies and Perceptions of the School Environment." Causey, David L., and Eric F. Dubow. Co-published simultaneously in *Prevention in Human Services* (The Haworth Press, Inc.) Vol. 10, No. 2, 1993, pp. 59-81; and: *Prevention and School Transitions* (ed: Leonard A. Jason, Karen E. Danner, and Karen S. Kurasaki) The Haworth Press, Inc., 1993, pp. 59-81. Multiple copies of this article/chapter may be purchased from The Haworth Document Delivery Center. Call 1-800-3-HAWORTH (1-800-342-9678) between 9:00 - 5:00 (EST) and ask for DOCUMENT DELIVERY CENTER.

© 1993 by The Haworth Press, Inc. All rights reserved.

coping strategies and favorable perceptions of the school environment were associated with higher levels of perceived coping effectiveness and general adaptation to junior high school, while the use of avoidance coping strategies was associated with lower levels of perceived coping effectiveness and general adaptation. Hierarchical regressions revealed prospective effects for initial levels of coping strategies in predicting *later* perceived coping effectiveness.

As children move into adolescence, they experience many potentially stressful transitions, including social, physiological, and cognitive changes that provide opportunities for positive development and/or adjustment difficulties (Felner, Farber, & Primavera, 1983; Petersen & Hamburg, 1986). One of the more common transitions that children typically face is the normative transition from elementary school into middle or junior high school (Crockett, Petersen, Graber, Schulenberg, & Ebata, 1989). Following the life transitions model proposed by Felner et al. (1983), beginning junior high school may be viewed as a "marker" of an ongoing process (i.e., transition period) of adaptation to daily school-related stressors (e.g., more difficult school work, being picked on by older students) (Elias, Ubriaco, Reese, Gara, Rothbaum, & Haviland, 1992). The life transitions model also emphasizes resource variables (e.g., coping strategies, environmental factors, social support) that enhance the individual's ability to adapt to the transition. The present study examines the contributions of students' use of coping strategies and their perceptions of the school environment to predicting their adaptation to the junior high school transition.

Recent studies have investigated the role of normative school transitions in the development of maladaptive symptoms and/or positive growth. For example, Felner, Primavera, and Cauce (1981) found that the transition from eighth grade to high school had a significant negative effect on grade-point averages and attendance. Blyth, Simmons, and Bush (1978) and Blyth, Simmons, and Carlton-Ford (1983) reported that girls who faced the junior high school transition decreased in self-esteem, whereas boys experienced more victimizations (i.e., assault, theft, or robbery). Students undergoing the junior high school transition were also less likely to participate in extracurricular activities. Hirsch and Rapkin (1987) reported that students' overall attitudes toward the new junior high school environment became increasingly negative during the seventh grade year.

Some studies, however, have indicated mixed findings regarding children's adjustment to this transition. For example, Hirsch and Rapkin (1987) found that students' self-esteem did not change during the junior high school transition. They also found that although girls increased in symptoms of depression and hostility, boys *decreased* in their reports of these symptoms during the transition. Nottleman (1987) reported that students *increased* in perceived competence during the transition.

In attempts to clarify these mixed findings, some researchers have suggested that children's reliance on resources (e.g., coping strategies, attitudes about the school) may differentiate those who adapt well to the school transition from those who do not. Resources have been defined as "traits, abilities, or means, both material and human, which can be used to meet demands" (Patterson & McCubbin, 1987, p. 167). Jason et al. (1992) suggest that adjustment to the transition may be viewed as a transaction between children, resources, and stressful situations. Children's coping skills and their perceptions of the school environment are resources that are viewed as important to their adaptation to the normative school transition (Crockett et al., 1989; Elias et al., 1992). Children's coping abilities, or how they respond to stressful circumstances, may be conceptualized as "approach" strategies in which thoughts or behaviors are directed toward the stressor (e.g., seeking support to solve the problem), and "avoidance" strategies in which thoughts or behaviors serve to avoid the problem or its emotional impact (Roth & Cohen, 1986). Approach strategies appear to be related to positive functioning (e.g., higher self-concept) in youngsters, whereas avoidance strategies are more often related to poorer adjustment (e.g., higher anxiety) (Causey & Dubow, 1992; Ebata & Moos, 1989).

Some studies have assessed children's coping with the normative school transition. Elias, Gara, Ubriaco, Rothbaum, Clabby, and Schuyler (1986) implemented a social problem-solving skills intervention to enhance children's coping with the transition into middle school. Compared to a no-intervention control group, children exposed to this program reported fewer stressors upon entry into middle school; and, children with better developed social problem-solving skills reported experiencing fewer adjustment difficulties in response to the transition. Social support, another important coping resource (Compas, 1987), has also been examined in children making the transition into junior high school. Hirsch and DuBois (1992) found that initial (end of sixth grade) peer support predicted symptomatology assessed as children began the seventh grade.

Perceptions of the school environment (e.g., attitudes about teachers) have also been viewed as important in children's adaptation to school transitions (Elias et al., 1992; Elias et al., 1986). Domains of the school environment include the physical setting, organizational factors, student characteristics, and social interactions (Moos, 1979). Children's perceptions of their schools appear to accurately reflect actual aspects of the school environment (Horwitz, 1979; Lunenburg & Schmidt, 1989; Stewart, 1979). Furthermore, students' *perceptions* of the school environment have been linked to such factors as self-concept, grade-point averages, absenteeism, and anxiety about school (Epstein & McPartland, 1976; Moos & Moos, 1978; Nelson, 1984). Felner and Adan (1988) described a prevention program that emphasized reorganizing the school environment in order to reduce the flux and facilitate adjustment during the transition into high school. Compared to control students, project students exhibited more positive perceptions of the school environment, and had fewer absences and higher grade-point averages.

The above findings support Jason et al.'s (1992) recommendation to study the relations among stress, coping, and other resources to improve our understanding of children's adaptation to school transitions. Negotiating the junior high school transition is a dynamic process. As such, we used a "prospective" approach (Holahan & Moos, 1981); that is, we collected data at two time points, and examined whether resources used *initially* to cope with the transition predicted change over time in adaptation. The resources we measured were coping strategies the students used in response to the most problematic transition-related stressor they experienced since entering junior high school, and their perceptions of the school environment. Significant prospective results are important in identifying resources to target in school transition intervention programs, and perhaps in determining whether the initial use of certain types of coping strategies (e.g., avoidance) places the student at risk for later adaptation problems. We also examined whether changes over time in the resource variables predicted concomitant changes in adaptation.

In terms of the adaptation, or criterion, variables, the present study used both a global and a specific measure. First, we assessed students' self-reported experience of a range of school-related difficulties encountered since entering junior high school (e.g., being picked on by older students, having more and harder teachers). This criterion measure reflects global adaptation problems experienced in the new school. In addition, the importance of considering the *specific* outcome of one's coping efforts has been noted (Griffith, 1992). Thus, the second criterion measure sought the children's perceptions of how effectively they dealt with the specific transition-related stressor that they chose as most problematic for them. We expected that initial use of coping strategies (i.e., higher levels of approach and lower levels of avoidance coping) would predict improved adaptation (especially for the specific measure of coping effectiveness) over time. In addition, initial positive perceptions of the school environment were expected to predict decreases in general adaptation problems over time. We also hypothesized that *changes* in resources over time would predict concomitant changes in adaptation (e.g., increases in the use of avoidance coping would predict increases in adaptation problems).

Finally, it has been noted that an individual's perceived control over the stressor will likely influence the outcome for coping with that stressor (Lazarus & Folkman, 1984). Reliance on approach coping strategies for stressors perceived as controllable may increase the likelihood of a more positive outcome, whereas reliance on avoidance coping strategies for stressors perceived as controllable may increase the likelihood of a negative outcome (Causey & Dubow, 1992; Compas, Malcarne, & Fondacaro, 1988). Thus, we examined the possibility that students' perceptions of control over a specific transition-related stressor would moderate the relation between use of coping strategies in response to that stressor and perceptions of how effectively they dealt with the stressor.

METHOD

Subjects and Procedures

The subjects were seventh graders who transferred from five different elementary schools into the local junior high school of a semi-rural industrial midwestern community (population approximately 15,000). There were 270 eligible subjects. However, 3% of the parents declined consent for their children's participation, 2% of the children declined consent, 27% either moved or were absent for one or both testing sessions, and 8% were dropped from the analyses for failure to follow instructions in completing the measures (e.g., they did not complete the coping measure in response to the same stressor at both time points). The final sample of 162 students included 51% female and 86% White children (of the 22 non-White children, 8 (5%) were Hispanic and 14 (9%) were Black). Regarding the subjects' families, 71% of the parents were married, the average socioeconomic status was lower-middle class (mean = 46.94, SD = 15.29 on Hollingshead's two-factor index of social position; see Miller, 1977), and the mean number of children in the family was 2.53.

In terms of the effects of subject attrition, when compared with the sample of children who participated at Time 1 only (n = 37), the children who participated at both time points were more likely to be white, $\chi^2(1, N = 199) = 14.46, p < .01$, less likely to be from single parent homes, $\chi^2(1, N = 199) = 8.46, p < .01$, were higher in socioeconomic status, $t(173) = 3.33, p < .01$, and reported lower levels of general adaptation problems associated with the school transition, $t(197) = 2.86, p < .01$.

Children completed paper-and-pencil questionnaires in group sessions during school hours. Time 1 testing occurred three weeks into the new school year, a time when students report a variety of salient transition-related stressors (Elias, Gara, & Ubriaco, 1985). Time 2 testing occurred three months later to provide sufficient time to assess students' progress in negotiating the transition.

Measures

Demographic questionnaire. Students provided their gender, race, number of siblings, and parental marital, educational, and occupational statuses. For each student, a family socioeconomic score (SES) was computed using Hollingshead's two-factor index of social position (Miller, 1977), which takes into account parental education and occupation status. In two parent families, the SES was the higher of the two parents' scores.

Coping strategies. Students completed a 34-item measure (Causey & Dubow, 1992) designed to examine five coping strategies based on Roth and Cohen's (1986) approach/avoidance conceptualization of coping. The Approach scale includes seeking social support (e.g., talk to someone about how it made you feel) and problem solving (e.g., try to think of different ways to solve it). The Avoidance scale consists of distancing (e.g., make believe nothing happened), externalizing (e.g., curse out loud), and internalizing (e.g., worry too much about it). Students were asked to choose one transition-related stressor from the survey of daily school stressors (to be described below) that had been most problematic for them since beginning junior high school. *In response to this specific stressor at both Time 1 and Time 2,* the students indicated how often they used each of the 34 coping strategies on a 5-point scale (1 = never, 5 = always) to the lead question, "When this problem happens to me, I. . . ." Scores for each coping subscale reflect the sum of the responses to items on that subscale.

Causey and Dubow (1992) found factor analytic support for the five specific coping strategies, and adequate internal consistency, test-retest reliability, and validity (e.g., correlations with peer-ratings of students' coping strategies). In the present study, a principal components analysis with a promax rotation was computed on the five coping subscales. As hypothesized, a two-factor solution (approach and avoidance) emerged, accounting for 69% of the variance (eigenvalues were 2.20 and 1.27). Internal consistencies, using Cronbach's alpha, were: approach coping, .89 and .88 for Time 1 and Time 2, respectively; and avoidance coping, .82 and .77 for Time 1 and Time 2, respectively.

In addition, *perceived controllability over the stressor* was assessed by having the students respond to the following question on a 5-point scale (1 = never, 5 = always), "When this problem happens to you, how often do you think you can do something to change the situation?" Using this item, Causey and Dubow (1992) found that perceived controllability over the stressor was positively associated with the use of approach strategies and negatively associated with the use of avoidance strategies.

Perceived quality of the school environment. Students completed the 27-item Quality of School Life scale (QSL; Epstein & McPartland, 1976). The measure contains 14 true-false items and 13 items that are rated on a 4-point or 5-point scale which are then dichotomously coded to reflect a positive or negative evaluation of a school experience. The measure assesses general satisfaction with school, commitment to classwork, and reactions to teachers (e.g., Most of my teachers really listen to what I have to say.). Given the moderate to high intercorrelations among the three subscales, and that the internal consistency for the total scale has ranged from .86-.90 across studies (Epstein & McPartland, 1976), only the total score was used in the present study (Cronbach's alphas were .86 and .87 at Time 1 and Time 2, respectively). The authors of the scale report positive correlations between the QSL and a number of measures of positive adjustment.

Survey of daily school stressors. Students completed the Survey of Adaptational Tasks of Middle School (Elias et al., 1992), a measure assessing perceived experience of the severity and frequency of 25 daily stressors specific to the junior high school transition. Subscales include: peer relationships (e.g., having trouble making new friends), conflicts with authority (e.g., not getting along with all your different teachers), academic pressures (e.g., getting too much homework), and problems related to the new, larger environment (e.g., having school farther away from home). Students rate the degree to which each stressor has been a problem for them on a 4-point scale (1 = not a problem, 4 = large problem). An Adaptational Difficulty score is obtained by summing the scores for the 25 items, reflecting a composite of the frequency and severity of problems experienced in the adaptation to seventh grade in general. Elias et al. (1992) reported a coefficient alpha of .92 for this measure (.88 at both time points in the present study), and moderate negative relations with self-concept.

Coping effectiveness for the specific transition-related stressor. At the end of the coping questionnaire, students responded to six items regarding their perceived effectiveness in coping with the stressor that they chose as the most problematic since beginning junior high school. The items were adapted from Aldwin and Revenson (1987) and Pargament et al. (1990) (e.g., I have learned from the event, I feel better about myself, I handled the event well given the circumstances; students respond on a 5-point scale, 1 = strongly disagree, 5 = strongly agree). Griffith (1992) reported internal consistencies ranging from .80-.86 in a sample of adolescents (in the present study, .77 and .83 at Time 1 and Time 2, respectively). Griffith also found that reliance on approach coping strategies was positively related to coping effectiveness, while reliance on avoidance coping was negatively related to coping effectiveness.

RESULTS

Preliminary Analyses

Characteristics of transition-related stressors. The 10 most problematic stressors (i.e., percent of students rating the stressor as a "medium" or "large" problem) three weeks into junior high school were: having to do harder work (26%); getting too much homework (23%); having a tough teacher (21%); missing friends from elementary school (17%); teachers expecting too much of you (16%); getting things stolen from you (13%); having school farther away from home (12%); dating members of the opposite sex (11%); leaving the wrong books/supplies in your locker and forgetting to bring them to class (11%); and kids trying to talk you into things you don't want to do (10%). Three months later, a few different stressors were among the 10 most problematic: having an argument with a teacher (18%); not getting along with all your different teachers (17%); getting into fights (14%); and being sent to the vice principal's office (14%).

Recall that students were asked to identify the single stressor that was most problematic for them since beginning junior high school: 40% ($n = 64$) chose a conflict with authority stressor, 23% ($n = 37$) chose a peer stressor, 21% ($n = 34$) chose a new/larger environment stressor, and 17% ($n = 27$) chose an academic pressure stressor. With one exception, ANOVAs showed that there were no significant relations between the type of stressor chosen and perceptions of the quality of the school environment, use of coping strategies, perceived control over the stressor, perceived coping effectiveness, and general adaptation to junior high school. (The ANOVA for use of avoidance coping at Time 2 was significant, $F(3,158) = 2.69, p < .05$; avoidance coping was used less often for academic stressors than for conflict with authority or peer stressors).

Demographic differences in the resource and criterion variables. A series of 2 (sex) X 2 (race: white/nonwhite) X 2 (parental marital status: married/single) ANOVAs were computed for each resource and criterion variable at each time point. There were no significant sex effects. Compared to white students, nonwhite students reported higher perceptions of control over the stressor at Time 1, $F(1,157) = 4.44, p < .05$. Compared to students from married families, students from single parent homes reported higher perceptions of control over the stressor at Time 2, $F(1,155) = 13.99, p < .01$, and used less approach coping at Time 2, $F(1,158) = 3.92, p < .05$.

Table 1 shows that number of siblings and SES were either weakly related or unrelated to the resource and criterion variables.

Given the few significant demographic effects, and the fact that there were no significant demographic effects on the same variable at both time points, no demographic variables were included as control variables in later regression analyses.

Correlations Among Resource and Criterion Variables

Cross-sectional correlations. Table 1 shows the intercorrelations of the resource and criterion variables at Time 1 above the diagonal and at Time 2 below the diagonal. Of particular interest, favorable perceptions of the school environment were positively related to perceptions of coping effectiveness for the specific transition-related stressor, and negatively related to general adaptation difficulties at each time point. In addition, the use of approach strategies to cope with the specific transition-related stressor was positively related to perceived coping effectiveness for that stressor (but not to general adaptation difficulty) at both time points. The use of avoidance coping strategies in response to the specific transition-related stressor was negatively related to coping effectiveness for that stressor at Time 2 only, but was related to general adaptation difficulty at

Table 1

Correlations Among Time 1 Variables (Above Diagonal) and Among Time 2 Variables (Below Diagonal)

Variables	1.	2.	3.	4.	5.	6.	7.	8.
1. Number of siblings		-.12	-.11	-.06	.13	.09	-.14	.20*
2. Socioeconomic status[a]	-.12		.02	-.04	-.12	-.11	-.11	.05
3. Perceived school environment	-.10	-.02		.29**	-.18*	.24**	.29**	-.28**
4. Approach coping	.00	-.03	.35**		.25**	.47**	.47**	.09
5. Avoidance coping	.16*	.00	-.16*	.31**		.08	-.09	.30**
6. Perceived control over the stressor	.14	.01	.28**	.42**	-.04		.39**	-.10
7. Coping effectiveness	-.04	.03	.46**	.33**	-.24**	.34**		-.07
8. General adaptation difficulty	.15	.10	-.27**	.05	.30**	-.09	-.20**	

Note. Analyses include only those students who participated at both Time 1 and Time 2. Due to incomplete data for some students, $\underline{N}$s vary across correlations, ranging from 157-162.

[a] Higher scores reflect lower levels of socioeconomic status.

*p<.05. **p<.01.

both time points. Finally, higher levels of perceived control over the specific transition-related stressor were positively related to coping effectiveness for that stressor at both time points.

Cross-lag correlations. Table 2 shows the correlations between the resource and criterion variables over time. The values along the diagonal show that there was moderate to high stability over three months in perceptions of the school environment, the use of coping strategies, perceived coping effectiveness, and general adaptation difficulties in junior high school. However, there was only modest

Table 2

Correlations Between the Time 1 and Time 2 Variables

	Time 1 variables					
	Resource variables				Criterion variables	
	1.	2.	3.	4.	5.	6.
Time 2 variables						
Resource variables						
1. Perceived school environment	(.63**)	.27**	-.17*	.17*	.23**	-.17*
2. Approach coping	.17*	(.57**)	.18*	.27**	.20*	.09
3. Avoidance coping	-.11	.15	(.62**)	-.05	-.17*	.19*
4. Perceived control over the stressor	.15	.31**	-.17*	(.25**)	.21**	-.05
Criterion variables						
5. Coping effectiveness	.31**	.33**	-.20**	.20*	(.48**)	-.05
6. General adaptation difficulty	-.25**	-.02	.19*	-.19*	-.14	(.67**)

Note. Due to incomplete data, Ns range from 157-162. Correlations in parentheses along the diagonal represent the stability of the variable from Time 1 to Time 2.
*p<.05. **p<.01.

stability *(r = .25)* in perceptions of control over the specific transition-related stressor.

Correlations between the resource variables at Time 1 and the criterion variables at Time 2 were generally consistent with the cross-sectional results presented above. Favorable perceptions of the school environment at Time 1 were related to higher levels of coping effectiveness for the specific transition-related stressor and to better general adaptation at Time 2. The initial use of approach strategies to cope with a transition-related stressor was related to higher levels of coping effectiveness for that stressor three months later, while the initial use of avoidance coping strategies was related to lower levels of coping effectiveness for that stressor and to poorer general adaptation three months later. In addition, higher levels of perceived control over the stressor at Time 1 were related to higher levels of coping effectiveness and better general adaptation at Time 2.

The results presented in Table 2 also point to the possibility of bidirectional effects, for example, the possibility that initial effectiveness of coping with a specific transition-related stressor and initial general adjustment to the junior high school transition influence students' use of coping stategies and their perceptions of the school environment.

Hierarchical Regressions: Relations Between the Resource and Criterion Variables

Prediction of changes in the criterion variables. We used a hierarchical regression model to analyze potential prospective effects of the resource variables on the criterion variables, and to assess whether changes over time in the resource variables were related to changes over time in the criterion variables. Two sets of regressions were computed, one predicting each criterion measure. In step one of the hierarchical procedure, the Time 1 criterion variable was entered as a predictor of the corresponding Time 2 criterion in order to control for the stability of the criterion variable. In step two, the Time 1 resource variables and perceived controllability over the specific stressor were entered. Significant findings at this step suggest that students' standing on these variables (i.e., perceptions of the school environment, approach and avoidance coping, and perceived controllability over the specific stressor) at Time 1 predicts change in the criterion variable over time. In the third step, the Time 2 resource variables were entered. Significant findings at this step suggest that changes in the resource variables over time are related to concomitant changes in the criterion variables, as significant findings represent the residual effects of the resource variables after controlling for initial levels of the resource and criterion variables (Dubow et al., 1991; Holahan & Moos, 1981).

Table 3 shows that in step one, students' ratings of how effectively they were coping with the specific transition-related stressor three weeks into the junior high school transition accounted for 23% of the variance in their ratings of coping effectiveness for that same stressor three months later. In addition, their initial general

Table 3

Hierarchical Multiple Regressions of the Time 2 Criterion Variables on the Time 1 Criterion, Time 1 Resource Variables, and Time 2 Resource Variables

	Time 2 criterion variables			
	Coping effectiveness		General adaptation difficulty	
Predictor variables	R^2	Beta	R^2	Beta
Step 1: Time 1 criterion	.23	.48**	.45	.67**
F-value (for step)		$F(1,154)=46.21**$		$F(1,159)=130.14**$
Step 2: Time 1 resource variables and				
perceived control over stressor	.08		.03	
Perceived school environment		.11		−.04
Approach coping		.18+		−.02
Avoidance coping		−.20*		.00
Perceived control over stressor		−.09		−.16+
F-value (for step)		$F(4,151)=3.13*$		$F(4,156)=1.34$
Step 3: Time 2 resource variables	.10		.07	
Perceived school environment		.19*		−.14+
Approach coping		.18*		.04
Avoidance coping		−.11		.19*
F-value (for step)		$F(3,152)=5.53**$		$F(3,157)=3.88**$

Note. Only those students with complete data for all variables were included in each analysis.

+$p<.10$. *$p<.05$. **$p<.01$.

adaptation difficulty during the transition accounted for 45% of the variance in their later adaptation difficulty.

In step two, the block of Time 1 resource variables and perceived control over the stressor accounted for an additional and significant 8% of the variance in coping effectiveness. Specifically, initial reliance on avoidance coping in response to the specific transition-stressor was related to decreased coping effectiveness for that stressor over time, while initial reliance on approach strategies was related to increased coping effectiveness. Initial level of coping strategies in response to the specific transition-related stressor and perceptions of the school environment did not account for changes in general adaptation to junior high school.

In step three, the block of Time 2 resource variables accounted for an additional and significant 10% of the variance in coping effectiveness and 7% of the variance in general adaptation difficulty. Specifically, increases over time in the use of approach strategies and increases in positive perceptions of the school environment were related to increases in ratings of coping effectiveness for the specific transition-related stressor. Increases in the use of avoidance strategies and decreases in positive perceptions of the school environment were related to increases in general adaptation difficulty during the transition.

Examination of the possible moderating role of perceptions of control over the stressor. To examine the possibility that perceived control over the specific transition-related stressor would moderate the relation between type of coping strategy used and adaptation, the above regressions were recomputed. The first two steps of the hierarchical procedure were identical to the original regressions. However, in the third step, the interaction terms of Time 1 approach coping X Time 1 perceptions of controllability and Time 1 avoidance coping X Time 1 perceptions of controllability were entered. These interaction terms failed to reach significance. Thus, initial perceptions of control over the specific transition-related stressor failed to moderate the relation between initial coping strategies and changes in the criterion variables.

Prediction of changes in the resource variables. The possibility of a reverse causal effect, that is, that initial adaptation might influence changes in resource variables over time, has been suggested (Felner et al., 1983). For example, a student's initial perceptions that he or she coped effectively with a specific transition-related stressor might influence an increase in the use of approach coping strategies as well as more favorable perceptions of the school environment. To examine this possibility, three additional hierarchical regressions were computed in which changes in the resource variables (approach and avoidance coping, and perceptions of the school environment) were predicted by initial levels of coping effectiveness and adaptational difficulty. In step one, the Time 1 resource variable was entered to predict the corresponding Time 2 resource variable. In step two, the Time 1 criterion variables were entered. This block of Time 1 criterion variables (initial levels of coping effectiveness and adaptation difficulty) failed to account for significant changes over time in approach and avoidance coping strategies or perceptions of the school environment.

DISCUSSION

Resources that influence adjustment to school transitions need to be investigated so that the process of adaptation can be better understood (Simmons, Carlton-Ford, & Blyth, 1987). The correlational findings of the present study supported the hypothesized relations: the resource variables (higher levels of approach coping and lower levels of avoidance coping, and positive perceptions of the school environment) were generally associated with positive adaptation to junior high school (both the specific outcome of one's coping efforts and general adaptation to the new junior high school). However, correlational findings limit interpretations regarding causality among variables. The strength of the present study lies in its prospective design which allows for a more adequate clarification of potential causal relations among the resource and adaptation variables (i.e., does *initial* reliance on resources influence changes over time in adaptation?). Our design also allowed us to examine whether changes over time in reliance on resources predicted concomitant changes in students' adaptation.

Coping Strategies as a Resource

Previous studies have shown prospective relations between initial coping efforts and changes in adjustment (Glyshaw, Cohen, &

Towbes, 1989; Holahan & Moos, 1986). In the present study, there were no prospective effects for coping strategies on changes in *general* adaptation to the junior high school transition. Perhaps this null finding should not be so surprising. The coping measure was stressor-specific, assessing children's coping strategies in response to the most problematic transition-related stressor they experienced since entering junior high school, while the adaptation measure was of a global nature, assessing a broad range of problems experienced in junior high school. Similarly, previous coping research has often mixed the level of analysis (e.g., situation-specific coping measures, but global outcome measures) (Compas et al., 1988; Ebata & Moos, 1989). Griffith (1992) has shown that when the outcome of a specific stressor is used as the criterion variable, coping strategies in response to that stressor account for much more variance than when a global criterion measure (e.g., state anxiety) is used.

In fact, significant prospective results *were* obtained for coping strategies as predictors of changes in students' ratings of how effectively they handled the *specific* stressor. Higher levels of approach coping and lower levels of avoidance coping in response to the most problematic transition-related stressor early in the transition, predicted improvement over time in ratings of effectiveness in coping with that stressor. These significant findings are especially noteworthy in light of the relatively strong stability in ratings of coping effectiveness, and suggest that the repertoire of coping strategies that students *initially* bring into a transition-related stressful situation influences later perceptions of how effectively they handled that stressor. A student who initially avoids the stressor may miss out on the opportunity to develop needed coping resources (e.g., building a social support network) and to learn useful ways of handling a given problem. In turn, the problem may worsen and coping efforts would increasingly be perceived as less effective. Conversely, a student who initially uses approach strategies may develop additional coping resources and be exposed to success experiences that foster perceptions of coping effectiveness. These prospective findings provide some indication of causality. Following other researchers (Dubow et al., 1991; Compas, Howell, Phares, Williams, & Giunta, 1989), we examined possible bidirectional effects. We found that early levels of adaptation *did not* influence changes over time in the use of coping strategies.

The critical aspect of resources may not simply be the *initial* levels of the resources that are brought to the situation, but also the *change* in these resources from baseline levels. In the present study, increases in the use of approach coping predicted increases in positive perceptions of coping effectiveness for the specific transition-related stressor. This is similar to other studies which suggest that changes in children's coping skills are predictive of changes in adjustment (e.g., Dubow et al., 1991). Perhaps the development of approach coping skills in response to a specific stressor creates ongoing opportunities for mutually satisfying experiences with teachers and peers, which in turn fosters perceptions that the stressor was handled effectively. In contrast, changes in avoidance coping were *not* related to changes in coping effectiveness. Perhaps as the process of coping with a specific problem continues, children pay increasingly more attention to the active strategies they use, and become less aware of their reliance on avoidant behaviors, when making judgments about how effectively they coped with the stressor.

Changes in approach coping were not related to changes in general adaptation problems. This may suggest that approach coping efforts in response to a *specific* transition-related stressor do not generalize to, or have substantial impact on, students' *general* adaptation to junior high school. However, it seems particularly noteworthy that increases over time in avoidance coping in response to the most problematic transition-related stressor *were* significantly related to increases in general adaptation problems. Following conclusions from previous research (Holahan & Moos, 1985), this may suggest that students' increasing reliance on avoidance coping strategies in response to one significant stressor is either diagnostic of, or has a substantial impact on, their more global distress during the junior high school transition. For example, increasing avoidance of a problematic stressor may lead the student to experience ongoing feelings of frustration or failure, which may generalize to other areas of school adaptation.

Perceptions of the School Environment as a Resource

There were no prospective effects for initial perceptions of the school environment in predicting changes in adaptation to the junior high school transition. It may be that students' initial perceptions of the school include both positive (e.g., opportunities to make new friends) and negative (e.g., more difficult school work) expectations. Thus, their initial perceptions may not be particularly relevant to changes in adaptation. However, as students' perceptions are modified and solidified over time, these perceptions may be more closely associated with their adjustment (Felner et al., 1983). The present study found that viewing the school environment more positively over time was related to improved adaptation. Perhaps as students perceive the school environment as more manageable and less threatening over time, their perceived self-competence improves (Nelson, 1984), in turn facilitating adaptation.

The Role of Perceptions of Controllability over the Stressor

There has been some suggestion that perceptions of controllability over a stressor may moderate the relation between coping strategies and later adaptation (Causey & Dubow, 1992; Lazarus & Folkman, 1984). For example, when a stressor is perceived to be controllable, reliance on approach coping strategies may be more predictive of positive adjustment than when the stressor is perceived to be uncontrollable. In the present study, however, initial perceptions of controllability over a specific transition-related stressor failed to moderate the relation between initial use of coping strategies and changes in adaptation. Such nonsignificant findings may in part be due to the low degree of stability over time in students' ratings of controllability over the stressor ($r = .25$). That is, because students substantially changed their perceptions of how controllable the stressor was from Time 1 to Time 2, it may be somewhat unreasonable to expect that perceptions of control assessed at Time 1 would play a significant role in the relation between initial coping efforts and later adaptation.

Limitations and Implications

Although the prospective findings of this study suggest a causal role of coping strategies in determining changes in the specific outcome of a problematic transition-related stressor, the findings cannot confirm causality (Cohen, Burt, & Bjorck, 1987; Dubow et al., 1991). To further address the issue of causality, future research could evaluate the effects of an intervention designed to vary the level of resources (e.g., coping skills) provided early in the transition to groups of students experiencing different levels of transition-related distress. Another limitation of the present study is the sole reliance on student self-report measures. For example, perhaps students' perceptions of the school environment fail to measure certain objective aspects of the school environment that might also affect adaptation (e.g., size of school, organizational structure of the administration) (Stewart, 1979). Nevertheless, the necessity of assessing students' perceptions of their environment, their coping strategies, and their adaptation has been emphasized; significant adults in the children's lives may actually underestimate the impact that stressors have on children (Colton, 1985; Moos, 1979).

This study has implications for prevention efforts to aid students undergoing the normative junior high school transition. First, it is important to assess not only *general* adaptation to junior high school, but also how students negotiate *specific* problematic stressors that they experience. The junior high school transition presents different challenges to different students; 40% identified conflict with authority stressors as the most problematic transition-related stressors, 23% identified peer stressors, 21% identified difficulties associated with the larger school, and 17% identified academic stressors. Thus, prevention programs should focus on helping students cope with a range of specific transition-related stressors. Second, the notion that the transition is an ongoing process must be recognized (Felner et al., 1983; Jason et al., 1992). We found that changes over time in the use of coping skills and perceptions of the school environment were related to changes in students' adaptation during the first semester of junior high school. Finally, interventions should train students to rely on approach coping skills, discourage the use of avoidant coping skills, and perhaps attend to environmental modifications that would improve students' perceptions of the new school (see Felner & Adan, 1988). Because the impact of the junior high school transition is sufficient enough to elicit referrals to special services for some students (Elias et al., 1985), efforts should be made to make this transition as smooth as possible.

REFERENCES

Aldwin, C. M., & Revenson, T. A. (1987). Does coping help? A reexamination of the relation between coping and mental health. *Journal of Personality and Social Psychology, 53*, 337-348.

Blyth, D. A., Simmons, R. G., & Bush, D. (1978). The transition into early adolescence: A longitudinal comparison of youth in two educational contexts. *Sociology of Education, 51*, 149-162.

Blyth, D. A., Simmons, R. G., & Carlton-Ford, S. (1983). The adjustment of early adolescents to school transitions. *Journal of Early Adolescence, 3*, 105-120.

Causey, D. L., & Dubow, E. F. (1992). Development of a self-report coping measure for elementary school children. *Journal of Clinical Child Psychology, 21*, 47-59.

Cohen, L. H., Burt, C. E., & Bjorck, J. P. (1987). Life stress and adjustment: Effects of life events experienced by young adolescents and their parents. *Developmental Psychology, 23*, 583-592.

Colton, J. A. (1985). Childhood stress: Perceptions of children and professionals. *Journal of Psychopathology and Behavioral Assessment, 7*, 155-173.

Compas, B. E. (1987). Coping with stress during childhood and adolescence. *Psychological Bulletin, 101*, 393-403.

Compas, B. E., Howell, D. C., Phares, V., Williams, R. A., & Giunta, C. T. (1989). Risk factors for emotional/behavioral problems in young adolescents: A prospective analysis of adolescent and parental stress and symptoms. *Journal of Consulting and Clinical Psychology, 57*, 732-740.

Compas, B. E., Malcarne, V. L., & Fondacaro, K. M. (1988). Coping with stressful events in older children and young adolescents. *Journal of Consulting and Clinical Psychology, 56*, 405-411.

Crockett, L. J., Petersen, A. C., Graber, J. A., Schulenberg, J. E., & Ebata, A. (1989). School transitions and adjustment during early adolescence. *Journal of Early Adolescence, 9*, 181-210.

Dubow, E. F., Tisak, J. Causey, D., Hryshko, A., & Reid, G. (1991). A two-year longitudinal study of stressful life events, social support, and social problem-solving skills: Contributions to children's behavioral and academic adjustment. *Child Development, 62*, 583-599.

Ebata, A. T., & Moos, R. H. (1989, April). *Coping and adjustment in distressed and healthy adolescents.* Paper presented at the meeting of the Society for Research in Child Development, Kansas City, MO.

Elias, M. J., Gara, M., & Ubriaco, M. (1985). Sources of stress and support in children's transition to middle school: An empirical analysis. *Journal of Clinical Child Psychology, 14*, 112-118.

Elias, M. J., Gara, M., Ubriaco, M., Rothbaum, P. A., Clabby, J. F., & Schuyler, T. (1986). Impact of a preventive social problem solving intervention on children's coping with middle school stressors. *American Journal of Community Psychology, 14*, 259-275.

Elias, M. J., Ubriaco, M., Reese, A. M., Gara, M. A., Rothbaum, P. A., & Haviland, M. (1992). A measure of adaptation to problematic academic and interpersonal tasks of middle school. *Journal of School Psychology, 30*, 41-57.

Epstein, J. L., & McPartland, J. M. (1976). The concept and measurement of the quality of school life. *American Educational Research Journal, 13*, 15-30.

Felner, R. D., & Adan, A. M. (1988). The school transitional environment project: An ecological intervention and evaluation. In R. H. Price, E. L. Cowen, R. P. Lorion, & J. R. McKay (Eds.), *Fourteen ounces of prevention: A casebook for practitioners* (pp. 111-122). Washington, D. C.: American Psychological Association.

Felner, R. D., Farber, S. S., & Primavera, J. (1983). Transitions and stressful events: A model for primary prevention. In R. D. Felner, L. A. Jason, J. N. Moritsugu, & S. S. Farber (Eds.), *Preventive psychology: Theory, research, and practice* (pp. 199-215). NY: Pergamon.

Felner, R. D., Primavera, J., & Cauce, A. M. (1981). The impact of school transitions: A focus for preventive efforts. *American Journal of Community Psychology, 9*, 449-459.

Glyshaw, K., Cohen, L. H., & Towbes, L. C. (1989). Coping strategies and psychological distress: Prospective analyses of early and middle adolescents. *American Journal of Community Psychology, 17*, 607-624.

Griffith, M. A. (1992). *Developmental differences in adolescent coping with family, school, and peer stressors.* Unpublished doctoral dissertation, Bowling Green State University, Bowling Green, OH.

Hirsch, B.J., & DuBois, D.L. (1992). The relation of peer support and psychological symptomatology during the transition to junior high school: A two-year longitudinal analysis. *American Journal of Community Psychology, 20*, 333-347.

Hirsch, B. J., & Rapkin, B. D. (1987). The transition to junior high school: A longitudinal study of self-esteem, psychological symptomatology, school life, and social support. *Child Development, 58*, 1235-1243.

Holahan, C. J., & Moos, R. H. (1981). Social support and psychological distress: A longitudinal analysis. *Journal of Abnormal Psychology, 90*, 365-370.

Holahan, C. J., & Moos, R. H. (1985). Life stress and health: Personality, coping, and family support in stress resistance. *Journal of Personality and Social Psychology, 49*, 739-747.

Holahan, C. J., & Moos, R. H. (1986). Personality, coping, and family resources in stress resistance: A longitudinal analysis. *Journal of Personality and Social Psychology, 51*, 389-395.

Horwitz, R. A. (1979). Effects of the "open classroom." In H. J. Walberg (Ed.), *Educational environments and effects: Evaluation, policy, and productivity* (pp. 275-292). CA: McCutchan.

Jason, L. A., Weine, A. M., Johnson, J. H., Warren-Sohlberg, L., Filippelli, L. A., Turner, E. Y., & Lardon, C. (1992). *Helping transfer students: Strategies for educational and school readjustment.* San Francisco: Jossey-Bass.

Lazarus, R. S., & Folkman, S. (1984). *Stress, appraisal, and coping.* New York: Springer.

Lunenburg, F. C., & Schmidt, L. J. (1989). Pupil control ideology, pupil control behavior, and the quality of school life. *Journal of Research and Development in Education, 22,* 36-44.

Miller, D. C. (1977). *Handbook of research design and social measurement.* NY: David McKay Company, Inc.

Moos, R. H. (1979). *Evaluating educational environments.* San Francisco: Jossey-Bass.

Moos, R. H., & Moos, B. S. (1978). Classroom social climate and student absences and grades. *Journal of Educational Psychology, 70,* 263-269.

Nelson, G. (1984). The relationship between dimensions of classroom and family environments and the self-concept, satisfaction, and achievement of grade 7 and 8 students. *Journal of Community Psychology, 12,* 276-287.

Nottleman, E. D. (1987). Competence and self-esteem during the transition from childhood to adolescence. *Developmental Psychology, 23,* 441-450.

Pargament, K. I., Ensing, D. S., Falgout, K., Olsen, H., Reilly, B., VanHaitsma, K., & Warren, R. (1990). God help me: Religious coping efforts as predictors of the outcomes to significant negative life events. *American Journal of Community Psychology, 18,* 793-824.

Patterson, J. M., & McCubbin, H. I. (1987). Adolescent coping style and behaviors: Conceptualization and measurement. *Journal of Adolescence, 10,* 163-186.

Petersen, A. C., & Hamburg, B. A. (1986). Adolescence: A developmental approach to problems and psychopathology. *Behavior Therapy, 17,* 480-499.

Roth, S., & Cohen, L. J. (1986). Approach, avoidance, and coping with stress. *American Psychologist, 41,* 813-819.

Simmons, R. G., Carlton-Ford, S. L., & Blyth, D. A. (1987). Predicting how a child will cope with the transition to junior high school. In R. M. Lerner, & T. T. Foch (Eds.), *Biological-psychosocial interactions in early adolescence* (pp. 325-375). Hillsdale, NJ: Erlbaum.

Stewart, D. (1979). A critique of school climate: What it is, how it can be improved, and some general recommendations. *The Journal of Educational Administration, 17,* 148-159.

Trajectory Analysis of the Transition to Junior High School: Implications for Prevention and Policy

Barton J. Hirsch

Northwestern University

David L. DuBois

University of Missouri

Ann B. Brownell

Northwestern University

SUMMARY. There are important limitations to analysis of variance (ANOVA) as a method for longitudinal prevention research. We consider in particular the limitations of ANOVA for identifying different courses of adjustment during life transitions and the proportion of the population who manifest each course. To complement traditional ANOVA, we argue for the use of cluster analytic techniques to uncover differences in longitudinal trajectory. This method is illustrated with two-year longitudinal data on self-esteem during the transition from elementary school to junior high school. Four contrasting trajectories are identified: Consistently High (35%), Chronically Low (13%), Steeply Declining (21%), and Small Increase (31%).

[Haworth co-indexing entry note]: "Trajectory Analysis of the Transition to Junior High School: Implications for Prevention and Policy." Hirsch, Barton J., David L. DuBois, and Ann B. Brownell. Co-published simultaneously in *Prevention in Human Services* (The Haworth Press, Inc.) Vol. 10, No. 2, 1993, pp. 83-101; and: *Prevention and School Transitions* (ed: Leonard A. Jason, Karen E. Danner, and Karen S. Kurasaki) The Haworth Press, Inc., 1993, pp. 83-101. Multiple copies of this article/chapter may be purchased from The Haworth Document Delivery Center. Call 1-800-3-HAWORTH (1-800-342-9678) between 9:00 - 5:00 (EST) and ask for DOCUMENT DELIVERY CENTER.

© 1993 by The Haworth Press, Inc. All rights reserved.

The identification of the Steeply Declining trajectory is considered especially important for prevention. The trajectory approach yields distinctive information for identifying and understanding at-risk groups, for informing the design of prevention and policy options, and for increasing the specificity of evaluation efforts. Though not without limitations, the results are considered promising enough to warrant use of this approach for studying a wide array of outcomes and life transitions.

Longitudinal research is critical to formulating prevention and policy options. It is only with longitudinal research that we can understand the course of problems to prevent and adaptive processes to enhance. Similarly, longitudinal data play an important role in evaluating the effectiveness of programs and services. Given this importance, there is a need to attend more carefully to the limitations of existing methods of longitudinal analyses and to consider the potential substantive contributions of alternative statistical approaches. In this paper we explore the potential benefits of using clustering procedures to identify contrasting longitudinal trajectories. Three questions guide this inquiry. First, does a trajectory approach increase our understanding of at-risk groups? Second, can this approach inform the design of prevention and policy options? Third, is this approach likely to strengthen evaluation efforts? Our exploration is based on a two-year longitudinal analysis of self-esteem trajectories during the transition from elementary school to junior high school.

We begin by considering some limitations of analysis of variance (ANOVA) as a method for longitudinal research. Although a variety of multivariate procedures have been developed to address causal relations over time (especially LISREL), ANOVA remains the principal analytic method for studying the direction of change in a variable over time. If we want to know whether school grades, mental health, family support, and so forth, have gone significantly up or down, we typically employ ANOVA to find out. ANOVA is concerned with changes in the sample mean over time (i.e., average change across all subjects). It identifies the modal trajectory. Unfortunately, such findings can obscure subgroup differences that are important for prevention. For example, let us assume that using ANOVA we find no significant change in mental health over the course of a life transition. We do not know from ANOVA whether this is because there was no fluctuation in mental health, there was a balancing of respondents who gained slightly with those who declined slightly, or there was a balancing of respondents who gained considerably with those who declined considerably. Even in the absence of a significant average decline, preventive intervention might be indicated if a substantial number of individuals suffered a serious decline in mental health.

Similar problems arise for other possible results. For example, a significant but slight average decline in mental health only begins to tell the story. The type of preventive intervention to be designed might differ considerably depending on whether there was a slight decline among all respondents versus a substantial decline among one group coupled with little change in others.

Some increase in useful information is obtained by looking at how factors such as gender or race interact with time. However, the limitations just discussed remain. For example, let us assume that the mental health of girls is found to decline significantly more over the transition than that of boys (an important issue in studying school transitions in adolescence). We still need to know whether we are talking about a slight general decline among girls or whether instead there are subgroups of girls with markedly different trajectories, including some whose mental health has deteriorated substantially. In the latter case, we would want to know how many girls suffered such a decline, the factors associated with the decline, the implications of such a severe decline on other areas of functioning, and so on.

In this paper we focus on the transition to junior high school to examine the potential benefits of analyses that focus on identifying different longitudinal trajectories. This particular life transition is unusually well suited for this task. Students typically go from smaller, neighborhood-based schools to larger, more geographically distant and often less personal schools. But this is more than just a school change. There are also profound changes in physical, social, and personal development which have either begun or are on the near horizon. The school transition, in short, heralds the end of childhood and the beginning of adolescence. Although *sturm und drang* (storm and stress) might not characterize adolescence in general, if there were upheaval, it might well occur at this time.

Initial research on the transition to junior high school suggested that this period was a time of heightened risk for the emotional well-being of girls. In a landmark study conducted in the 1970s, white girls who went from elementary to junior high were found to have lower self-esteem than girls who stayed in the same school (K-8), with the self-esteem effects lasting into high school (Simmons & Blyth, 1987, is the most comprehensive report). Findings on self-esteem change from subsequent longitudinal studies have been mixed (Abramowitz, Petersen & Schulenberg, 1984; Berndt & Hawkins, 1988; Crockett, Petersen, Graber, Schulenberg, & Ebata, 1989; Hirsch & Rapkin, 1987; McCarthy & Hoge, 1982; Nottleman, 1987; Wigfield, Eccles, MacIver, Reuman & Midgley, 1991). Although it might be tempting to conclude from these mixed results that there is little change in self-esteem at this time, our previous discussion reminds us that there may well be substantial subgroups of adolescents whose self-esteem changes substantially at this time. These analyses provide few clues. Given the developmental and ecological significance of this transition, it seemed important to discover whether different trajectories could be identified and then to consider the implications of such findings for prevention and policy.

IDENTIFICATION OF CONTRASTING SELF-ESTEEM TRAJECTORIES

Our study involved 128 adolescents who entered a single junior high school from six feeder elementary schools. Longitudinal data were obtained on four occasions over a two-year period: end of 6th grade, in elementary school (Time 1); middle of 7th grade, in junior high school (Time 2); end of 7th grade (Time 3); and end of 8th grade (Time 4). We focused on global self-esteem as the criterion variable given its salience in prior developmental research and its intrinsic importance as a summary measure of overall psychological well-being. We emphasize, however, that we are using self-esteem trajectories in this paper primarily to *illustrate* the potential benefits of a trajectory analysis. Readers with primary interests in other substantive domains (e.g., school grades, psychological symptoms, social support, etc.) are encouraged to think of possible trajectories in those areas.

Rosenberg's (1965) widely used 10-item scale was employed to tap overall self-esteem. Self-report measures at all four assessments were obtained on self-esteem, peer social support, quality of school life, and psychological symptomatology. Problem behaviors and competence behaviors were assessed via teacher ratings at Time 1 only. A measure of academic competence utilizing a standard test battery was obtained at Time 1 only (further details about the measures and procedures are reported in Hirsch & Rapkin, 1987, and Hirsch & DuBois, 1991).

A *k*-means clustering algorithm (Hartigan, 1975) was employed to differentiate subgroups of adolescents who had contrasting self-esteem trajectories across the four times of measurement. This procedure seeks to minimize within-cluster variance on criterion variables (i.e., self-esteem scores at Time 1, Time 2, Time 3, and Time 4), while maximizing differences between clusters. There is no single clustering procedure which has achieved universal acceptance; in general, the *k*-means approach seems to meet with approval from a variety of statistical experts. For prevention purposes, *k*-means has the advantage, in contrast to some other procedures, of being sensitive to extreme profiles and thus does not mask atypical patterns in order to achieve similarly sized groups.

As in determining the number of factors to retain in factor analysis, there are no universally agreed upon guidelines for deciding how many clusters to extract. In our research we were guided by conceptual and applied considerations, as well as by an empirical decision rule that Hartigan (1975) has suggested for determining the number of clusters to retain when applying the *k*-means algorithm. When applying Hartigan's decision rule to our sample, we found strong empirical justification for choosing a solution with as many as 4 clusters, but only marginal support for moving to a 5- or 6-cluster solution. We chose the 4-cluster solution over the 5- and 6-cluster solutions because these more refined partitions of the sample did not produce any trajectories that were sufficiently different substantively from those already contained in the 4-cluster solution, and because the 5- and 6-cluster solutions each included two clusters with 10 or fewer students and thus presented practical concerns for further analyses.

The 4-cluster solution that emerged is presented in Figure 1. Cluster 1 is the Consistently High group. The 45 students (35%) in this cluster invariably reported higher self-esteem than adolescents in each of the other three clusters. The self-esteem of students in Cluster 2 was Chronically Low. These 16 students (13%) reported the lowest self-esteem of any cluster at each point in time. Cluster 3 is the Steep Decline group. These 27 students (21%) reported a high level of self-esteem at Time 1 (6th grade). However, their self-esteem declined steadily and severely after entering junior high school. By the end of 8th grade (Time 4), the self-esteem of the Steep Decline group was not significantly different from the Chronically Low group. Finally, Cluster 4, the Small Increase group, contained 40 adolescents (31%) who reported a modest net increase in self-esteem.

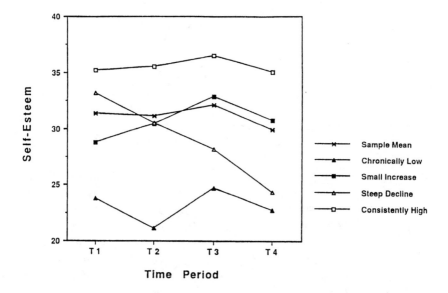

Figure 1. Self-esteem trajectories during the transition to junior high school.

Source: Hirsch & DuBois (1991)

We then turned to consider how students in these four self-esteem trajectories differed on variables other than self-esteem. The results of between-group analyses at Time 1 are summarized below.

Students in the Consistently High self-esteem trajectory were doing quite well across all of the other domains that we assessed. They had the highest scores on peer support, quality of school life, and academic competence. They reported the fewest psychological symptoms of any group.

The Chronically Low self-esteem group was not doing well in most other areas. They reported little satisfaction with school and the poorest level of peer social support. Their academic competence was average on national norms, though somewhat lower (nonsignificantly) than the other three clusters. Adolescents in this cluster reported the highest level of psychological symptomatology, which worsened over the course of this study. For example, they moved from the 85th percentile at Time 1 to the 94th percentile at Time 4 on norms for depressive symptoms.

The Small Increase group was closest to the sample mean on self-esteem. They tended to be in the mid-range on most of the other variables as well.

Students in the Steeply Declining self-esteem trajectory scored high on measures of peer social support and academic competence. Their scores in these domains were not significantly different from the Consistently High group. The only area in which the Steeply Declining group showed signs of possible difficulty was in their level of psychological symptoms. This was the one domain where their scores at Time 1 differed significantly from the Consistently High group. In comparison to the latter group, the Steeply Declining group reported more somatic, obsessive-compulsive, and depressive symptoms. Steep Declining students reported fewer symptoms in these areas at Time 1 than Chronically Low students. The Steep Decliners were at the 60th percentile for depressive symptoms at Time 1 (by Time 4 their scores had risen to the 80th percentile).

In order to explore in more detail how the three symptom indices noted above can differentiate between the Steep Decline and Consistently High trajectories, we conducted a discriminant function analysis on the two groups using the Time 1 scores on those symptom variables as predictors. Of particular interest to us was the utility of these symptom variables in identifying students in the Steep Decline group at Time 1. The findings of the discriminant analysis revealed one significant function (canonical $R = .48$) in which all three symptom indices had high loadings (standardized loadings of .35 or greater). This function correctly classified 73.5% of the students into the Consistently High and Steep Decline groups. However, the function was much better at correctly classifying students in the Consistently High group (92.9% correctly classified) in comparison to students in the Steep Decline group (42.3% correctly classified). These findings suggest that using symptom scores alone would be of only modest help in identifying students who may be at-risk for developing self-esteem problems during the school transition despite reporting relatively high initial levels.

In addition to the analyses of cluster differences on Time 1 variables, we tested for longitudinal differences between self-esteem clusters on patterns of change in peer support and quality of school life across the four time points of the study. These repeated-measures ANOVA revealed a significant difference between clusters in their pattern of change on the peer support measure over time. As can be seen in Table 1, the Steep Decline group reported declining levels of peer support. In contrast, each of the other three groups either increased or had little net change. No significant Cluster by Time interactions were found on our measures of the quality of school life.

IMPLICATIONS FOR PREVENTION AND POLICY

Given these findings, let us consider the distinctive contributions that the trajectory approach might yield for prevention and policy concerns. We address the three questions posed at the beginning of the paper.

Does a Trajectory Approach Increase Our Understanding of At-Risk Groups?

Any response must be predicated on an understanding of "risk." In this paper, we have focused on self-esteem due to our prior work

Table 1
Peer Support Trends for the Self-Esteem Trajectories[a]

Groups	Time 1	Time 2	Time 3	Time 4
Consistently High				
M	10.06	10.49	10.80	10.80
SD	2.01	1.52	1.46	1.33
Chronically Low				
M	7.31	7.55	8.23	8.22
SD	3.10	2.57	2.95	2.90
Steep Decline				
M	10.02	9.82	9.81	9.22
SD	1.81	1.43	1.84	3.09
Small Increase				
M	9.52	10.03	10.30	9.80
SD	2.32	1.97	1.49	1.71

[a]Ns: consistently high = 44; chronically low = 16; steep decline = 27; small increase = 40.

Source: Hirsch & DuBois (1991)

on delineating longitudinal trajectories in this domain. It thus makes the most sense, for purposes of illustration, to focus on risk for self-esteem decline. It is possible that a group not at risk for self-esteem decline may be at risk for other negative outcomes (e.g., school failure), but we do not have the data to consider such possibilities extensively.

The research findings focus our attention on adolescents in the Steeply Declining group. Findings from the cluster analysis tell us how many adolescents are at risk and the seriousness of their decline in self-esteem. In this particular instance, 21% of students in the sample (the Steeply Declining group) suffered a decline in self-esteem that should be considered serious. This information is quite different from the results of an ANOVA. For example, in an earlier publication based on data from the first three time points, we reported no change in self-esteem from Time 1 to Time 2, followed by a *rise* in self-esteem from Time 2 to Time 3 (Hirsch & Rapkin, 1987). During this Time 1 to Time 3 period, adolescents in the Steeply Declining trajectory were already reporting a substantial drop in their self-esteem. There is no way to tell from the ANOVA how many adolescents reported a decline in self-esteem, nor the extent of their decline. Indeed, in standard practice we would be unlikely to even *think about* such a possibility; instead, we would be likely to focus entirely on the rise in self-esteem scores. That was exactly the nature of our discussion in the earlier article.

Our identification of the Steeply Declining trajectory bears comparison with results from a study of psychological adjustment over an 8-year period beginning with the first year of junior high school (Offer and Offer, 1975). This study found an identical proportion of adolescents who displayed a pattern of increased psychological disturbance. Confidence in our finding is increased given that this earlier study employed different sample selection methods, a broader assessment procedure involving multiple data sources, and different statistical methods.

Whereas parts of our approach (and some findings) are similar to those of Offer and Offer (1975) in examining change over time, we differ from the approach utilized by Simmons and Blyth (1987). The latter study was concerned with self-esteem changes during the transition to junior high school, but focused only on the *amount* of self-esteem gain or loss, without attending to the *absolute level* of self-esteem. For preventive and policy purposes, it seems critical to know, for example, whether the decline in self-esteem is severe enough to seriously consider intervention.

In this study, the decline from initial self-esteem was not only steep and continuous, but the final level of self-esteem reported was quite low. By the end of 8th grade (Time 4), the self-esteem of the Steep Decliners was slightly below the scale midpoint. Although no definite norms are available for interpreting scores on the Rosenberg self-esteem instrument that we used, most community samples of junior high school-age youth, including our own, have reported an average level of self-esteem that is approximately a full standard deviation above the scale midpoint on this and on other similar measures of self-esteem (e.g., McCarthy & Hoge, 1982; Harter,

1988). Thus, the level of self-esteem eventually reported by students in this trajectory appears to be substantially lower than that of most young adolescents. The self-esteem decline was also accompanied by a notable increase in depressive symptoms so that by the final assessment they fell within what could be considered an at-risk range (80th percentile). We further specified that the number of adolescents who demonstrated such a trajectory was a rather substantial subgroup of the school.

Although we were successful in identifying a group that might well merit preventive intervention, we were less successful in identifying those adolescents prior to the school transition. The longitudinal analyses were also of limited usefulness in understanding the process(es) which underlie the self-esteem change of the Steeply Declining group. This trajectory was the only one to demonstrate a significant decline in peer support scores over time. However the sequencing of changes for support and self-esteem left the direction of causality unclear. In particular, whereas most of the decline in support for the Steeply Declining group occurred between Time 3 and Time 4, these students had already demonstrated a decline in self-esteem from Time 1 to Time 2 and from Time 2 to Time 3. We discuss the reciprocal relation of peer support and psychological adjustment more extensively in Hirsch and DuBois (1992).

This research does highlight the need to understand the processes which underlie such a marked decline in self-esteem. It is possible that the factors which lead to a severe decline in self-esteem may be different than those which affect self-esteem for the sample as a whole. In some respects, identifying the need to understand such a decline process is as important of a contribution as any of our more specific findings.

The other trajectory that is of interest for this discussion is the Chronically Low cluster. The longitudinal analyses suggest that the low self-esteem of these adolescents is a chronic problem and not one that has arisen during the school transition or upon exposure to the junior high school environment. It is possible that some of the Chronically Low students may have moved from merely having low self-esteem and high symptoms to having sufficient symptomatology to warrant a clinical diagnosis. In that sense, they may be a group at risk for clinical levels of disturbance; however, we are unable to address this question with this kind of self-report data. This group may also be at risk for a variety of other outcomes (e.g., school failure). Thus, although the Chronically Low trajectory does not appear relevant to prevention of self-esteem decline, it will remain of interest to policy makers.

Do Trajectory Data Inform the Design of Prevention and Policy Options?

The discussion of prevention efforts will focus on the Steeply Declining group. We then consider the implications of these findings for other policy options.

We know that the self-esteem scores for the Steeply Declining adolescents suffer a serious drop. The broadest question in designing interventions is whether a strong intervention is required or whether a relatively weak one will suffice. In this instance, the nature of the decline is so steep and continuous that strong prevention efforts are necessary. This effectively eliminates weaker interventions that involve only efforts to orient students to a new school.

Orientation programs have been one of the most frequently reported prevention interventions at times of school transition (Cornille, Bayer, & Smyth, 1983). The underlying assumption of these programs appears to be that the most problematic aspect of school transition is the anxiety produced by lack of awareness of what attending the new school will entail. Interventions, which commonly include school tours, information sessions, and peer buddy assignments, are generally implemented during the last few weeks of elementary school, the intervening summer, or the first few weeks of junior high school. The effectiveness of these programs (for any school transition, not just the junior high transition) is often not evaluated (Jason et al., 1992). Some data suggest that these programs by themselves do not result in significant decreases in anxiety or stronger peer ties, as measured by sociometric ratings (Jason & Bogat, 1983).

Given the nature of the decline we have documented for the Steeply Declining group, it is difficult to imagine how such a limited intervention could effectively prevent this profound of a decline. Unfortunately, our analysis did not reveal much about the nature of the decline process, but whatever is producing such a substantial decline in self-esteem must be fairly powerful. Orientation programs may have some value in facilitating social support or competence in dealing with the new school environment. Nevertheless, we have difficulty constructing a plausible account that would have such a powerful impact for orientation programs on support, school competence, or any other adaptive resource.

Our data more generally calls into question the potential effectiveness of interventions that seek to facilitate adjustment to school transition by increasing levels of peer social support. Such support may be less relevant to preventing decline in self-esteem than might previously have been thought. Scores on peer social support in 6th grade differentiated only the Chronically Low group from the other three groups. Ratings of peer support did not differentiate the Steeply Declining group from either the Consistently High group or the Small Increase group. This suggests that initial high levels of support have limited ability to sustain global self-esteem over time. Although the absence of some minimal level of peer support may contribute to the impoverishment of self-esteem, support above this minimal threshold may have relatively little impact on self-esteem (see also Hirsch & DuBois, 1992).

We wish that we could go beyond identifying limitations in existing interventions to suggest what should be included in prevention efforts for Steep Decliners. Based on our data we can only suggest the need for a strong intervention; we do not have findings which indicate the need for any specific intervention component. Unfortunately, we were unable to include an assessment of factors such as family life or problem-solving ability, either of which could provide the basis for strong interventions.[1] We should also note that while we have expressed skepticism about the value of pure orientation programs for preventing severe declines, it might be valuable to include an orientation intervention as a component of a broader strategy that might include, for example, ongoing academic tutoring (Jason et al., 1992) or other intensive, longer lasting training or services.

On a more speculative level, we might consider the hypothesis that the Steeply Declining group suffers most from the alleged developmental mismatch between the needs of early adolescents and the structure of the traditional junior high school (e.g., Eccles et al.,

1993; Epstein & MacIver, 1990; Lipsitz, 1977). In comparison to elementary school, students in junior high reported less opportunity for classroom input, fewer opportunities for cooperative peer interaction, and teachers who were less caring, friendly, and supportive. This situation contrasts markedly with the developmental needs of early adolescents. As adolescents move toward greater independence, the school environment ought to provide more rather than fewer opportunities for input. Fewer settings for cooperative interaction may constrain the development of peer friendships. As adolescents seek increased distance from their parents, they need to develop strong ties to nonfamily adults, but it will be difficult for teachers to assume this role if they are seen as less caring. These considerations suggest that fundamental change in the structure of the school may be indicated for the modal adolescent and especially for adolescents in the Steeply Declining trajectory.

The principal policy option for restructuring schools for the middle grades is the creation of middle schools. Middle schools were created as an alternative to the junior high school. In theory (though often not in practice), middle schools include interdisciplinary instructional teams, correlated instruction across subject areas, more varied use of group formats, more flexible time periods, greater stability of peer groups across classes, and increased assumption of counseling functions by teachers (see Cuban, 1992, for a good historical and critical review). In terms of a need for a strong intervention, the middle school would certainly appear to qualify. Middle schools are designed to restructure the school environment in order to increase teacher and peer support and to provide increased opportunities for autonomy and positive feedback. In addition, teacher team meetings can be used as an early warning system for detecting student problems and developing coordinated response strategies. Do these trajectory analyses, though clearly not designed to address the broader middle school option, provide any relevant data? Let us look at our results on quality of school life and peer social support, as both of these variables were obtained in 7th and 8th grade. The setting of our research was a single school which was organized as a junior high school (an obvious research design limitation for this issue).

In our initial examination of changes in the self-reported quality of school life (Hirsch & Rapkin, 1987), we found a profound drop in each of the three scales, involving satisfaction with school, commitment to classwork, and reactions to teachers (F values for elementary school vs. junior high time effects ranged from 57 to 144). Further analyses revealed that scores on satisfaction and reaction to teachers stabilized, at low levels, between Time 3 and Time 4. There was a positive increase in reaction to teachers during this latter time period, although scores still remained substantially depressed as compared to elementary school levels. We did not find a significant Cluster by Time difference on these scores, suggesting that regardless of self-esteem trajectory, students perceived substantial inadequacies and that major reforms need not be predicated solely on the needs of a small minority. This finding may also be of political value in promoting change in that it is in the interest of better functioning students as much as any other group. Middle school may engender more support as a "universal" prescription than if targeted only at problem adolescents (however defined).

There was no overall change in peer social support among our sample. However, as previously discussed, adolescents in the Steeply Declining trajectory were the only ones to report a decline in peer support over this time; the other clusters were essentially unchanged. As the middle school, or conceptually related interventions (e.g., Felner, Ginter, & Primavera, 1982), are designed in part to increase levels of peer support, this could be a useful intervention for the Steeply Declining group. However, it is unclear to what extent the middle school organizational structure will actually lead to enhanced peer social support. Moreover, even if such effects do occur, our prior discussion suggests that the adaptive impact of peer support during this period may be more circumscribed than previously considered.

What would be most useful would be to directly compare trajectories in junior high and middle schools, something we were unable to do. These and other evaluation issues raised by a trajectory approach are considered next.

Is a Trajectory Approach Likely to Strengthen Evaluation Research?

If a trajectory approach is to make distinctive contributions to evaluation research, it will be because it points to the impact of interventions on distinct subgroups. There are two principal trajectory outcomes that are of interest. First, does the intervention change the slope of the trajectory? Second, does the intervention increase or decrease the number (proportion) of youth who manifest the trajectory? Let us consider these issues as they would apply to each of the trajectories that we identified in our research.

Presumably, a primary objective of any preventive intervention that is focused on facilitating adjustment to a school transition would be to effect desirable changes in either the slope of the Steeply Declining trajectory or the number of youth who exhibit this type of trajectory. An intervention could affect the *slope* of the Steeply Declining trajectory in several ways. Instead of a steep decline, there may be only a moderate or slight decline. Alternatively, it may be that a sharp decline levels out quickly or there may even be a rebound after an initial decline. The precise alternative would depend on a greater understanding of the decline process and how the intervention is designed to address the underlying factors. Another type of positive outcome would be to reduce the *number* (proportion) of adolescents who manifest a declining trajectory. This outcome involves reducing the number of adolescents with either a severely declining trajectory or one of the modified declining trajectories just described. These kind of data would address the specific aims of a preventive intervention much more directly than would results from the more typical ANOVA.

Change in trajectory slope and number of adolescents in the trajectory are also relevant to evaluating the effectiveness of programs that address students whose self-esteem might otherwise be Chronically Low. Here we would hope to see either a rise in self-esteem scores or fewer adolescents who manifest this trajectory.

In designing an intervention to strengthen at-risk or problem adolescents, we do not wish to negatively impact other adolescents. Fear of such unintended consequences can be a factor leading school staff or parents to oppose change efforts. Therefore it is important to address these concerns directly; trajectory analysis is well suited to this objective. For the Consistently High group, we would not want the intervention to result in a trajectory in which self-esteem declined from prior high levels. Nor would we want to see fewer adolescents who reported Consistently High self-esteem.

On the other hand, a successful intervention might increase the number of adolescents with a Consistently High profile. Similarly, with the Small Increase group, our concern would be whether the intervention had either a negative impact (less of an increase in slope) or a positive one (rise in self-esteem gains).

Given that the trajectory approach has not yet been applied to evaluation research in these ways, the methodological and statistical details of how this would be accomplished are not entirely clear. One important issue relates to how cluster analysis or alternative procedures for identifying contrasting trajectories would be implemented within the context of using an experimental or quasi-experimental design to evaluate program effectiveness. One possible approach would be to conduct separate cluster analyses for control and intervention groups. Using this approach, one could then compare and contrast the trajectories that are identified for each group. In doing so it would also be important to consider the numbers (proportion) of adolescents who manifest various types of trajectories in each group. However, because there would not necessarily be a one-to-one correspondence between the trajectories that are identified for control and intervention groups, it might not be possible to make direct comparisons between groups in the number of adolescents who manifest various types of trajectories. An alternative procedure that would address this concern would be to perform a single cluster analysis on the entire sample and then test for differences in the numbers (proportion) of intervention and control group students who manifest each type of trajectory. However, this approach would have the limitation of potentially obscuring trajectories that are associated primarily with only the intervention or control group. Although neither of the above approaches is without possible limitations, we suspect that the statistical and methodological issues could be resolved satisfactorily if there is enough interest in the substantive questions that can be addressed using trajectory analysis as an aid in evaluation research.

CONCLUSION

We have presented a method for conducting longitudinal trajectory analyses and illustrated its use with self-esteem data over the transition from elementary school to junior high school. These analyses provided distinctive and useful information for identifying and understanding at-risk groups, for informing the design of prevention and policy options, and for increasing the specificity of evaluation efforts. Nonetheless, there were limitations to the findings, particularly with respect to processes underlying the severe decline in self-esteem of one trajectory. Whether this was a limitation of this study only or instead a weakness in the approach is unclear. We consider the results promising enough to warrant utilization of this method of analysis for studying a wide array of other outcomes and life transitions. Trajectory analyses should not replace other more traditional analytic strategies but should instead be employed to complement them and increase our ability to utilize findings from longitudinal research.

NOTE

1. We had originally included an assessment of the family social environment in our study. However, objections to parts of this material by one teacher at the very last minute initiated a series of events which led to our removing all family questions from the research.

REFERENCES

Abramowitz, R. H., Petersen, A. C., & Schulenberg, J. E. (1984). Changes in self-image during early adolescence. In D. Offer, E. Ostrov, & K. Howard (Eds.), *Patterns of adolescent self-image* (pp. 19-28). San Francisco, CA: Jossey-Bass.

Berndt, T. J., & Hawkins, J. A. (1988). *The contribution of supportive friendships to adjustment after the transition to junior high school.* Unpublished manuscript. W. Lafayette, IN: Purdue University.

Cornille, T. A., Bayer, A. E., & Smyth, C. K. (1983). Schools and newcomers: A national survey of innovative programs. *Personnel and Guidance Journal, 62,* 229-236.

Crockett, L. J., Petersen, A. C., Graber, J. A., Schulenberg, J. E., Ebata, A. (1989). School transitions and adjustment during early adolescence. *Journal of Early Adolescence, 9,* 181-210.

Cuban, L. (1992). What happens to reforms that last? The case of the junior high school. *American Educational Research Journal, 29,* 227-251.

Eccles, J., Midgley, C., Wigfield, A., Buchanan, C., Reuman, D., Flanagan, C., & MacIver, D. (1993). Development during adolescence: The impact of stage-environment fit on young adolescents' experiences in schools and in family. *American Psychologist, 48*, 90-101.

Epstein, J. L. & MacIver, D. J. (1990). Education in the middle grades: Overview of a national survey of practices and trends. (Rep. No. 45). Baltimore, MD: Johns Hopkins University Center for Research on Elementary and Middle Schools.

Felner, R. D., Ginter, M., & Primavera, J. (1982). Primary prevention during school transitions: Social support and environmental structure. *American Journal of Community Psychology, 10*, 277-290.

Harter, S. (1988). *Manual for the Self-Perception Profile for Adolescents.* Denver, CO: University of Denver.

Hartigan, J. A. (1975). *Clustering algorithms.* New York: Wiley.

Hirsch, B. J., & DuBois, D. L. (1991). Self-esteem in early adolescence: The identification and prediction of contrasting longitudinal trajectories. *Journal of Youth and Adolescence, 20*, 53-72.

Hirsch, B. J., & DuBois, D. L. (1992). The relation of peer social support and psychological symptomatology during the transition to junior high school: A two-year longitudinal analysis. *American Journal of Community Psychology, 20*, 333-347.

Hirsch, B. J., & Rapkin, B. D. (1987). The transition to junior high school: A longitudinal study of self-esteem, psychological symptomatology, school life, and social support. *Child Development, 58*, 1235-1243.

Jason, L. A., & Bogat, G. A. (1983). Evaluating a preventive orientation program. *Journal of Social Service Research, 7*(2), 39-49.

Jason, L. A., Weine, A. M., Johnson, J. H., Warren-Sohlberg, L, Filippelli, L. A., Turner, E. Y., & Lardon, C. (1992). *Helping transfer students: Strategies for educational and school readjustment.* San Francisco: Jossey-Bass.

Lipsitz, J. (1977). *Growing up forgotten.* Lexington, MA: D. C. Heath.

McCarthy, J. D., & Hoge, D. R. (1982). Analysis of age effects in longitudinal studies of adolescent self-esteem. *Developmental Psychology, 18*, 372-379.

Nottleman, E. D. (1987). Competence and self-esteem during transition from childhood to adolescence. *Developmental Psychology, 19*, 257-268.

Offer, D., & Offer, J. (1975). *From teenage to young manhood.* New York: Basic.

Rosenberg, M. (1965). *Society and the adolescent self-image.* Princeton, NJ: Princeton University Press.

Simmons, R. G., & Blyth, D. A. (1987). *Moving into adolescence: The impact of pubertal change and school context.* New York: Aldine De Gruyter.

Wigfield, A., Eccles, J. S., MacIver, D., Reuman, D. A., & Midgley, C. (1991). Transitions during early adolescence: Changes in children's domain-specific self-perceptions and general self-esteem across the transition to junior high school. *Developmental Psychology, 27*, 552-565.

Restructuring the Ecology of the School as an Approach to Prevention During School Transitions: Longitudinal Follow-Ups and Extensions of the School Transitional Environment Project (STEP)

Robert D. Felner
Stephen Brand
Angela M. Adan
Peter F. Mulhall
Nancy Flowers
Barbara Sartain

University of Illinois

David L. DuBois

University of Missouri

SUMMARY. Normative school transitions are often accompanied by deterioration in students' socio-emotional, behavioral and academic adjustment, and poorer outcomes in later adolescence and young adulthood. The current paper describes a preventive interven-

---

[Haworth co-indexing entry note]: "Restructuring the Ecology of the School as an Approach to Prevention During School Transitions: Longitudinal Follow-Ups and Extensions of the School Transitional Environment Project (STEP)." Felner, Robert D. et al. Co-published simultaneously in *Prevention in Human Services* (The Haworth Press, Inc.) Vol. 10, No. 2, 1993, pp. 103-136; and: *Prevention and School Transitions* (ed: Leonard A. Jason, Karen E. Danner, and Karen S. Kurasaki) The Haworth Press, Inc., 1993, pp. 103-136. Multiple copies of this article/chapter may be purchased from The Haworth Document Delivery Center. Call 1-800-3-HAWORTH (1-800-342-9678) between 9:00 - 5:00 (EST) and ask for DOCUMENT DELIVERY CENTER.

© 1993 by The Haworth Press, Inc. All rights reserved.

tion for students experiencing normative transitions into middle grade schools and junior and senior high schools–the School Transitional Environment Project (STEP). The program is based on a transactional-ecological model of preventive intervention that employs a school restructuring and transformation approach in order to prevent the deleterious effects of school transitions and create school environments that are developmentally enhancing. Core features of STEP seek to change the ecological characteristics of the school setting in ways that: (a) reduce the adaptational demands of coping with flux and complexity in new school settings; (b) increase access to and the provision of important emotional and academic/instrumental support and guidance from school staff and other students; and (c) increase the students' sense of connectedness and belonging within the school. The present paper reviews findings from prior trials of the School Environment Transition Project, and presents the results of two additional STEP studies. The first reports on a long-term follow-up of STEP students who received the project in a large, urban high school that served students whose families were largely on public assistance. Results of this study revealed approximately 50% reductions in drop-out rates and significant positive effects on school performance and attendance patterns. The second study reports on an extension of STEP to junior high schools and middle grade students. Consistent with earlier studies, during the transition year, students in STEP schools reported more positive experiences in school environment dimensions that STEP sought to impact, and better adjustment outcomes than non-STEP students across academic, socio-emotional, and behavioral domains.

Prevention efforts in educational settings are now well into their third generation (Felner & Felner, 1989). Critical distinctions among these generations have been the ways in which they answer the questions of; (1) What are the program's goals? (2) Who does the program target? and (3) What and where is the focus of intervention (Felner & Felner, 1989)? Initial prevention efforts in educational settings would be best characterized as a "secondary prevention" (Zax & Specter, 1974). These programs target specific students who have been identified through screening procedures as displaying "preclinical" levels of symptoms and adaptive difficulties (e.g., academic delays and/or behavioral problems). The goals of these efforts are to reverse these problems or at least keep them from becoming worse. As part of efforts to refine the concept of prevention it has been suggested that such efforts are better labeled "early intervention" (Felner, Felner, & Silverman, 1993a; Seidman, 1987).

From these early efforts emerged programs that strove to be more truly preventive in their focus. These not only differ in their timing but also in their targeting. In these interventions the emphasis is no longer on the identification or remediation of early signs of problems in selected individual students. Rather, they typically center on efforts to enhance the competencies of groups of students, such as decision making/problem solving skills (Caplan & Weissberg, 1989; Shure & Spivack, 1982) or refusal skills (Rotherman, 1988), in order to increase the levels of resiliency of groups of students. These programs typically take the form of curriculum based instruction, at times accompanied by experiential elements, to teach the skills to the students and provide practice opportunities. As in early intervention efforts the primary targets of change in these programs are again students rather than the environments in which they function.

By contrast, third generation prevention efforts in educational and other settings seek to modify the ecology of educationally relevant contexts and settings that shape the developmental pathways of students. By contrast to the previous approaches the first order goals of these prevention efforts are: (1) the modification or removal of conditions of risk in the environment that may be developmentally hazardous and predispose to the acquisition of vulnerabilities and/or that precipitate the onset of adaptive difficulties; and (2) The enhancement of conditions in educational and interrelated contexts that increase the probability that students will "naturally" acquire the competencies and strengths that will make them more resilient in the face of life's challenges. A core aspect of these efforts is the intent to modify the elements of the school environment's structure, regularities and organization to make them more appropriate to the competencies and developmental requirements of most students. Unfortunately, efforts to address prevention's goals by following these routes have been often dismissed as overly difficult, and at least, when "conservative" definitions of prevention programs are employed, these are the least frequently attempted of all prevention research efforts, especially in educational contexts.

However, if we broaden our view of prevention efforts beyond those that traditional mental health and human service professionals might label as such, and include school reform and transformation efforts that intentionally seek to enhance the socio-emotional, educational, and related life outcomes of children and youth, then there are far more such efforts that may be included. This is not to say that all school reform efforts should somehow be labeled as prevention programs, even if a "side effect" is that they are somehow preventive. As Cowen (1980) has noted, a key feature of prevention efforts is that they are "intentional." That is, a central aspect in the design and development of any effort that is labeled prevention must be that it has systematically targeted for change those risk and protective factors that empirical research and prior theory has shown should produce positive changes in the adaptive outcomes of students of concern.

School reform efforts, such as those espoused by the recent *Turning Points* report of the Carnegie Corporation's Task Force on the Education of Young Adolescents (1989), with its focused recommendations on making middle grade educational settings more developmentally appropriate in order to enhance the socio-emotional, physical, and academic well-being of youth, certainly fall into this category. So too do such educational reform and transformation efforts as the creation of "schools within schools," those that seek to create positive alternative settings for those students for whom more traditional school contexts are not congruent with their values and skills (Trickett, 1991), and others that seek to change the social ecology and culture of schools to make them more developmentally sensitive and enhancing (Kelly, 1986; Sarason, 1982).

In considering this new generation of prevention efforts it may be helpful to consider their primary targets of change employing the metaphor of developmental pathways. From such a perspective what we can see is that these efforts "back up" one step further in the evolution of adaptive difficulties of youth than do those that directly seek to teach students competencies and resiliencies. Based on transactional and ecological models of human development (Bronfenbrenner, 1979; Sameroff & Fiese, 1989) these contextually focused prevention efforts reflect the understanding that modification of the primary contexts in which youth engage in daily transactions may lead them to naturally acquire the competencies that second generation program efforts seek to bring to students. Similarly, they also reflect the understanding that when educational and other primary developmental contexts are developmentally inappropriate and hazardous, students may both fail to gain such competencies and have those competencies they do have, which may be more than appropriate for their developmental level, be overwhelmed by developmentally inappropriate levels of demands (Felner & Felner, 1989).

Environmentally-focused programs also do not see the individual as "to blame" for their being at risk. Instead, from this perspective it is far more appropriate to view students as being *"at risk"* rather than as *high risk students*. In this case *students are not high risk, circumstances are*. It is the reduction of the exposure of students to these high risk circumstances, and increasing their exposure to developmentally enhancing conditions, that is the concern of environmentally-focused prevention programs (Felner & Felner, 1989). Put another way, "the underlying perspective of these programs is that *any "normal" or "typical" child or adolescent,* when exposed to these conditions, may begin to show the emergence of problematic developmental outcomes and disorder" (Felner & Felner, 1989, p. 37).

The present paper presents findings from a prevention program that is based in Transactional-Ecological (**T-E**) models of development (Felner & Felner, 1989; Felner et al., 1993a) and that sought to enhance adaptational outcomes during school transitions by restructuring the environmental characteristics of school settings. Specifically, we discuss findings from a five year follow-up of the initial experimental trial and replications of the School Transitional Environment Project (**STEP**). We also present the initial results of a further replication and extension of STEP to middle and junior high school contexts and students.

Normative school transitions, such as moving from elementary schools to middle/junior high schools, or from junior to senior high school, are among the most pervasive and important ecological transitions (Bronfenbrenner, 1979) facing adolescents. These transitions bring with them marked shifts in the relationship between the person and the social environment. Because of their developmental significance, times of ecological transition in person's lives are particularly opportune for prevention efforts. Transitions may be accompanied by the rapid growth of coping skills and enhancement of developmental outcomes.

Unfortunately, for many students, school transitions are instead accompanied by marked deterioration in social, emotional, behavioral and academic adjustment (Blyth, Simmons, & Bush, 1978; Blyth, Simmons, Carlton-Ford, 1983; Felner & Adan, 1988; Felner, Ginter, & Primavera, 1982; Felner, Primavera, & Cauce, 1981; Hirsch & Rapkin, 1987; Simmons, Burgeson, Carlton-Ford, & Blyth, 1987). Further, these changes in students' adaptation during school transitions are not merely short-term, transitory conditions. They may also have enduring consequences for adaptation. The linkage between adaptive difficulties in early adolescence and subsequent dysfunction in later adolescence and early adulthood is well documented. Illustratively, lower grades and absenteeism, increased behavioral problems, and lower self-esteem, adaptive changes that may frequently follow the normative transition to junior or senior high school, especially among high risk youth (Felner & Adan, 1988), have been found to relate consistently to later school failure and dropout, substance abuse, delinquency, crime, poorer vocational outcomes, and welfare dependency (Bachman, Green & Wirtanen, 1971; Cowen, Pederson, Babigian, Izzo, & Trost, 1973; Galloway, 1985; Kellam, Branch, Agrawal, & Ensminger, 1975; Newcomb & Bentler, 1988; U.S. Department of Health, Education and Welfare, 1975).

A number of factors may contribute to the adaptive significance of school transitions for adolescents. These transitional events typically occur when individuals are also experiencing developmental transitions (Erikson, 1959) that occur as a function of the organism's growth and biological maturation, and that bring with them dramatic changes in the developmental demands and challenges adolescents confront. Thus, both the developmental significance of school transitions and the degree to which they place adolescents "at risk" may be far greater than for ecological transitions that are not accompanied by these other milestones. This co-occurrence of developmental and ecological transitions can significantly lower the "threshold of vulnerability" (Felner & Adan, 1988) of all youth experiencing such normative school transitions.

It is also the case that all adolescents experiencing normative school transitions are not equally vulnerable. Students or populations of students may have differential levels of coping skills and resources that influence their threshold of vulnerability during this transition. Students who are economically or socially disadvantaged, and those with relatively low levels of family support for educational accomplishment are more likely to show significant declines in school performance following these transitions than those students who have greater compensatory and protective resources in their other developmental contexts (Felner, Brand, DuBois, Adan, Mulhall & Evans, 1993b; Felner et al., 1981; Felner et al., 1982; Hirsch & Rapkin, 1987; Simmons et al., 1987). The co-occurrence of other life stresses (Felner, Farber, & Primavera, 1983; Simmons et al., 1987) and the level of educational preparation a student has received in the school they are coming from, as well as the degree to which this level "matches" that of other students who are entering from other feeder schools, also influence the degree of risk and vulnerability (Felner, Schroeder, & Brand, 1993c; Jason, Weine, Johnson, Warren-Sohlberg, Filippelli, Turner, & Lardon, 1992).

Similarly, not all school transitions are equally risk producing. Illustratively, when only one small elementary school "feeds" into one small middle school, and there are no other feeder schools, the level of risk will be far less than when two or more fairly large elementary schools feed into an even larger middle school and, in turn, students from several of these large middle schools feed an even larger high school. That is, the *characteristics and regularities of the school setting that the student enters may have a profound effect on the levels of risk that students experience when they enter the new setting.* Previous discussions of the impact of school transitions have often puzzled over the sometimes inconsistent findings pertaining to the impact of school transitions, with some studies finding such efforts and others failing to do so, at least to the same extent. The answer, of course, is the degree to which they will have such effects depends in large part on identifiable characteristics of both the students and the settings they are leaving and entering (Felner & Adan, 1988). Thus, the degree of difficulty that students experience in mastering transitional tasks is a function of both sides of the transactional equation, and their interaction with either or both "sides" of the equation being appropriate points to target for change through prevention efforts. Efforts to change setting-level variables (i.e., school characteristics) must be sensitive to the ways in which program elements have differential effects on adaptation as a function of students' varied levels of coping resources and exposure to risk factors outside of school. An understanding of these school and student dimensions that relate to the degree of differential risk and vulnerability are critical to guiding prevention efforts since the "first order" target for change by prevention efforts is the reduction of conditions of risk and the enhancement of protective factors (Felner et al., 1993a).

SCHOOL TRANSITIONS: GUIDING FRAMEWORKS

As noted above, from a T-E perspective for prevention (Felner et al., 1983; Felner et al., 1993a), modification of developmentally hazardous environmental features in the school environment are seen as the primary locus with which to start prevention efforts. These interventions start with the question of whether there are conditions in educational environments that make developmental adaptation difficult and that can be shifted to make the setting more developmentally appropriate and enhancing for students. Although this may not always be possible, there are many instances in which the regularities of schools are not ones that are necessary. Instead they may serve little purpose, and in fact, if modified will not only make the setting more developmentally appropriate but may also enhance other activities that are occurring in the school, such as instruction (Carnegie Corporation, 1989).

Applying this perspective to traditional junior and senior high schools, we see that students' efforts to cope with the transitional tasks that accompany entry into these settings are constrained by at least two factors, the heightened complexity and developmental demands of the new school setting and the inability of the school to provide needed supports, resources, and information (Felner et al., 1982; Felner & Adan, 1988). Levels of developmental hazard and risk increase to the extent that schools have higher levels of flux and disorganization, require greater understanding of new expectations and regularities, and confront the student with unfamiliar and problematic social and academic demands. These conditions are typical of the transition to traditional junior and senior high schools. They are particularly marked in schools in which large numbers of students are entering from multiple feeder schools. Suddenly students are confronted throughout the school day by a continuously changing group of often unfamiliar peers as they move from class to class, by short periods with each teacher, and by a new set of rules that may vary dramatically from teacher to teacher. Students are also confronted with developmental challenges and pressures posed by older students who are already present in the school, to higher levels of systemic flux due to the large numbers of students entering the school, and to the demands posed by an academic setting in which the expectations and requirements may be significantly greater than they were in the prior school context.

The capacity of the school to be responsive to, and supply needed supports for students during these times of transition, just when students may need them most is, unfortunately, often at its lowest levels. The large numbers of new and unknown students in the entering class make it difficult for teachers and other school staff to get to know individual students and provide information and resources appropriate to the students' individual needs. Similarly, the traditional regularities (Sarason, 1982) of junior and senior high schools, in which students have multiple teachers, generally for only one brief subject period each day, impede the creation of positive bonds between students and teachers and make it difficult for students to gain access to necessary adult support. These teachers also often have little interaction with each other, further exacerbating difficulties in coordinating efforts to reach and understand students, or to develop uniform rules and norms across classes.

THE SCHOOL TRANSITION ENVIRONMENTAL PROJECT

STEP seeks to facilitate successful adaptation to the transition from elementary to middle and secondary schools by reducing the adaptational demands imposed by these transitions, and to increase coping resources available to students. It accomplishes these goals by modifying specific elements of the ecology of the school context that we have identified above as particularly salient to mastering the tasks associated with these transitions. That is: (a) reorganizing the regularities of the school environment to reduce the degree of flux and complexity that the entering student confronts; and (b) restructuring the roles of homeroom teachers and guidance staff so that they and may provide greater support for entering students. Figure 1 graphically displays the central elements and pathways of influence that are incorporated into the design of STEP.

Reorganizing the school social system. STEP first seeks to reorganize the social system that the student is entering in order to reduce the degree of flux and complexity that the student confronts, create smaller learning environments within larger schools, and provide a stable and consistent set of classmates and peers at school. Towards these ends, all STEP students are assigned to classes so that all primary academic subjects (e.g., English, mathematics) and homeroom are taken only with other students in the STEP project. The actual implementation of STEP has characteristically involved assigning 60-100 incoming students to a STEP "team," then assigning students to classes so that each STEP "core" class is comprised of students from the same STEP "team." The restructured STEP school no longer requires students to adapt to, and cope with, a continually changing peer group in each core class, in marked contrast to the traditional practice of assembling classes randomly from the full set of entering freshmen. This program element should reduce the difficulty of mastering the transitional task of reestablishing a stable and satisfying peer support network and increase the students' sense of belonging in the school. By reducing flux and complexity, this STEP program element should also provide a school climate that students experience as well-organized, understandable and cohesive.

To undergird the reorganization of the school social system, STEP also focuses on restructuring the physical environment of the school. Within the school building, efforts are made to locate STEP classrooms in close physical proximity to each other (e.g., in the same part of one wing or floor). Minimizing distances between classes helps students to feel comfortable in, and familiar with the new school setting, and increases opportunities for informal social interaction among STEP classmates between class periods. Such change in the physical environment of the school may serve to reduce students' sense of the school as an unmanageable, chaotic, and forbidding place, particularly in large schools whose vast size is often overwhelming to entering students. In addition, to the extent that STEP students no longer pass through other parts of the school building, entering students are no longer exposed to social pressures (e.g., intimidation) from older students, a factor which may contribute to the onset of problem behaviors during the school transition.

Restructuring homeroom teacher's roles and increasing teacher support. The second STEP element involves assigning incoming students to a homeroom in which the role of the teacher has been redefined so that the homeroom period becomes part of a teacher-advisory program. Characteristically, STEP units of 60-100 students have four to five homerooms, each consisting of 20-30 students. In each homeroom, the teacher serves as the primary administrative/counseling link between the students, their parents, and the rest of the school. Homeroom teachers also perform many of the guidance and administrative duties that, in traditional schools, are carried out by counselors and other school staff (e.g., choosing classes, counseling for school and personal problems). When the student is absent, the STEP homeroom teacher often is the one who contacts the family and follows up on excuses. Finally, all STEP team teachers participate in regular meetings with other staff in the same STEP unit that generally occur several times or more each week. During these team meetings, staff attempt to identify any students who may require some additional assistance or support from teachers or guidance counselors, or communication between the school and the family. Team members can then develop integrated efforts to teach and/or otherwise assist students that extend across significant portions of the school day. In implementing this redefined role, teachers receive consultation and supervision, when necessary, from school guidance staff, as well as training in team-building and student advisory skills.

The goal of the changes in homeroom teachers' roles are fourfold: (1) to make the transitional task of acquiring and reorganizing formal support less difficult and to increase the amount of support students receive and perceive as being available from school staff; (2) to reduce the difficulty with which students can gain access to

FIGURE 1

CORE ELEMENTS OF THE SCHOOL TRANSITIONAL ENVIRONMENT
PROJECT AND ILLUSTRATIVE PATHWAYS OF ECOLOGICAL
DEVELOPMENTAL INFLUENCE

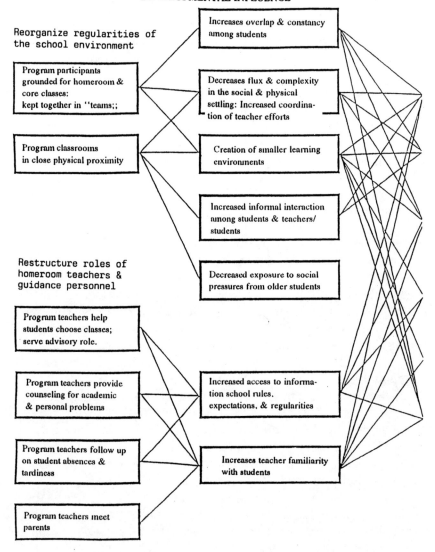

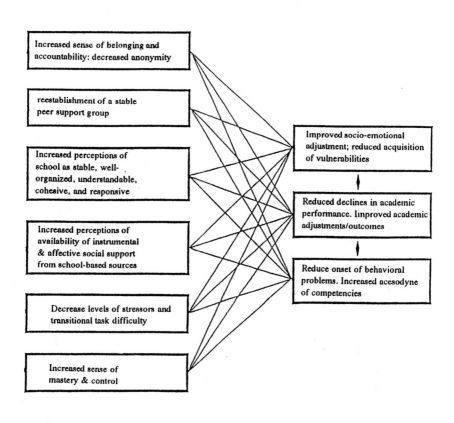

important information about school rules, expectations, and regularities; (3) to increase students' sense of accountability and belongingness, and reduce their sense of anonymity; and (4) to increase the extent to which teachers are familiar with students and reduce the overload that teachers often experience in gaining familiarity with large numbers of entering students.

FIVE-YEAR LONGITUDINAL FOLLOW-UP OF STEP

The initial experimental trial of STEP was conducted in a large urban high school in which students entering ninth grade were primarily from low socio-economic status and/or minority backgrounds. Evaluation data were obtained from STEP program participants and a matched control sample. A number of significant findings indicated that STEP program participation was associated with better short-term academic and social adjustment (Felner et al., 1982). By the end of the first project year, control students showed marked decreases in grades, attendance, and self-concept. This pattern of deteriorating adjustment is similar to that found among students who made the transition in the same school setting in previous years (Felner et al., 1981). By contrast, STEP students in this school setting exhibited stable levels of academic performance (e.g., grades), attendance and self-concept, showing no such decline in adjustment. These data suggest that STEP accomplished one of the primary goals of an effective prevention program, that is, to keep negative changes from occurring.

In addition to these outcome indicators, several process measures were employed in the first year evaluation to assess the extent to which STEP program elements were actually experienced as intended by students, and the degree to which these elements were associated with the obtained differences in academic and socioemotional adjustment. These process data supported the view that the elements of the school environment that had been proposed as hazardous were indeed associated with differential developmental outcomes in the expected directions. When compared with control students, STEP students perceived the school environment as more stable, understandable, well-organized, involving and supportive, and reported higher levels of support from teachers and other school personnel. By contrast, control group students exhibited systematic declines in their ratings of school climate and staff support. The overall pattern of these findings suggests that STEP participation affected students' school experiences as intended and, in turn, these differential school experiences worked to prevent deteriorating outcomes during the transition year.

Long-Term Follow Up–The Results

Five years following the initial transition into the high school the students' school records were employed to track the samples in the initial STEP experimental trial (Felner & Adan, 1988). For over 90% of the students in the initial samples, school records included sufficient data to establish whether students had graduated, transferred, or dropped out while failing. Both groups remained matched on demographics and pre-transition levels of school adjustment. Primary information available at this five year follow-up point related to whether or not students had dropped-out of school prior to graduation or graduated, their ongoing grades, and their attendance records.

Drop-out rate. Perhaps the most striking finding concerned the differential drop-out rate for the two groups. Table 1 reveals the cumulative drop-out rates for the two groups. From the second year forward, students in the comparison group had significantly higher drop-out rates than did STEP students (all Chi squares < .05). Indeed, from the second year forward drop-out rates of the former group were approximately twice those in the STEP group. By the end of the first four years, the traditional period it takes for graduation to occur, students in the control group showed a 43% drop-out rate, and another three (3) percent were in alternative educational settings. This rate is similar to the drop-out rates found for schools in the community serving similar student populations and for students in the target school in previous years. By contrast, STEP students exhibited a 24% drop-out rate, approximately half of the comparison group.

Academic achievement and absenteeism. Paralleling the drop-out rates for students in the two groups was evidence that STEP had enduring effects on academic achievement and absenteeism. These data also demonstrate the program's effectiveness in keeping stu-

TABLE 1. School transition project: Five year follow-up on high school sample. Drop-out rates: Cumulative at end of each academic year.

GROUPS	9TH	10TH*	11TH**	12TH**
DROP-OUT (CUM. PERCENT) PROJECT	7.3%	11.4%	19.1%	24.3%
CONTROLS	10.7%	18.5%	31.6%	42.7%

YEAR BY YEAR DIFFERNECE INCREMENTS AND
CUMULATIVE DIFFERENCES BOTH SIGNIFICANT AT P ≤ .05

*DIFFERENCES AT P < .01

dents above their threshold of vulnerability and in preventing the development of more serious problems. In these analyses we employed both the weighted quality grade point average (QPAs) employed by the school as well as the students grades in core subjects. As can be seen in Table 2, although having approximately equal grades during the pre-transition eighth grade year, students in the STEP program had significantly higher weighted QPA and core grades in the first two years following the transition to high school. The two groups began to approximate each other more closely in the third and fourth years–indeed control students had directionally higher core grades and QPAs in the third year. Absenteeism rates paralleled the findings for grades in the pre-transition and first two post-transition years. But, by contrast to grades, absenteeism rates continued to be far worse for comparison students throughout the four years.

The closing of the gap on grades across the groups was not, however, due to poorer performance by STEP students nor more positive performance by comparison students in these years. Rather, it reflected the differential drop-out rates of the two groups. The significant differences in the first two years reflected the fact that more comparison students than controls did poorly after the transition. But, many of these poorly performing students, especially among the comparison group, dropped out by the end of the third year.

Giving further weight to this explanation and the hypothesis that the STEP program would be particularly helpful to students nearest their threshold of vulnerability, further analyses revealed that students in the comparison sample who remained in school at the end of the third year, and beyond, had significantly higher pre-transitions grades and lower rates of absenteeism than did STEP students who still remained in school, even though there were no initial overall grade differences between the two groups. Thus, it appears that in this trial STEP did differentially help somewhat poorer students to remain above their thresholds of vulnerability. Recall that STEP students remained in the program for only the first year. Thus, any long term effects of the program are due to enduring effects of that intervention and not to any continuing program involvement.

TABLE 2. School transitional environment project: Five year follow-up of high school program. Comparison of step and comparison groups: Grades—eight through twelfth grade.

				GRADE		
	GROUPS	8TH	9TH*	10TH*	11TH	12TH
OVERALL QPA (WEIGHTED)	STEP	2.56	2.77	2.48	2.53	3.19
	CONTROLS	2.61	1.97	2.18	2.74	3.12
CORE GPA	STEP	1.94	1.72*	1.46*	1.43	1.62
	CONTROLS	2.07	1.22	1.30	1.62	1.58
ABSENCES	STEP	12.3	16.7*	15.8*	17.2*	14.7*
	CONTROLS	12.9	25.1	24.6	26.4	19.3

* = GROUP DIFFERENCES SIGNIFICANT AT P < .05

STEP REPLICATIONS

Several replications and generalization trials of STEP have been mounted prior to the current work (Felner, Adan, & Evans, 1987; Felner & Adan, 1988). One replication study was carried out in two high schools and three junior high schools serving predominantly rural and small urban communities serving students from predominantly lower to middle class socioeconomic backgrounds. In this work a broader range of outcome measures were employed than in the initial work, including indices of depression and other emotional difficulties, self-concept, school behavior problems, delinquency, substance abuse, grades, achievement test scores, and absences. The scope of process measures was also expanded and enriched, as were measures bearing on the differential effectiveness of program participation for students with diverse coping skills and stress experiences. Results from this replication study were generally consistent with and expand on the findings of the initial STEP evaluation. STEP students entering junior and senior high school were more likely than control students to avoid significant declines in academic performance and self-concept than those in comparison samples. Control students also showed more emotional (e.g., depression, self-concept), behavioral (e.g., substance abuse, delinquency) and academic dysfunction (e.g., dropping out) following the transition than did STEP students. A second comparison group in this replication study focused on the relative efficacy of STEP when compared with more individually focused interventions (e.g., transition task focused training in coping and social problem-solving skills). Students receiving individually-focused training exhibited somewhat better outcomes than control students. But, they did not adapt as well to the transition as STEP students, particularly in academic domains.

The Current Replication and Extension

Whereas the initial STEP trials focused extensively on students making the transition to high school, subsequent replications have attempted a downward extension of these findings to students entering junior high and middle schools. The conditions of risk during the high school transition are also found during the transition to junior high school. Indeed, some (Carnegie Corporation, 1989) have suggested that this transition may be even more developmentally important due to the students' ages, the close association of this transition with the onset of puberty, and the fact that this represents the initial transition of children to the demands of adolescents. It is also the first time many students have experience with a school that is segmented into departmentalized classes, with making choices about courses of study to follow, and with changing classes and teachers often. Further, the shift in expectations and demands between elementary school and junior high school may be more discontinuous than between junior and senior high schools. Illustrative of the potential impact of these transitions, beyond those discussed above, is the findings of a series of studies of urban junior high schools conducted by Simmons and colleagues (Blyth et al., 1978; Simmons & Blyth, 1987; Simmons, Blyth, VanCleave, & Bush, 1979). They found marked declines in socio-emotional and academic adjustment during this transition. In the longer term, difficulties in adjustment during the middle grade years may be followed by increasing levels of problem behavior and poor adjustment in high school and beyond (Rutter, 1980).

Thus, the following study expands on the field trials examining the efficacy of STEP program elements by focusing further on students entering middle and junior high school.

METHOD

Sample

In this replication, we report on the first two years of longitudinal data for this cohort of students. Participating students were those in the entry grade who attended four schools that had adopted core STEP elements, as described above, as part of moving toward broader school transformations, and four comparison non-STEP schools, who were also moving toward similar school transformations. Overall, these schools represent a wide range of geographic, demographic and structural characteristics. Included in the present sample are: (a) urban, suburban and rural schools; (b) schools serving lower income and minority students as well as those with students from more affluent backgrounds; (c) schools in which students enter in the sixth grade and those in which the transition occurs in grade seven; and (d) schools of varying sizes and numbers of feeder schools. A critical feature of this replication was, however, that the overall level of risk of students in these schools was far lower than in the relatively high risk schools employed in the first trials. This sample is comprised of 1204 students in four STEP schools and 761 students in four non-STEP comparison schools. Overall, 17% of participants are minorities, and 44% came from a household in which the highest level of parental education is high school graduation. Students made the transition to junior high school in either the sixth grade (58%) or the seventh grade (42%).

The samples include all non-special education students in each school, and the demographic/socio-economic characteristics and per pupil expenditures of the participating schools are not significantly different. If there are any differences between the sample it is that the schools in the STEP sample were generally larger (Mean entering class sizes 295 versus 179; overall sizes of 880 for STEP versus 434 for comparisons) and had somewhat more feeder schools (a mean for STEP schools of 6.25 "feeders" versus 3.8 for comparison schools). To the extent that larger school size and multiple feeder schools increase levels of peer group flux and student stress during the transition, any bias resulting from the non-equivalence of these samples would work against finding positive results for the STEP schools relative to the non-STEP schools.

Procedures

The broader study from which the current sample is drawn (Felner, Mulhall, Sartain, Standiford, Brand, & Kasak, 1992) employs data from multiple sources, including student self-report, teacher ratings of classroom adjustment, teacher ratings of curricular elements, instructional practices and work experiences, administrator reports of program implementation, and school records. The present study focuses on the academic and socio-emotional differences between STEP and non-STEP schools employing student self-report measures and teacher behavioral ratings, the students' permanent grade record, and student report of their experiences of the school environment. Students' self-report measures were administered in their classroom by teachers during regular school hours in the Spring semester. To ensure that students' relative reading ability would not interfere with their ability to answer any item, all of the instructions and individual items were read aloud by the teacher. Usable and reliable survey data were obtained from over 85% of the potential participants. In addition, ratings of classroom behavioral adjustment were obtained for each student from teachers who instructed the student in "core" academic classes on a regular basis. Principal and teacher reports were employed to establish the degree to which each school had implemented STEP elements and to determine school characteristics (e.g., size, number of feeder schools).

Measures

There were two primary sets of measures employed in the present study. These are: (1) process measures of school dimensions that, in the STEP program, are the immediate target of change (i.e., quality of middle school life, school regularities and social environment, social support) and; (2) measures of program outcomes including shifts in critical mediating conditions in the school environment (i.e., school transition stresses), and, most importantly, student adjustment (e.g., psychological distress, behavior problems, academic expectations, and classroom behavioral adaptation).

Process Measures

The *Perceived School Climate Scale (PSCS)* was adapted from Moos' (1979) classroom environment scale and a previous version employed by Felner et al. (1982). The current 61 item version of the PSCS provides information regarding a students' perception of the school's social climate on eight factorially derived subscales: Student Affiliation, Negative Student Interactions, Positive Teacher-Student Relations, Harshness, Student Participation in Decision-Making, Innovative Curriculum, Structure/Clarity, and Achievement Emphasis/Commitment.

Outcome Measures Included:

1. *School Transition Stress (STS)*. Students completed a measure of stress associated with the transition from elementary school

to the junior high school/middle school, consisting of 13 items drawn from prior studies of stress during the middle school transition (Elias, Gara, & Ubriaco, 1985) and extensive fieldwork by the authors. The overall scale demonstrated high internal consistency (alpha = .85);
2. *Psychological Distress* was assessed in three areas: depression, anxiety, and low self-esteem. To assess levels of depression, the Children's Depression Inventory was used (Kovacs, 1981). To measure children's experiences of anxiety, the Revised Children's Manifest Anxiety Scale (Reynolds & Richmond, 1978) was employed. The Self Evaluation Questionnaire (SEQ) was employed (DuBois, Felner, & Brand, 1993) to assess self-esteem in the critical life domains of family, school and peer interactions, as well as overall general self-esteem. Scales demonstrated high internal consistency ranging from (alpha = .84 − .90);
3. *Behavior Problems.* To assess behavioral difficulties students completed a measure consisting of twelve items from the Delinquency scale of the Youth Self-Report (Achenbach & Edelbrock, 1987). Students indicated how often they engaged in each behavior in the past six months. This scale exhibited high internal consistency (alpha = .90);
4. *Academic Expectations.* Student's expectancies about their own academic performance were assessed by having students complete a nine item measure of academic expectations from the student, parents and teachers;
5. *Classroom Behavioral Adaptation* was assessed by asking teachers to rate each student on three problem behavior scales from the Teacher-Child Rating Scale (Hightower, Work, Cowen, Lotyzewski, Spinell, Guare, & Rohrbeck, 1986), i.e., the Acting Out, Moody-Shy and Learning Difficulties scales.

RESULTS

Assessment of Program Process Intervention

To understand any adaptive differences that might be obtained between STEP and comparison students it was first important to understand whether we could establish that the: (1) STEP students actually experienced the school differently in the ways intended due to the participation in STEP; and (2) that these dimensions were significantly associated with the differential adjustment.

Multiple analysis of variance (MANOVA) and subsequent univariate analysis of variance (ANOVA) procedures were employed to test the degree to which STEP students rated the school environment in the predicted and more favorable directions than did those in the comparison sample. These MANOVAs tested the overall effects of program participation testing the unique contribution of participation in STEP to process measures, after partialling out the effects of student race, sex and parental education. The MANOVA for process measures found that STEP participation had significant unique effects upon student's experiences of the school environment and levels of support they received after partialling out student background ($F = 10.57$; $p < .001$). As can be seen in Table 3 across all dimensions of the PSCS patterns supporting the significant differential and more favorable effect of program participation were present. Further, in several instances there were significant effects for time, such that consistent with the initial Felner et al. (1982) work there were declines in the students experience of the setting across both years, with STEP students retaining a somewhat more positive experience. Finally, in two instances, the experience of school climate harshness and negative interactions with teachers, group by time effects were found, with STEP students showing increased difficulties in these areas in the second year. These changes may have occurred due to STEP students moving out of STEP into the more general school environment in their second year and lend support to the notion that these students were not simply more positive students.

To test the overall assumption that the school environment/context variables targeted for change by STEP program elements are associated with student outcomes, correlational analyses were also carried out to examine the extent to which PSCS dimensions were related significantly to student outcomes across both STEP and comparison samples. Of 112 correlations only eleven (11) were non significant, with the most consistent non-association being between ratings of student decision making and the adjustment dimensions

TABLE 3. Comparison of step versus non-step groups on process measures: Middle grade replications.

		Means		F		
	Groups	Transition Year	Second Year	Group	Time	Group X Time
SCHOOL EXPERIENCES						
Harshness	STEP Non-STEP	17.8 20.5	18.7 19.7	46.47**	.01	21.74**
Negative Interactions	STEP Non-STEP	18.0 20.7	18.6 19.2	47.12**	8.78**	41.72**
Teacher Support	STEP Non-STEP	21.2 19.3	20.7 19.3	26.88**	1.76	1.76
Student Decision-Making	STEP Non-STEP	13.5 12.6	13.4 12.5	12.32**	.18	.00
Innovative Instruction	STEP Non-STEP	11.9 10.7	12.0 11.1	26.83**	3.10	1.88
Structure	STEP Non-STEP	22.7 21.7	22.4 21.6	5.95*	1.39	.23
Peer Affiliation	STEP Non-STEP	17.9 17.0	17.7 16.7	26.17**	11.37**	5.80*
Commitment	STEP Non-STEP	24.4 22.2	23.2 20.8	75.55**	59.08**	.35

* $p < .05$; ** $p < .01$

(five of 14 were non-significant and several others were significant but quite weak). Overall average correlations were generally moderate, in the r = .20 to .30 range. Better scores on each student adjustment scale and subscale were correlated significantly with more positive levels of school climate dimensions. Taken together these findings indicate that STEP students did experience the school environment significantly more in the ways sought, and these dimensions do appear to be significantly associated with student adjustment and performance.

STEP versus Non-STEP Schools

A critical concern in the present study is the degree to which students in STEP schools differ from those in comparison schools due to participation in STEP program elements. The MANOVA for students' self-reports of socio-emotional adjustment and teacher ratings of student behavioral adjustment found a significant unique effect of STEP after partialling out student background variables (F = 2.84; d.f. = 14, 629; $p < .001$). Thus, participation in STEP is associated with both more favorable school experiences and with more positive student adjustment over and above any differences that may be explained by differences in student background characteristics.

Subsequent univariate ANOVAs were conducted on each of the variables that comprised the MANOVAs in order to clarify more specific STEP effects (see Table 4). Significant group effects were found across all analysis sets. Compared with students in non-STEP schools, STEP students reported significantly lower levels of school transition stress and better adjustment on measures of school, family and general self-esteem, depression, anxiety, delinquent behavior, and higher levels of academic expectations. Further, teachers reported these students to have significantly more favorable classroom behavioral adjustment on each of the classroom behavioral problem dimensions. Finally, STEP student grades and attendance patterns were significantly more favorable than those in non-STEP schools.

These findings provide additional support for the STEP project as an effective prevention approach. As noted above, these schools are relatively "low risk" schools, especially the comparison schools in which one entering class is less than 100 and two of the other three are less than 125 students. By contrast, none of the STEP schools had entering classes of less than 250 students. Further, neither set of schools had the extent of high risk, low income students present in the first two trials (e.g., the original high school trial took place in a setting in which approximately 85% of the students' families were receiving public assistance). Despite these conditions, all of which should have worked to reduce effect sizes, the significant differences favoring the schools with STEP elements in place during the transition year were found for almost all process and outcome variables. Particularly noteworthy is that STEP program effects were found across converging indices of adaptation, across multiple domains of functioning, and that were drawn from multiple sources (i.e., student self-report, teacher ratings, grade/attendance records).

DISCUSSION

The STEP project and its evaluation underscore the potential for developing inexpensive but effective contextually-focused, developmentally informed, preventive and school transformation efforts. Given STEP's relatively low cost (Felner & Adan, 1988) and the enormous costs to society of many of the problems that it seems to be effective in reducing, these additional program findings and replications reported in the current paper should be encouraging to those who seek to establish that preventive efforts for mental health and academic difficulties can be established. Further, by contrast to most preventive efforts, STEP appears to have effects that are as robust, if not more so, for students from high risk backgrounds and home environments, as for students from lower risk family/community contexts.

An additional feature of the STEP program is that it is not only unobtrusive and minimally disruptive to the host setting–the school–but it is also one that is associated with improved job satisfaction and lower levels of burn-out for teachers (Felner et al., 1992). These features are critical ones in efforts to develop prevention programs that are not only effective when done well, but also that have the potential to actually be done well when implemented

TABLE 4. Comparison of step versus non-step groups on outcome measures: Middle grade replications.

		Means			F		
	Groups	Transition Year	Second Year	Group	Time	Group X Time
STRESS						
Transition Stress	STEP Non-STEP	20.1 21.3	19.8 21.1	23.78**	1.81	.25
SELF-ESTEEM						
Peer	STEP Non-STEP	22.7 22.9	23.2 23.6	1.01	11.59**	.29
School	STEP Non-STEP	22.6 21.0	22.7 20.7	28.14**	.60	.83
Family	STEP Non-STEP	25.5 24.3	25.8 24.2	18.61**	.31	.90
General	STEP Non-STEP	23.8 22.8	24.0 23.1	10.24**	1.95	.01
SOCIO-EMOTIONAL ADJUSTMENT						
Depression	STEP Non-STEP	9.1 11.1	10.1 12.0	12.91**	9.13**	.02
Anxiety	STEP Non-STEP	10.2 11.9	9.0 10.9	19.42**	28.23**	.11
Behavior Problems	STEP Non-STEP	20.6 23.3	21.2 23.3	25.04**	.76	.59

EXPECTATIONS					
Self	STEP	12.9	13.0	27.24**	.19	2.20
	Non-STEP	12.3	12.2			
Parent	STEP	13.3	13.2	36.53**	4.03*	.95
	Non-STEP	12.6	12.4			
Teacher	STEP	12.3	12.4	36.59**	4.39*	.19
	Non-STEP	11.3	11.5			
Total	STEP	38.6	38.7	27.37**	.00	.30
	Non-STEP	36.6	36.5			
CLASSROOM BEHAVIOR					
Acting-Out	STEP	7.6	7.7	24.88**	.20	.05
	Non-STEP	8.9	9.0			
Moody-Shy	STEP	7.8	7.7	9.43**	.75	.80
	Non-STEP	8.4	8.2			
Learning Difficulties	STEP	8.8	9.8	26.38**	4.30*	5.48*
	Non-STEP	11.2	11.1			
Total	STEP	24.2	25.1	28.61**	.92	1.67
	Non-STEP	28.5	28.4			
ACADEMIC ADJUSTMENT					
Grade Point Average	STEP	3.9	3.9	117.60**	2.13	4.40*
	Non-STEP	3.2	3.3			

* $p < .05$; ** $p < .01$

in the "real world." Increasingly, research on the implementation of prevention efforts has shown that the fidelity and dosage with which programs are implemented are critical determinants of their potential efficacy. Indeed, at least some of the disappointing results that have been obtained in employing more individually focused, curriculum models may be due to such implementation difficulties. At least some of these failures appear to result from the fact that teachers typically do not implement these programs effectively, if at all. Furman and his colleagues, (Furman, Giberson, White, Gravin, & Wehner, 1989) note, "It is quite common for 25% or more of teachers to be non-users of a *required* innovation, even in the second or third year of implementation . . . Among those who implement a program there is marked variation in how well they implement it."

The STEP project has several advantages on these dimensions. First, the fact that teachers are working in teams increases the probability that each will participate more fully and with greater fidelity. Second, due to the fact that the program is one that teachers actually find makes their lives better, increases their satisfaction with teaching, and requires little initiative from them to continue it once it is in place, all increase the probability that it will happen as intended. Further, since it does not take away from instructional time it is not a competitor for this critical resource as are many other efforts. Finally, many aspects of the STEP project are consistent with the reforms being recommended for increasing instructional and school efficacy (cf. Carnegie Corporation, 1989). The extent to which mental health and human service interventions are able take place in ways and of a form that is consistent with the other missions of the educational setting will greatly increase the potential that these programs will take place.

Additional replications and extensions of STEP that incorporate additional school reform and transformation are currently being conducted and evaluated. Combined with the current results these efforts should lead to increased emphasis on the development of preventive efforts that seek to restructure and modify both instructional regularities and practices, as well as the social and physical organization of educational contexts, so as to make them more developmentally appropriate, thus creating "user friendly schools" and enhancing the social, academic, and emotional well-being of students. Given the interrelatedness of each of these domains, preventive efforts that yield such comprehensive impacts will be far more effective than those that target single outcomes (Felner et al., 1993a).

AUTHOR NOTE

Robert D. Felner, Stephen Brand, Angela M. Adan, Peter F. Mulhall, Nancy Flowers, Barbara Sartain, and David L. DuBois wish to thank the Association of Illinois Middle Schools, those students and staff at schools participating in Project Initiative Middle Level, Saverio Mungo, PhD, and Deborah Kasak, for their assistance and support with the middle grades element of this paper. We also wish to thank Roger P. Weissberg, PhD, and his research staff for their assistance in collecting the follow-up data from the initial high school cohort, and students and staff at all participating schools whose assistance and cooperation made this project possible. We also appreciate the assistance of Julia Brenner, Susan Standiford, Christine Kerras, Susan Wolf, and David Baysinger in various phases of the data collection and analyses and the preparation of this paper.

This project was supported in part through a grant from the Carnegie Corporation of New York to Robert Felner.

Address correspondence to Robert D. Felner, PhD, Director, Center for Prevention Research and Development, Institute of Government and Public Affairs, University of Illinois, 1002 W. Nevada, Urbana, IL 61801.

REFERENCES

Achenbach, T.M., & Edelbrock, C. (1987). *Manual for the Youth Self-Report and Profile*. Burlington, VT: University of Vermont Department of Psychiatry.

Bachman, J.G., Green, S., & Wirtanen, I.D. (1971). *Youth in Transition* (Vol. 3). Ann Arbor: Survey Research Center, Institute for Social Research.

Blyth, D.A., Simmons, R.G., & Bush, D.M. (1978). The transition into early adolescence: A longitudinal comparison of youth in two educational contexts. *Sociology of Education, 51*, 149-162.

Blyth, D.A., Simmons, R.G., & Carlton-Ford, S. (1983). The adjustment of early adolescents to school transitions. *Journal of Early Adolescence, 3*, 105-120.

Bronfenbrenner, U. (1979). *The ecology of human development: Experiments by nature and design*. Cambridge, MA: Harvard University Press.

Caplan, M.Z., & Weissberg, R.P. (1989). Promoting social competence in early adolescence: Developmental Considerations. In B.H. Schneider, G. Attili, J. Nadel, & R.P. Weissberg (Eds.), *Social Competence in Developmental Perspective* (pp. 371-386) Boston: Kluwer Academic Publishers.

Cowen, E.L. (1980). The wooing of primary prevention. *American Journal of Community Psychology, 8,* 258-284.

Cowen, E.L., Dorr, D., Clarfield, S., Kreling, B., McWilliams, S.A., Pokracki, F., Pratt, D.M., Terrell, D., & Wilson, A. (1973). The AML: A quick-screening device for early identification of school maladaptation. *American Journal of Community Psychology, 1,* 12-35.

Cowen, E.L., Pederson, A., Babigian, H., Izzo, L.D., & Trost, M.A. (1973). Long-term follow-up of early detected vulnerable children. *Journal of Consulting and Clinical Psychology, 41,* 438-446.

DuBois, D.L., Felner, R.D., & Brand, S. (1993). Self Evaluation Questionnaire. Unpublished manuscript University of Illinois, Center for Prevention Research and Development, Urbana.

Elias, M.J., Gara, M., & Ubriaco, M. (1985). Sources of stress and support in children's transition to middle school: An empirical analysis. *Journal of Clinical Child Psychology, 14,* 259-275.

Erikson, E.H. (1959). Identity and the life cycle. *Psychological Issues Monograph 1.* New York: Universities Press.

Felner, R.D., & Adan, A.M. (1988). The school transitional environment project. In R.H. Price, E.L. Cowen, R.P. Lorion, J. Ramos-McKay, & B. Hitchins (Eds.), *Fourteen Ounces of Prevention: A Casebook of Exemplary Primary Prevention Programs.* Washington, D.C.: American Psychological Association.

Felner, R.D., Adan, A.A., & Evans, E. (1987). *Evaluation of school-based primary prevention programs.* Unpublished manuscript.

Felner, R.D., Brand, S., DuBois, D.L., Adan, A.M., Mulhall, P.F., & Evans, E.G. (1993b). *Poverty and educational disadvantage: Environmental mediators of socioemotional and academic adjustment in early adolescence.* Manuscript submitted for publication.

Felner, R.D., Farber, S.S., & Primavera, J. (1983). Transitions and stressful life events: A model for primary prevention. In R.D. Felner, L.A. Jason, J.N. Moritsugu, & S.S. Farber (Eds.), *Preventive psychology: Theory, research, and prevention* (pp. 191-215). New York: Pergamon.

Felner, R.D., & Felner, T.Y. (1989). Primary prevention programs in the educational context: A transactional-ecological framework and analysis. In L.A. Bond & B.E. Compas (Eds.), *Primary prevention and promotion in the schools* (pp. 13-49). Newbury Park, CA: Sage.

Felner, R.D., Felner, T.Y., & Silverman, M.M. (1993a). Primary prevention: Conceptual and methodological issues in the development of a science of prevention in mental health and social intervention. In J.Rappaport and E.Seidman (Eds.), *Handbook of Community Psychology.* New York: Plenum Press.

Felner, R.D., Ginter, M., & Primavera, J. (1982). Primary prevention during school transitions: Social support and environmental structure. *American Journal of Community Psychology, 10,* 277-290.

Felner, R.D., Mulhall, P., Sartain, B., Standiford, S., Brand, S., & Kasak, D. (1992). *The evaluation of the impact of middle grades restructuring on school regular-*

ities, climate, and student outcomes. Presentation to Annual Meeting of the National Middle School Association, San Antonio, Texas.

Felner, R.D., Primavera, J., & Cauce, A. (1981). The impact of school transitions: A focus for preventive efforts. *American Journal of Community Psychology, 9,* 449-459.

Felner, R.D., Schroeder, T., & Brand, S. (1993c). *RICCA High Risk Youth Project.* Unpublished manuscript, University of Illinois, Center for Prevention Research and Development-IGPA, Urbana.

Furman, W., Giberson, R., White, A.S., Gravin, L.A., & Wehner, E.A. (1989). Enhancing peer relations in school systems. In B.H. Schneider, G. Attili, J. Nadel, & R.P. Weissberg (Eds.), *Social Competence in Developmental Perspective* (pp. 355-370) Boston: Kluwer Academic Publishers.

Galloway, D. (1985). *Schools and persistent absentees.* New York: Pergamon Press.

Hightower, A.D., Work, W.C., Cowen, E.L., Lotyzewski, B.S., Spinell, A.P., Guare, J.C., Rohrbeck, C.A. (1986). The Teacher-Child Rating Scale: A brief objective measure of elementary children's school problem behaviors and competencies. *School Psychology Review, 15,* 393-409.

Hirsch, B.H., & Rapkin, B.D. (1987). The transition to junior high school: A longitudinal study of self-esteem, psychological symptomatology, school life and social support. *Child Development, 58,* 1235-1243.

Jason, L.A., Weine, A.M., Johnson, J.H., Warren-Sohlberg, L., Filippelli, L.A., Turner, E.Y., & Lardon, C. (1992). *Helping transfer students: Strategies for educational and social readjustment.* San Francisco: Jossey-Bass.

Kellam, S., Branch, J., Agrawal, K., & Ensminger, M. (1975). *Mental hygiene and going to school.* Chicago: University of Chicago Press.

Kelly, J.G. (1986). An ecological paradigm: Defining mental health consultation as a preventive service. *Prevention in Human Services, 4,* 1-36.

Kovacs, M. (1981). Rating scales to assess depression in school-aged children. *Acta Paedopsychiatry, 46,* 305-315.

Moos, R.H. (1979). *Evaluating educational environments.* San Francisco: Jossey-Bass.

Newcomb, M.D., & Bentler, P.M. (1988). Impact of adolescent drug use and social support on problems of young adults: A longitudinal study. *Journal of Abnormal Psychology, 97,* 64-75.

Reynolds, C.R. & Richmond, B.O. (1978). What I think and feel: a revised measure of children's anxiety. *Journal of Abnormal Child Psychology. 55,* 432-444.

Rotherman, M.J. (1988). The children's assertiveness training program. In R.H. Price, E.L. Cowen, R.P. Lorion, J. Ramos-McKay, & B. Hitchins (Eds), *Fourteen ounces of prevention: A casebook of exemplary primary prevention programs.* Washington, D.C.: American Psychological Association.

Rutter, M. (1980). *Changing youth in a changing society: Patterns of adolescent development and disorder.* Cambridge, MA: Harvard University Press.

Sameroff, A.J., & Fiese, B.H. (1989). Conceptual issues in prevention. In D.

Schaffer, I. Phillips, N.B. Enzer, M.M. Silverman, & V. Anthony (Eds.), *Prevention of mental disorders alcohol and other drug use in children and adolescents: OSAP Prevention Monograph-2* (pp. 23-54). DHHS Publication No. (ADM) 89-1646. Washington, D.C.: U.S. Government Printing Office.

Sarason, S.B. (1982). *The culture of the school and the problem of change* (2nd ed.). Boston: Allyn & Bacon.

Seidman, E. (1987). Toward a framework for primary prevention research. In J.A. Steinberg & M.M. Silverman (Eds.), *Preventing mental disorder: A research perspective*. DHHS Publication No. (ADM) 87-1492. Washington, D.C.: U.S. Government Printing Office.

Shure, M.B., & Spivack, G. (1982). Interpersonal problem-solving in young children: A cognitive approach to prevention. *American Journal of Community, 10*, 341-356.

Simmons, R.G., & Blyth, D.A. (1987). *Moving into adolescence: The impact of pubertal change and school context*. New York: Aldine De Gruyter.

Simmons, R.G., Blyth, D.A., VanCleave, E.F., & Bush, D.M. (1979). Entry into early adolescence: The impact of school structure, puberty, and early dating on self-esteem. *American Sociological Review, 44*, 948-967.

Simmons, R.G., Burgeson, R., Carlton-Ford, S., & Blyth, D.A. (1987). The impact of cumulative change in early adolescence. *Child Development, 58*, 1220-1234.

Task Force on Education of Young Adolescents. (1989). *Turning points: Preparing American youth for the 21st century*. Washington, D.C.: Carnegie Corporation of New York, Carnegie Council on Adolescent Development.

Trickett, E.J. (1991). *Living an idea: Empowerment and the evolution of an alternative high school*. Brookline Books.

U.S. Department of Health, Education, and Welfare (1975). *Dropout Prevention*. Washington, D.C.: Educational Resources Information Center, (ERIC Document Reproduction Service No. ED 105 354).

Zax, M., & Specter, G.A. (1974). *An introduction to community psychology*. New York: Wiley & Sons.

Identifying High-Risk Students During School Transition

Olga Reyes
Don Hedeker

University of Illinois at Chicago

SUMMARY. A preventive, community-based program was designed to facilitate high school transition and reduce dropout. Participants in the study were ninth grade, predominantly Hispanic inner-city students. School absence was used as a variable to identify students who were at high risk for failure. Compared with low- and middle-absence groups, the high-absence groups' failures and class rankings deteriorated consistently across time points. In addition, over time, high-absence group students experienced more pronounced increases in school absence and decreases in academic achievement relative to low- and middle-absence counterparts. Findings are discussed in terms of their implications for dropout prevention programming.

Nationwide, high school dropout rates are alarmingly high, while effective solutions to the problem are not readily forthcoming. One novel approach to the dropout problem involves focusing on the

---

Address correspondence to: Olga Reyes, Psychology Department (M/C 285), UIC, Box 4348, Chicago, IL 60680.

[Haworth co-indexing entry note]: "Identifying High-Risk Students During School Transition." Reyes, Olga, and Don Hedeker. Co-published simultaneously in *Prevention in Human Services* (The Haworth Press, Inc.) Vol. 10, No. 2, 1993, pp. 137-150; and: *Prevention and School Transitions* (ed: Leonard A. Jason, Karen E. Danner, and Karen S. Kurasaki) The Haworth Press, Inc., 1993, pp. 137-150. Multiple copies of this article/chapter may be purchased from The Haworth Document Delivery Center. Call 1-800-3-HAWORTH (1-800-342-9678) between 9:00 - 5:00 (EST) and ask for DOCUMENT DELIVERY CENTER.

© 1993 by The Haworth Press, Inc. All rights reserved.

transition period between elementary school and high school, a period clearly shown to be one of increased vulnerability for school maladjustment (Felner, Ginter, & Primavera, 1982). It has been found that after children enter high school, some may experience significant decreases in academic performance and increases in absenteeism (Felner, Primavera, & Cauce, 1981), both factors which have been previously identified as strong predictors of later school failure or "dropping out" (Lloyd, 1978). Several other studies have indicated that although minorities and low-income individuals are typically at heightened risk for school failure, they are increasingly more susceptible during the transition to high school (Cervantes, 1965; Elliot, Voss, & Werdling, 1966; Gad & Johnson, 1980; U.S. Department of Health, Education, & Welfare, 1975).

Elias, Gara and Ubriaco (1985) have listed the challenges posed by transitions. They encompass students' coping (i.e., cognitive self-appraisal, problem solving) with the transition. In addition, social and academic adaptation involve: (a) shifts in role definition, (b) changes in membership and position in social networks, (c) reorganization of personal and social support resources, (d) restructuring the way one perceives one's world, and (e) management of stress resulting from uncertainty about expectations and goals and one's ability to accomplish the transition tasks. In addition, students must also gain their new teachers' acceptance and adapt to a new set of school rules and academic standards (Holland, Kaplan, & Davis, 1974). Additional logistical tasks to be mastered if students are to succeed in high school include: (a) locating classes in the new building, (b) understanding how classes are programmed, (c) identifying graduation requirements, (d) understanding prerequisites for classes, (e) finding the right office or individual to go to with scheduling problems or academic difficulties, and (f) finding out about locker assignments and lunch procedures (Reyes & Jason, 1991).

Felner, Ginter, and Primavera (1982) designed a program to facilitate the transition to high school for freshmen students, which aimed at increasing the level of social support available to students as well as reducing the degree of flux and complexity in the school setting. The project's two primary components involved a redefinition of the homeroom teachers' role, and a reduction in the overall complexity of the setting for students. Participants in the Felner et al.

project were found to have significantly better attendance records, grade point averages, and more stable self-concepts compared to matched counterparts at the end of the school year. A long-term, follow-up study using school records further attested to the program's enduring effects (Felner & Adan, 1988). Project participants were found to exhibit a lower dropout rate compared with controls. In addition, project participants were found to earn significantly higher grades and fewer absences than control counterparts during their first and second years of high school. These differences were smaller by the third and fourth years as a result of differential dropout rates for the two groups (Felner & Adan, 1988).

In Chicago, a group of motivated teachers at an inner-city high school were also concerned with easing the transition for incoming freshmen at their highly gang-active, high dropout rate, low-income school. Though unaware of it, the teachers' Dropout Prevention Program design closely resembled the intervention developed and implemented by Felner et al. (1982). In the program's first year, for example, the teachers of the Dropout Prevention Program identified program components similar to those targeted by Felner et al. (1982). They also chose to restructure the role of the homeroom teacher and reorganize the school environment to reduce system flux. However, unlike Felner et al. (1982), program teachers also decided to include an attendance monitoring component in which a freshmen attendance counselor investigated students' absences.

Like Felner et al.'s (1982) teachers, program teachers also provided incoming freshmen students with a homeroom teacher whose role included guidance and counseling components. In addition, the student population of the homerooms was comprised solely of project participants for each of the programs.

Both programs also attempted to modify school complexity and largeness by reorganizing the social system of the setting. For both of the respective programs, this reorganization involved placing participants together in several of their classes. However, Felner et al. took this component one step further than Chicago program teachers by also locating Transition Project students' classes in a "wing" of the building. Thus, their travel about the school was limited to a restricted area, which further reduced the school's complexity and largeness.

Thompson (1987) evaluated the Chicago Dropout Prevention Program at the end of its first year. Comparison of participant and control students on academic and attendance variables indicated only one significant difference between the groups, where controls earned higher grade point averages in the final quarter of the school year. Both groups performed below average academically throughout the school year. Thompson offered several reasons for the failure of this program, including teachers' inexperience with the novel program and teachers' inability to meet together regularly as they had initially planned in order to discuss and address program issues.

The second year the program was implemented attempts were made to strengthen the intervention, while retaining the same basic goals and components, and the program's similarity to the Felner et al. (1982) Transition Project. First, the attendance monitoring component was replaced by an academic progress feedback component. This feedback component was absent from the Felner et al. (1982) Transition Project. Finally, in the social system reorganization component, teachers modified the number of classes program students shared.

In an evaluation of the project, Reyes and Jason (1991) found that both the Experimental and Control students experienced decreases in grades and overall class rank, and increases in course failures, absenteeism and class cutting over the course of the treatment year.

The evaluations (Reyes & Jason, 1991; Thompson, 1987) of both versions of the Dropout Prevention Program clearly indicated that the experimental and control groups appear to be at similar risk for school failure. Although a number of reasons were offered for the program's lack of effect, the overwhelming and threatening nature of the Dropout Prevention Program setting was considered to be a primary influencing factor in the program's general failure. In this light, it was considered that even though both experimental and control students were similarly at risk, there might be an especially high-risk group of students who is more acutely susceptible to failure in such an overwhelming setting.

The present study attempts to identify those students who may be at particularly high risk for failure based on their school absence in the eighth grade. Absence and truancy are well-known precursors to school failure (Bachman, Green, & Wirtanen, 1971; Conrath, 1984; Howell & Frese, 1982; Ziesner, 1984). One prediction study found absence to be one of the best predictors of school failure and dropout (Pallas, 1984). Researchers have found that the attendance of dropouts begins to decline as early as the sixth grade, touching off a process of disengagement from school that becomes accelerated in the later junior high years and in the transition to high school (Roderick, 1992). That is, dropouts evidence significant decreases in attendance compared with the stable attendance of counterparts who ultimately graduate from high school. Specifically, eighth grade absence emerges as an important predictor of early school leaving (Roderick, 1992).

In the present study, school absence was used to further distinguish the groups. The results of this re-examination of the Dropout Prevention Program are reported here.

METHOD

Design/Participants

Participants were ninth grade students, half of whom comprised the Experimental Group (E), the other half, the Control Group (C). (See Reyes & Jason, 1991, for a complete description of this sample). During the summer prior to the ninth grade, all program eligible students (at the time only 130 students were identified as meeting program criteria) were randomly assigned to the E or C conditions. The entire Experimental group ($n = 77$) was drawn from this pool at the time, due to the school's policies with regard to "special programs." (The school requires that any students participating in special programming are to have their class schedules done first.) The remaining 53 students from this initial pool were assigned to the C Group with 24 additional eligible students who did not enroll in the school until September, for a total of 77 C group students. All students were entering a large urban high school (total enrollment of approximately 2800) that had a high dropout rate (60%), and served a predominantly Hispanic (77%) and low-income student body (56%) (City of Chicago, Board of Education, 1985).

Students were identified as at risk for dropping out of school on the basis of three criteria: (a) being from low-income families, (b) residing in an ethnic minority and low-income neighborhood, and (c) transitioning from grade school (kindergarten through eighth grade) to high school. Because of the primary preventive nature of the study, only academically average students were targeted. Satisfaction of this criterion was based on students' eligibility for regular education status in English and Mathematics, as defined by the City of Chicago, Board of Education (1985). Eligibility for regular education status was determined by students' eighth grade scores on the Iowa Test of Basic Skills (Hieronymous, Hoover, & Lindquist, 1988). Students were classified in terms of their total eighth grade year absence into one of three groups: (1) a low-absence group with five or fewer absences, (2) a middle-absence group with 6-10 absences, and (3) a high-absence group missing school 11 days or more.

Project Description

As indicated earlier, three components were emphasized: (a) redefining the role of the homeroom teacher, (b) reorganizing the school environment to reduce system flux, and (c) providing parents with feedback on student progress. As in the Felner et al. (1982) study, the E's homeroom teacher served as a primary source of information about the school and as a link between the students, parents, and the other sections of the school. Additionally, the homeroom teacher provided E students with guidance around school difficulties or concerns (i.e., problems with other teachers or other students, class scheduling issues). Homeroom teachers also contacted parents by telephone in order to introduce themselves and address any questions they had about the program. In addition, the homeroom teachers mailed a letter to parents at the beginning of the school year, encouraging them to maintain close contact with the homeroom teacher.

The structural reorganization of the school's social system was intended to reduce the degree of change that E students encountered and to facilitate the restructuring and reestablishment of peer supports. Also similar to the Felner et al. (1982) study, E students in this program were assigned to classes only with other E students. However, whereas Felner et al.'s (1982) participants shared four primary academic classes throughout their day (English, Mathematics, Social Studies, and Science), E students in the present study saw fellow participants in only three primary subjects (English, Mathematics, and Social Studies). In both studies, E students were also grouped only with project participants in their respective homerooms. This restructuring component was designed to provide students with the stability of a peer group in three of their classes as well as in their homeroom. Thus, there was no longer a constantly shifting peer group in several of students' classes throughout the school day, as was the case for the rest of the freshman class. Furthermore, as in the Felner et al. (1982) study, the homeroom teacher also taught one of the students' main subjects. This component of the intervention was designed to enhance students' sense of belonging as well as to reduce the complexity of the school environment.

The final component of the intervention, absent in the Felner et al. (1982) study, featured a feedback system to keep parents informed of students' performance. Parents received progress reports on students' performance approximately every five weeks. Although initially the intent was to send progress reports every two weeks, teachers chose to extend the period between reports because they felt that insufficient academic information was available on students at the twice-monthly rate. Project teachers and the researcher collaborated on the design of the progress report. However, at midyear, teachers modified the progress report as the original version proved too taxing and time consuming. E homeroom teachers encouraged parents to contact homeroom teachers to discuss their children's progress and how they might facilitate their children's achievement. Control students (Cs) did not participate in any of these components. Instead, these students followed procedures typical for that school and most public high school students. Their six classes (four primary, and two minor) were composed of a mixture of the remaining incoming freshmen as well as sophomore students repeating their freshmen year. Additionally, homeroom teachers' role was not extended to include guidance and counseling responsibilities, as did E homeroom teachers. Further, C homeroom teachers did not contact students' parents, either by letter or phone. Finally, the parents of the C students did not receive regular progress reports detailing the academic performance and progress of the students, as did E parents.

Measures

Data were obtained on E and C students' academic and behavioral adjustment to school in the ninth grade. Data was gathered from students' academic records and relevant departmental sources (i.e., attendance office, counseling office).

Academic Adjustment Measures. E and C students' ninth grade records served as the primary source of data. From first and second semesters of the ninth grade, data was gathered on E and C students': grade point averages for English, Mathematics, and Social Studies; number of course failures in these subject areas; absenteeism rates; and number of classes not attended when students had been present in their homeroom. Students' rank position within the freshmen class was also collected. Rank position was calculated by determining students' class standing using a four-point scale: 1 = bottom quarter of class, 2 = bottom half of class, 3 = top half of class, 4 = top quarter of class. For example, a student ranking 300 in the class of 1166 would fall into the top half of the class or into category 3.

Behavioral Adjustment Measures. Dropout and counseling referral data were also gathered from students' ninth grade records at the end of the school year.

RESULTS

To examine the change across timepoints in those variables repeatedly measured, for the subgroups defined by condition (E vs. C) and rate of absenteeism (low, middle, high), repeated measures analysis of co-variance (ANCOVA) models (Winer, 1971) were used. For the dichotomous variables, which were assessed only at the end of the school year (school-leaving and counseling referral rates), a logistic regression was used to analyze condition and condition by absence-group effects. In all of these analyses, covariate-adjustment of the eighth grade math levels (on Iowa Test of

Basic Skills, Hieronymous, Hoover, & Lindquist, 1988) was performed in order to test for the effects of condition, absenteeism, and the interaction of condition by absenteeism, while statistically controlling for the effect of the eighth grade math levels. Eighth grade math scores were included as a covariate in the analyses because significant differences were found between groups on this measure in previous analyses (Reyes & Jason, 1991). Both the condition and absenteeism effects were examined using a-priori contrasts (Bock, 1975) in order to specifically assess: experimental vs. control group differences, low- vs. middle-absence differences, and high- vs. middle- and low-absence differences. Finally, with only two timepoints for the repeated measures analyses (ninth grade first and second semesters), time-related effects were characterized as effects which were constant over time or those which differed between the two timepoints.

Group means and standard deviations on intervention variables for the two condition groups (experimental and control) by absenteeism are summarized in Table 1. In terms of GPA scores, the repeated measures ANCOVA revealed a significant absenteeism by time interaction ($F = 3.10$, $df = 2,115$, $p < .05$). Inspection of the specific contrasts revealed the difference to be attributable to a larger decrease in GPA scores across time for the high absenteeism group relative to the low- and middle-absence groups ($t = 2.20$, $p < .03$). A significant time effect was also observed, indicating a decrease in all students' GPA scores over time ($F = 27.17$, $df = 1,115$, $p < .001$).

For the analysis of average failures, the repeated measures ANCOVA indicated a significant absenteeism main effect ($F = 6.22$, $df = 2,113$, $p < .003$). Inspection of the contrasts revealed an increased rate of failure for the high absenteeism group as compared to the low- and middle-absence groups ($t = 3.52$, $p < .001$). This difference in the rate of failure for absenteeism groups was consistent across the two timepoints. An overall difference between the two timepoints was observed ($F = 42.47$, $df = 1,114$, $p < .001$), however, indicating a general increase in the failure rate among all students across time.

With respect to absence, the repeated measures ANCOVA analysis indicated a significant absenteeism main effect ($F = 6.47$, $df =$

Table 1.

Means and Standard Deviations on Criterion Measures at the Beginning and End of the Ninth Grade for Experimental and Control Groups by Absenteeism Rate

	Group											
	Experimental						Control					
			Group by Absenteeism Rate									
	Lo		Mid		Hi		Lo		Mid		Hi	
Variables	M	(SD)	M	(SD)	M	(SD)	M	(SD)	M	(SD)	M	(SD)
GPA 1st semester	2.8	(2.8)	2.5	(2.8)	3.0	(2.7)	1.0	(1.1)	1.1	(.9)	1.0	(1.0)
GPA 2nd semester	2.5	(2.7)	2.1	(2.6)	2.9	(2.1)	1.2	(1.1)	1.3	(1.1)	1.1	(1.2)
Failures 1st sem.	.7	(.9)	1.7	(2.0)	.5	(1.5)	1.3	(1.9)	1.8	(1.3)	.7	(2.1)
Failures 2nd sem.	1.6	(1.4)	3.1	(1.6)	1.0	(2.5)	2.1	(2.2)	2.6	(2.0)	1.2	(2.4)
Absences 1st sem.	3.9	(4.9)	8.5	(4.6)	2.9	(9.4)	5.2	(7.8)	8.5	(6.2)	2.7	(10.8)
Absences 2nd sem.	9.4	(10.4)	20.3	(10.3)	5.8	(20.3)	14.1	(20.0)	23.1	(15.8)	5.6	(21.8)
Class Cuts 1st sem.	2.3	(5.4)	5.3	(3.2)	3.6	(4.1)	3.7	(16.2)	9.4	(3.1)	3.5	(4.8)
Class Cuts 2nd sem.	9.7	(8.9)	18.6	(8.9)	9.2	(10.8)	10.6	(7.9)	18.1	(7.9)	10.3	(13.9)
Class Rank 1st sem.	3.5	(3.3)	2.7	(3.2)	3.6	(3.0)	1.4	(1.0)	1.2	(.5)	.5	(1.3)
Class Rank 2nd sem.	3.3	(3.1)	2.5	(3.3)	3.5	(2.8)	.8	(.8)	1.3	(.9)	.7	(1.3)
Couns. Referral Rate	0.0	(0.0)	0.0	(0.0)	0.1	(0.3)	0.0	(0.0)	0.0	(0.0)	0.1	(0.2)
School-Leave Rate	0.1	(0.3)	0.0	(0.0)	0.0	(0.0)	0.04	(0.2)	0.0	(0.0)	0.0	(0.0)

2,116, $p < .01$). The contrasts revealed the difference to be attributable to a significantly higher rate of absences for the high absenteeism group as compared to the low- and middle-absence groups (t = 3.60, $p < .001$). In addition, a significant absenteeism by time interaction (F = 2.99, df = 2,117, $p < .05$) was observed. Specific contrasts revealed the difference to be attributable to a larger increase in absences across time for the high absenteeism group relative to the low- and medium-absence groups (t = -2.39, $p < .05$). Finally, a significant overall difference between the two time points was found (F = 34.68, df = 2,117, p < .001), indicating a general increase in absence rate among all students.

For students' class rank, the repeated measures ANCOVA indicated a significant absenteeism main effect (F = 5.99, df = 2,113, $p < .01$). Specific contrasts indicated the difference was attributable to the high absence group's consistently lower class rank in relative to the low- and medium-absence groups (t = -3.44, $p < .001$). In addition, a time effect was observed, indicating all students' general decrease in class ranking (F = 8.03, df = 2,114, $p < .01$) over time.

Repeated measures analysis of class cuts revealed a significant time effect (F = 38.88, p = 2,116, p < .001), indicating all students' overall increase in class cuts over time.

Finally, the logistic regression on students' end-of-the-ninth-grade school-leave and counseling referral rates indicated no group or group by absence-group effects.

DISCUSSION

In their evaluation of the Dropout Prevention Program, Reyes and Jason (1991) considered the setting and its troubled nature in understanding the effects of the intervention. Specifically, the school's longstanding history of gang, drug, and other social problems were cited as factors that might have overwhelmed the intervention's potential. Youngsters who attend the school must contend with a host of pressures including whether to join a gang, whether to use drugs and alcohol, and whether to become sexually active and risk early parenthood. For example, in a previous study conducted in the same setting, students revealed a pervasive fear of physical harm, even death as a result of gang violence in the school.

In discussing gang pressures, almost every respondent reported experience with gang fear, pressure, or violence in the school or the neighborhood (Reyes & Jason, in press).

This background information on the school setting serves as a basis for understanding that all students who attend the present school are at some level of risk. Program and control students' performances deteriorated significantly across all measures by the program's end.

With respect to risk status, if allegedly academically able students all experienced deteriorated school performances by year's end, does that mean that risk is indistinguishable among these students? The findings from this study suggest not and point to a group of students whose risk status is distinctly high, based on their high rate of school absence in the eighth grade. On two well-known precursors for school failure, absence and academic achievement, high-absence students' performances worsened more over time compared with the low- and middle-absence groups. That is, though their peers' school absence and academic achievement also deteriorated over time, the decline was most pronounced for the high-absence group. If students do not attend classes, it is likely that they will not be achieving in those classes. Consequently, the high-absence students' susceptibility for school failure is heightened. In addition, with respect to course failures and class rank, the high-absence group experienced a consistent drop in performance on these measures compared with low- and middle-absence groups. That is, this descent was not evidenced as a function of time. Instead, from one time point to the next, students were consistent in their number of course failures and their decrease in class rankings.

The findings from this study provide implications for dropout prevention programming with students in transition and with high-absence, high-risk students. The literature on school transitions attributes declines in students' academic and behavioral performances to difficulties in adjustment to the new school level (Felner, Ginter, & Primavera, 1982; Reyes & Jason, 1991). This is one way in which the observed deteriorated performances of all the students in this study might be understood. In this case, the implication is that research should continue to focus on normative school transitions. This research should focus on identifying both the factors that heighten youngsters' vulnerability during this time and methods for effectively intervening.

The principal finding of this study is that there is a highly absent group who suffers pronounced declines in school performance relative to peers who miss school less. Such students might benefit from interventions that specifically target this high-risk behavior. That is, new freshmen who begin to evidence absence problems could be identified and reasons for their excessive school absence explored. Appropriate, relevant measures could then be taken based on these findings.

Another implication of the findings is that although high-absence students were advantaged by virtue of their average academic status, they began high school with other disadvantages. Eighth grade absence may in fact be masking other problems which affect students' general school performance and make them uniquely vulnerable during the school transition compared with their peers. Examination of these students' elementary school records may reveal a pattern of school absence or other difficulties. Students evidencing such a pattern might be targeted for more intensive interventions that are tailored to their specific needs.

Ideally, students with longstanding absence and other difficulties should be identified much earlier in their educational careers. For researchers and educators the task is then to develop measures for identifying students at the earliest sign of school difficulty. Preventive programs could be implemented with such youngsters and patterns of long-term poor achievement and school failure potentially averted.

REFERENCES

Bachman, J.G., Green, S., & Wirtanen, J.D. (1971). *Dropping out: Problem or symptom?* Ann Arbor, MI: Institute for Social Research.

Bock, R.D. (1975). *Multivariate Statistical Methods in Behavioral Research.* New York: McGraw-Hill.

Cervantes, L. (1965). *The Dropout: Cause and Cures.* Ann Arbor: The University of Michigan Press.

City of Chicago, Board of Education. (1985). *1984-85 Test Scores and Selected School Characteristics.* Chicago: Author.

Conrath, J. (1984). Snatching victory from the jaws of learning defeat: How one school fought the dropout blitz. *Contemporary Education, 56,* 87-95.

Elias, M.J., Gara, M., Ubriaco, M. (1985). Sources of stress and support in chil-

dren's transition to middle school: An empirical analysis. *Journal of Clinical Child, 14,* 112-118.
Elliot, D., Voss, H., & Werdling, A. (1966). Capable dropouts and the social milieu of high school. *Journal of Educational Research, 60,* 180-186.
Felner, R., & Adan, A. (1988). The school transitional environment project: An ecological intervention and evaluation. In R. Price, E. Cowen, R. Lorion, & J. Ramos-McKay (Eds.), *Fourteen ounces of prevention: A casebook for practitioners* (pp. 111-122). Washington, D.C.: American Psychological Association.
Felner, R.D., Ginter, M., & Primavera, J. (1982). Primary prevention during school transitions: Social support and environmental structure. *American Journal of Community Psychology, 10,* 277-290.
Felner, R.D., Primavera, J., & Cauce, A.M. (1981). The impact of school transitions: A focus for preventive efforts. *American Journal of Community Psychology, 9,* 449-459.
Gad, M., & Johnson, J. (1980). Correlates of adolescent life stress as related to race, SES, and level of perceived social support. *Journal of Clinical and Child Psychology, 9,* 13-16.
Hieronymous, A.N., Hoover, H.D., & Lindquist, E.L. (1988). Iowa Test of Basic Skills. Chicago: Riverside Publishing.
Holland, J.V., Kaplan, D., & Davis S. (1974). Inter-school transfers: A mental health challenge. *Journal of School Health, 44,* 74-79.
Howell, F.M., & Frese, W. (1982). Early transition into adult roles: Some antecedents and outcomes. *American Educational Research Journal, 19,* 51-73.
Lloyd, D.N. (1978). Prediction of school failure from third grade data. *Educational and Psychological Measurement, 38,* 1193-1200.
Pallas, A.M. (1984). *The determinants of high school dropout.* Unpublished doctoral dissertation, Johns Hopkins University, Maryland.
Reyes, O., & Jason, L.A. (1993). Pilot study examining factors associated with academic success for Hispanic high school students. *Journal of Youth and Adolescence, 22*(1), 57-71.
Reyes, O., & Jason, L.A. (1991). An evaluation of a high school dropout prevention program. *Journal of Community Psychology, 19,* 221-230.
Roderick, M. (1992). School transitions and school dropout: Middle school and early high school antecedents to school leaving. Manuscript submitted for publication.
Thompson, K. (1987). *Comparisons of achievement, attendance, and success between two groups of high school freshmen: TEAM '90 and Regular English I.* Unpublished master's thesis, National College of Education, Chicago.
U.S. Department of Health, Education, Welfare. (1975). *Dropout Prevention* (First in a Series of Three). Washington, D.C.: Education Resources Information Center. (Eric Document Reproductions Service No. ED 105 354).
Winer, B.J. (1971). *Statistical principles in Experimental Design (2nd Edition).* New York: McGraw-Hill.
Ziesner, C. (1984). Student and staff perceptions of truancy and court referrals. *Social Work in Education, 6,* 167-178.

Alternative Schools: A School Transition for Adolescent Mothers

G. Anne Bogat
Belle Liang
Robert A. Caldwell
William Davidson II
Martha Bristor

Michigan State University

Marian Phillips
Mary Suurmeyer

Lansing School District

SUMMARY. Pregnant adolescents experience many simultaneous life transitions: normal adolescent development issues, parenting, and school transitions. Whether a transition into an alternative school is academically beneficial to the teen or not is a question of some debate. Our study examined the post-partum effects of an alternative education setting on academic achievement and educational success for a sample of pregnant and parenting adolescents. Subjects were mainly from low socioeconomic families and had a history of poor academic performance prior to their pregnancy. Results showed

---

[Haworth co-indexing entry note]: "Alternative Schools: A School Transition for Adolescent Mothers." Bogat, G. Anne et al. Co-published simultaneously in *Prevention in Human Services* (The Haworth Press, Inc.) Vol. 10, No. 2, 1993, pp. 151-168; and: *Prevention and School Transitions* (ed: Leonard A. Jason, Karen E. Danner, and Karen S. Kurasaki) The Haworth Press, Inc., 1993, pp. 151-168. Multiple copies of this article/chapter may be purchased from The Haworth Document Delivery Center. Call 1-800-3-HAWORTH (1-800-342-9678) between 9:00 - 5:00 (EST) and ask for DOCUMENT DELIVERY CENTER.

© 1993 by The Haworth Press, Inc. All rights reserved.

that attending an alternative school had mixed effects on academic outcomes. Post-pregnancy educational success (e.g., graduation from high school) was not related to attendance; however, the teens' post-pregnancy grade point averages were positively related to attendance. Future directions for research are discussed.

INTRODUCTION

School transitions have been recognized as significant and potentially stressful life events. Unfortunately, little research has examined how pregnant and parenting adolescents may react when faced with this stress.

School transitions involve movement from one school to another. They may involve a *group* of students making a progressive and scheduled change (e.g., graduation from elementary to junior high school) or they may be lateral and unscheduled changes involving an *individual* student (e.g., transferring to a new elementary school because of a family residential move) (Jason et al., 1992). As with all life stresses, an individual's subjective appraisal of the event and the number of concurrent life stresses will influence whether or not and the degree to which stress is experienced (Lazarus & Folkman, 1984). The literature on school transitions suggests that the transition itself leads to adjustment difficulties only when it occurs in conjunction with other, significant life stresses (Simmons, Burgeson, Carlton-Ford, & Blyth, 1987).

Among adolescents, there are negative consequences for students who must adjust to both school transitions and other stressors at the same time (Simmons, 1987). All adolescents, regardless of whether they are pregnant or parenting, are subject to certain stressful life events that can exacerbate the stress of a school transition. First, there are individual, biological changes such as puberty. Second, many social changes occur, particularly the increasing importance of peers (e.g., Mazor & Enright, 1988). However, even though peer support increases in its importance during the adolescent years, the literature seems to suggest that family support remains consistently important for the good adjustment of adolescents (e.g., Fenzel & Blyth, 1978). These normative physical and social changes may exacerbate the stress associated with school transitions.

Many school transitions are particularly difficult for adolescents. Often there is not just a physical move to another school building, but the nature of school itself changes at this time. Typically, during adolescence the student must master an ecological transition from a small, child-centered elementary school to a large, subject matter oriented middle/high school (Simmons et al., 1987). In addition, the changing role of the student is accompanied by changing expectations of teachers, parents, and peers. In combination, these changes can overwhelm an adolescent's coping ability.

> Children appear less able to cope if at the same time they are uncomfortable with their bodies because of physical changes, with family because of changes in family constellation, with home because of a move, with school because of great discontinuity in the nature of the school environment, and with peers because of the emergence of opposite-sex relationships and the disruption of prior peer networks. (Simmons et al., 1987, pp. 1231-1232)

Pregnant and parenting adolescents may find themselves undergoing a school transition (either a progressive, scheduled one into a middle school or high school, or a lateral, unscheduled one into an alternative school) at the same time as the transition to parenthood. Elster, McAnarney, and Lamb (1983) have noted that "adolescent parents, particularly younger ones, are faced with a variety of situational 'crises,' which are superimposed upon a maturational crisis (adolescence) . . . each of which may be associated with some degree of normal stress" (p. 497). Becoming a parent has long been recognized as a life transition involving some amount of stress (Holmes & Rahe, 1967; LeMasters, 1968). However, when such transitions occur earlier or later than socially prescribed norms dictate, higher levels of stress may result (Russell, 1980). For example, the physical stress of pregnancy is greater among school-aged women than older women; younger women are more likely to experience medical complications such as prematurity, toxemia, anemia, and difficult labor (Ahmed, 1990; Klerman & Jekel, 1973). Indeed, adolescent pregnancy and childbirth are associated with greater health risks for both the mother and the child (Morbidity & Mortality Weekly Report, 1991; Phipps-Yonas, 1980).

Adolescent pregnancy also puts the mother at greater social risk. Pregnancy inevitably interrupts the schooling of adolescents, whether for a short time (e.g., immediately prior to and following birth) or permanently (e.g., dropping out). The degree of disruption may place the adolescent mother at both a vocational and financial disadvantage (Moore & Waite, 1977). For example, studies find that women who are or were adolescent mothers are more likely to receive financial assistance from the government as compared to nonadolescent mothers (Klerman & Jekel, 1973). This economic disadvantage is often compounded by the fact that women who have children as adolescents "tend to have more children, more unintended births, more nonmarital births, and closer spacing of births compared to those who delay childbearing" (Popovich, 1990, p. 14).

Many pregnant adolescents now have a choice of staying in their home school during the pregnancy or attending an alternative school. It is not known whether pregnant adolescents who transfer to an alternative educational setting undergo more or less academic stress. On the one hand, transfer students are faced with the stress of readjusting to a new environment and the accompanying new expectations and roles. Research with the general adolescent population has provided some evidence that students who experience many school transitions exhibit greater scholastic difficulties than those who transfer less often (Benson, Haycraft, Steyaert, & Weigel, 1979; Brockman & Reeves, 1967; Levine, Wesolowski, & Corbett, 1966; Schaller, 1976). On the other hand, there is also evidence that the number of transfers does not affect scholastic performance (Cramer & Dorsey, 1970; Marchant & Medway, 1987; Perrodin & Snipes, 1966) or may actually enhance academic performance and adjustment for some students (Goebel, 1981; Jones & Thornburg, 1985; Whalen & Fried, 1973). Socioeconomic status (SES) may influence whether the effects of multiple school transitions are positive or negative; higher SES students continue their good academic performances whereas lower SES students' performances decline (Felner, Primavera, & Cauce, 1981; Morris, Pestaner, & Nelson, 1967). However, the transition to an alternative school for pregnant adolescents may be more academically beneficial than the school transfers typically investigated. Alternative schools offer smaller classes, greater individualized attention from faculty and staff, as well as peer support from a more homogeneous student body.

Historically, alternative schools provided a mechanism to isolate pregnant adolescents from their nonpregnant cohorts. Early schools for "unwed mothers," in effect, negatively stigmatized the pregnant adolescent and protected other adolescents from learning more about sex, pregnancy, and childbirth. These early practices reflected the negative societal attitudes towards young, unmarried, pregnant women. By the late 1960's many of these attitudes were changing (Becker, 1989). "No longer did it seem important to punish . . . women's nonmarital sexual activity. . . . Visiting the 'sins' of the parents on the child seemed arbitrary, even cruel. 'Illegitimacy,' as an important and debilitating status, became suspect" (Becker, 1989, p. 497).

The current impetus for alternative schools stems from interest in prevention and early intervention. Few adolescents who carry to term opt for adoption. The National Research Council (1987) estimated that during 1982, 91% of white adolescent mothers and 95% of black adolescent mothers chose to keep their child. Furthermore, in 1986, for every 1,000 women who either had a baby out of wedlock or who aborted, there were only 10 who selected adoption (Waldrop, 1989). During the last 20 years, the availability of abortion and more tolerant attitudes toward single parenting have combined to dramatically reduce the number of adolescents who give their babies up for adoption (Popovich, 1990; Resnick, Blum, Bose, Smith, & Toogood, 1990). Thus, alternative schools play an important role for an increasing number of teens (and pre-teens) who become parents. These programs are viewed as (a) early childhood intervention programs where the initial attitudes and behaviors of young mothers toward their children can be influenced and (b) secondary intervention programs for the young mothers themselves, to keep them from dropping out of school and adversely affecting their postpregnancy lives.

Although many alternative high schools for pregnant and parenting adolescents exist throughout the country, few have been systematically evaluated. In an early study, Osofsky and Osofsky (1970) found that students attending an alternative high school had better academic and health outcomes than a comparison group of student mothers. Seitz, Apfel, and Rosenbaum (1991) found that length of attendance at an alternative high school was negatively related to repeat births. For poorer students, postpartum academic achievement was enhanced the longer the adolescent spent in the alternative school. Length of stay was unrelated to academic achievement for the better students.

The goal of this study was to describe the academic performance of adolescents who transferred into an alternative high school for pregnant and parenting adolescents. It was hypothesized that academic achievement (as measured by classroom grades and reading and math scores on the Stanford Achievement Test) and school attendance would improve as a result of participation. Furthermore, it was hypothesized that both post-pregnancy academic achievement and post-pregnancy educational success (e.g., graduation, drop-out) would be predicted by pre-pregnancy academic achievement, amount of attendance at YPED, and the interaction of the latter two independent variables. The interaction term was added to the regression analyses in an attempt to replicate the results of Seitz et al. (1991), who found that high and low GPA students were differentially affected by the amount of time they attended an alternative school.

METHOD

Setting

The alternative school that is the subject of this paper, the Young Parent's Educational Development (YPED) program, is a branch of the Lansing (Michigan) School District's secondary education system and serves as an alternative educational program for pregnant or new teenage mothers in the greater Lansing area. Pregnant teens are typically referred to the program by their home school counselors, public health nurses, hospital maternal support programs, or a variety of community agencies. The program is voluntary–pregnant teens may choose to stay in their home school, or they may choose to attend YPED. YPED serves approximately 70 students per year. Students enroll while pregnant and have the option of remaining in the program for the duration of the school year in which they give birth. However, teens who deliver very late in the school year (and thus participate only minimally in the YPED program) may choose to return to YPED the following year. Because YPED is an interim program for pregnant teens, the permanent academic and attendance records of students are maintained by their home schools.

The curriculum at YPED includes the typical course requirements of the home school (e.g., math, English) as well as courses specifically designed to enhance parenting competencies (e.g., child growth and development, nutrition). YPED students attend basic academic requirement courses (e.g., math, English) through the Adult Education Division of the school district; thus, teens are in attendance with adults working to complete their high school diplomas. At any given time during the school year, YPED has an active enrollment of approximately 40 students, taught by 25 teachers (mostly adult education instructors). The average class size for standard academic courses is 20 (about 1/3 are YPED teens); parenting classes are somewhat larger.

Services available through the YPED program extend beyond academic ones and include on-site day care, transportation to and from school, two meals every school day, career planning and job placement services, academic advising, and a visiting public health nurse who is at YPED once a week. The parenting classes include instruction in personal living, nutrition, child growth and development, parenting skills, and birth preparation.

Sample

The study sample consisted of 33 expectant or new adolescent mothers. (It should be noted that some teens in this sample were excluded from certain analyses due to missing data.) At the time of their enrollment in the YPED program, the teens ranged in age from 14 to 20 years of age (Mean = 16.7, Median = 17). There were 11 African-Americans, 8 Hispanics, 13 Caucasians, and 1 Native American. The only socioeconomic status (SES) information available for our teen participants was *their* mother's educational level: 2 had completed junior high school, 12 had some high school education, 8 were high school graduates, 5 attended some college, and 1 was a college graduate. The average length of time that teens were enrolled in YPED was 45.77 days (N = 33, range: 3-135).

Measures

Demographic Information

Information regarding age, ethnicity, SES, and attendance was obtained from YPED intake interviews. Attendance was calculated as a percentage: number of days present divided by the number of possible school days.

Academic Record

Information regarding the participants' yearly grade point average (GPA) and yearly Stanford Achievement Test math and reading scores was obtained from the school district's permanent records. (Unfortunately, substantial missing Stanford Achievement Test data made subjects Ns too small to perform meaningful ANOVAs on these math and reading scores.)

Procedures

Two cohorts of YPED participants were identified: those attending YPED in the 1988-1989 academic year and those attending in 1989-1990. Records were searched to obtain the above measures for the two years prior to entry into YPED and for either one or two years post YPED, depending on the cohort. Thus, data for five time points were collected for the first cohort, and four time points for the second.

RESULTS

Pre-Pregnancy Academic Achievement

Most of the participants were performing poorly in school prior to their pregnancy and enrollment at YPED. The pre-pregnancy GPA and Stanford reading and math scores were calculated based on the average score for the two years prior to YPED. The pre-pregnancy GPA was 1.42 (out of a possible 4.00, range: 0.00-3.53). Both Stanford reading and math scores were reported as percentiles. Subjects' mean reading score was 38.64 (range: 15.40-53.10); their mean math score was 39.26 (range: 6.7-69.10). For all outcome measures, higher scores indicate better academic achievement.

Post-Pregnancy Academic Achievement and Success

Post-pregnancy GPA was calculated as a mean of the YPED-year score and, depending on the cohort, either one or two years post-YPED. Subjects' mean post-pregnancy GPA was 1.24 (range: 0.00-3.40). Reading and math post-pregnancy scores were calculated as the mean of the two years (or the one year) post-YPED. The mean reading score was 42.09 (range 13.10-73.25); the mean math score was 42.48 (range: 1.00-88.60).

Our subjects had mixed educational outcomes for the year(s) following their YPED experience. The school district uses 18 very specific classifications to code educational outcomes. We combined these into three broad categories: still in school or graduated (42%), no longer attending school and not graduated (30.5%), still enrolled but with failing grades (22.9%). For example, the first category combines students enrolled in or graduated from adult educational settings and home schooling with those enrolled in or graduated from traditional high schools. (Also, in order not to bias scoring against younger teens, who may have not been eligible to graduate at the final post-YPED time point, this category includes both likely and actual receipt of diploma.) Together, these three categories comprise a continuum of "educational success."

Comparisons of Pre- to Post-Pregnancy Academic Achievement

Three separate repeated measures analyses of variance (ANOVAs) were undertaken to determine whether there was a significant difference between pre-pregnancy and post-pregnancy GPAs and Stanford math and reading scores. Only 24 subjects had both pre- and post-pregnancy GPA scores. There was no significant difference between pre- and post-GPAs [$M = 1.66$; $M = 1.51$; respectively, $F(1, 23) = .98$]. As stated earlier, missing Stanford Achievement score data precluded our conducting ANOVAs on math and reading scores.

Predictors of Academic Achievement and Educational Success

Analyses were undertaken to determine what factors were predictive of academic achievement and educational success following the YPED experience. Because large numbers of subjects were missing post-pregnancy math and reading scores, only post-pregnancy GPA was used as the dependent variable for academic achievement. (School District personnel indicated that most missing information was a result of extended and frequent school absences.) "Educational success," the variable described above, was the second dependent variable. Two step-wise multiple regressions were conducted to predict each dependent variable. In both equations, GPA pre-pregnancy scores were entered as the first variable, attendance at YPED was entered second, and the interaction of these two variables was entered third. (Because age and SES were not significantly correlated to academic achievement or success, they were not used in the regressions.) See Table 1 for correlations among dependent and independent variables.

The first regression, using post-pregnancy GPA as the dependent variable, found that pre-pregnancy GPA and attendance at YPED were significant predictors ($\Delta R2 = .42$, $\Delta F = 14.75$, $p < .01$; $\Delta R2 = .15$, $\Delta F = 6.58$, $p < .05$; respectively, all corrected for shrinkage); the interaction was not significant. Students who had better pre-pregnancy GPAs, relative to those who had performed more poorly, also had better post-pregnancy GPAs. Furthermore, those who had a greater dosage of YPED (i.e., more days of YPED attendance) had better post-pregnancy scores than did those with a lesser YPED dosage even after the effect of pre-pregnancy GPA was controlled. See Table 2 and Figure 1 for results and a graph of the regression lines.

The second regression, using educational success as the dependent variable, found that only pre-pregnancy GPA was a significant predictor variable ($\Delta R2 = .18$, $\Delta F = 5.62$, $p < .05$, corrected for shrinkage). Attendance at YPED and the interaction did not account for a significant amount of variance. Those students with higher pre-pregnancy GPAs were more likely to achieve academic success (e.g., high school diplomas or equivalent or still enrolled with passing grades). See Table 2 and Figure 2.

Table 1

Pearson Product Moment Correlations Among Variables

	AGE	SES	GPAPRE	GPAPOST	ATTENDANCE
AGE	1.00				
SES	-.07 (N=29)	1.00			
GPAPRE	-.25 (N=30)	.27 (N=26)	1.00		
GPAPOST	.21 (N=26)	.18 (N=22)	.65** (N=24)	1.00	
ATTENDANCE	.09 (N=31)	.43 (N=26)	.44* (N=27)	.58** (N=24)	1.00
EXITCODE	.16 (N=33)	.24 (N=28)	.45 (N=30)	.49 (N=25)	.28 (N=30)

[a] $p<.05$ [b] $p<.01$

Table 2

Hierarchical Regressions with Pre-Pregnancy GPA and YPED Attendance Predicting Educational Success and Academic Achievement

	Academic	Success		
GPA Pre-Pregnancy (G)	14.75[b]	14.75[b]	.42	.65
YPED Attendance (A)	12.72[b]	6.58[a]	.15	.40
G x A	8.57[b]	.69	.00	.49
	Academic	Achievement		
GPA Pre-Pregnancy	5.62[a]	5.62[a]	.18	.43
YPED Attendance	3.40[a]	1.15	.04	.21
G x A	2.30	.30	.01	.39

*N=27 **N=22 [a]$p<.05$ [b]$p<.01$

FIGURE 1. GPA Post-Pregnancy Predicted by Pre-Pregnancy GPA and YPED Dosage

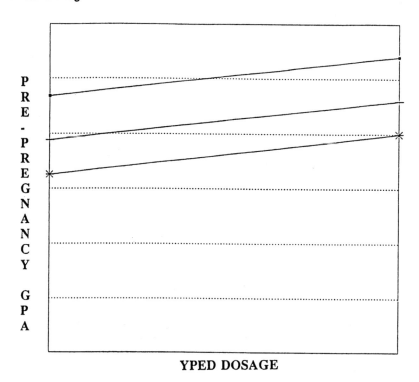

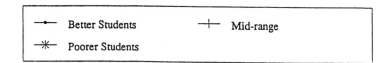

DISCUSSION

This paper was concerned with examining the relationship between attendance at an alternative school and pregnant adolescents' academic achievement and educational success. It should be noted that prior to their enrollment in YPED, the teens in our two cohorts were doing poorly in their academic work. Their attendance was

FIGURE 2. Educational Success as Predicted by YPED Dosage and Pre-Pregnancy GPA

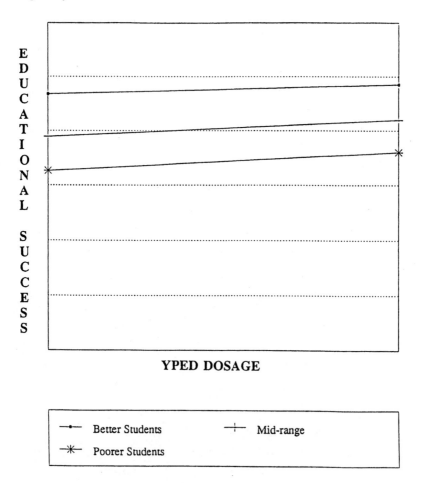

sporadic, and this may have resulted in the substantial amounts of missing data. Clearly, these teens were in academic trouble prior to their pregnancy.

The results of our analyses were mixed. Pre-pregnancy GPA is highly positively correlated with post-pregnancy GPA and educational success. ANOVAs for grades indicated no difference between pre- and post-pregnancy scores. Regressions indicated that the rate of attendance at YPED did not improve a student's chances of school completion or graduation; however, those students who attended YPED more often were better able to maintain their pre-pregnancy GPA.

The results reported here predicting academic success are different from those of Seitz et al. (1991) who found that the interaction between amount of intervention and pre-pregnancy academic achievement was significantly related to post-pregnancy academic success. In their study, poorer students benefitted most from higher intervention dosage. The disparity in the results of the two studies may result from initial differences in the samples as well as differences in the calculation of outcome variables. The pre-pregnancy GPA of Seitz et al.'s subjects was higher than ours. Seitz's subjects were also generally better school attenders prior to their pregnancy; in fact, absenteeism was considered high if students had missed more than 20 days of school. All teens in our study would have met this criterion. Furthermore, Seitz et al. analyzed most of their data using nonparametric statistics. Thus, intervention dosage was a categorical variable comprising either one, two, three, or four quarters of attendance. Our analyses were parametric and relied on continuous variables; in this case, intervention dosage was calculated based on actual days attended. Quarterly attendance is a generous indicator of dosage, but would have been particularly inaccurate in a population such as ours in which absenteeism was extremely high.

There are two possible explanations for the results of our study. First, because a comparison group of pregnant teens who stayed in their home schools was unavailable, it is difficult to confirm whether YPED had a substantial, positive impact upon our subjects. Subjects self-select into YPED, and it may be that the neediest and least academically-talented teens choose to attend. Therefore, one explanation of our results is that YPED is successful in maintaining pre-pregnancy academic performance (grades), an impressive feat given that this population is clearly well below normative academic standards.

Alternatively, one might argue that a longer time perspective is necessary in order to determine YPED's ultimate effects on teens' academic achievement. Our subjects were experiencing maturational crises coupled with a major role transition (parenting), all at about age 15 (mean age of subjects). The amount of stress from these crises may have exacerbated the stress that accompanied two significant schools transitions: transferring from the home school into YPED and then transferring out of YPED and back to the home school. It is likely that this amount of personal disruption cannot begin to dissipate within the one or two years in which we had data from our subjects. A longer time perspective may be necessary to ascertain YPED's success in fostering academic progress among these teens.

In conclusion, the mixed results of the YPED intervention indicate that alternative schools do not necessarily have a major, positive impact on pregnant and parenting teens. However, in the one and two years after the YPED intervention ends, teens generally maintain their pre-pregnancy achievement levels. Thus, the YPED school transition, although potentially stressful, may be worthwhile for such high-risk teens. Future research comparing pregnant teens who remain in their home schools (and do not undergo a school transition) with teens who choose to attend an alternative school is necessary in order to more fully understand the differential impact of the school transition and the pregnancy on the academic achievement and success of pregnant teens.

REFERENCES

Ahmed, R. (1990). Unmarried mothers as a high-risk group for adverse pregnancy outcomes. *Journal of Community Health, 15,* 35-45.

Becker, M. E. (1989). The rights of unwed parents: Feminist approaches. *Social Service Review, 63,* 496-517.

Bensen, G. P., Haycraft, J. R., Steyaert, J. P., & Weigel, D. J. (1979). Mobility in sixth graders as related to achievement, adjustment, and socioeconomic status. *Psychology in the Schools, 16,* 444-447.

Brockman, M., & Reeves, A. W. (1967). Relationship between transiency and test achievement. *Alberta Journal of Educational Research, 13,* 319-330.

Cramer, W., & Dorsey, S. (1970). Are movers losers? *Elementary School Journal, 70,* 387-390.

Elster, A. B., McAnarney, E. R., & Lamb, M. E. (1983). Parental behavior of adolescent mothers. *Pediatrics, 71,* 494-503.

Felner, R. D., Primavera, J., & Cauce, A. M. (1981). The impact of school transitions: A focus for preventive efforts. *American Journal of Community Psychology, 9,* 449-459.

Fenzel, L. M., & Blyth, D. A. (1986). Individual adjustment to school transitions: An exploration of the role of supportive peer relations. *Journal of Early Adolescence, 6,* 315-329.

Goebel, B. L. (1981). Mobile children: An American tragedy? *Psychological Reports, 48,* 15-18.

Holmes, T., & Rahe, R. H. (1967). The social readjustment rating scale. *Journal of Psychosomatic Research, 11,* 213-218.

Jason, L. A., Weine, A. M., Johnson, J. H., Warren-Sohlberg, L., Filippelli, L. A., Turner, E. Y., & Lardon, C. (1992). *Helping transfer students: Strategies for educational and school readjustment.* San Francisco: Jossey-Bass.

Jones, R. M., & Thornburg, H. D. (1985). The experience of school-transfer: Does previous relocation facilitate the transition from elementary- to middle-level educational environments? *Journal of Early Adolescence, 5,* 229-237.

Klerman, L. V., & Jekel, J. F. (1973). *School-age mothers: Problems, programs, and policy.* Hamden, CT: The Shoe String Press, Inc.

Lazarus, R. S., & Folkman, S. (1984). *Stress, appraisal, and coping.* New York: Springer Publishing Company.

LeMasters, E. (1968). *Sourcebook in marriage and family.* New York: Houghton Mifflin.

Levine, M., Wesolowski, J. C., & Corbett, F. J. (1966). Pupil turnover and academic performance in an inner city elementary school. *Psychology in the Schools, 3,* 153-160.

Marchant, K. H., & Medway, F. J. (1987). Adjustment and achievement associated with mobility in military families. *Psychology in the Schools, 24,* 289-294.

Mazor, A., & Enright, R. D. (1988). The development of the individuation process from a social-cognitive perspective. *Journal of Adolescence, 11,* 29-47.

Morbidity and Mortality Weekly Report. (1991). Trends in fertility and infant and maternal health–United States (1980-1988). *Journal of the American Medical Association, 266*(1), 24-25.

Moore, K. A., & Waite, L. J. (1977). Early childbearing and educational attainment. *Family Planning Perspective, 9,* 220-225.

Morris, J., Pestaner, M., & Nelson, A. (1967). Mobility and achievement. *Journal of Experimental Education, 35,* 74-79.

National Research Council. (1987). *Risking the future: Adolescent sexuality, pregnancy, and childbearing* (Vol. 1). Washington, D.C.: National Academy Press.

Osofsky, H. J., & Osofsky, J. D. (1970). Adolescents as mothers: Results of a program for low-income pregnant teenagers with some emphasis upon infants' development. *American Journal of Orthopsychiatry, 40,* 825-834.

Perrodin, A. F., & Snipes, W. P. (1966). The relationship of mobility to achievement in reading, arithmetic, and language in selected Georgia elementary schools. *Journal of Educational Research, 59,* 315-319.

Phipps-Yonas, S. (1980). Teenage pregnancy and motherhood: A review of the literature. *American Journal of Orthopsychiatry, 50,* 403-431.

Popovich, S. N. (1990). *The relationship of family environment, mothers' influ-*

ence, and pregnant adolescents' decisions to keep or release their babies for adoption. Unpublished doctoral dissertation, Michigan State University, East Lansing, MI.

Resnick, M. D., Blum, R. W., Bose, J., Smith, M., & Toogood, R. (1990). Characteristics of unmarried adolescent mothers: Determinants of child rearing versus adoption. *American Journal of Orthopsychiatry, 60,* 577-585.

Schaller, J. (1976). Geographic mobility as a variable in ex-post facto research. *British Journal of Educational Psychology, 46,* 341-343.

Seitz, V., Apfel, N. H., & Rosenbaum, L. K. (1991). Effects of an intervention program for pregnant adolescents: Educational outcomes at two years postpartum. *American Journal of Community Psychology, 19,* 911-930.

Simmons, R. G. (1987). Social transition and adolescent development. *New Directions in Child Development, 37,* 33-61.

Simmons, R. G., Burgeson, R., Carlton-Ford, S., & Blyth, D. (1987). The impact of cumulative change in early adolescence. *Child Development, 58,* 1220-1234.

Waldrop, J. (1989). The adoption option. *American Demographics, 11*(10), 11.

Whalen, T. E., & Fried, M. A. (1973). Geographic mobility and its effects on student achievement. *Journal of Educational Research, 67,* 163-165.

Easing Postpartum School Transitions Through Parent Mentoring Programs

Jean E. Rhodes

University of Illinois at Urbana-Champaign

SUMMARY. Alternative schools offer pregnant and parenting high school students smaller classes, a less stigmatizing environment, and specialized health and social services. Most alternative schools require that students return to their regular public high schools soon after they have delivered. Although students making this postpartum transition face extraordinary challenges, few supportive services are available. As a result, the academic performance of many postpartum students suffers and may eventually lead to high school drop out. Mentoring programs, which are initiated while students are still pregnant, may provide an important bridge between the alternative and regular school settings. Mentoring relationships can ease the stress associated with postpartum school transition and, ultimately, forestall or prevent the academic and social problems typically associated with adolescent pregnancy and parenthood.

Each year, ten percent of all 15 through 19 year old females in this country become pregnant and nearly half of these young women become school-age mothers (Ruch-Ross, Jones, & Musick, 1992). Some young mothers remain in high school, managing to

---

[Haworth co-indexing entry note]: "Easing Postpartum School Transitions Through Parent Mentoring Programs." Rhodes, Jean E. Co-published simultaneously in *Prevention in Human Services* (The Haworth Press, Inc.) Vol. 10, No. 2, 1993, pp. 169-178; and: *Prevention and School Transitions* (ed: Leonard A. Jason, Karen E. Danner, and Karen S. Kurasaki) The Haworth Press, Inc., 1993, pp. 169-178. Multiple copies of this article/chapter may be purchased from The Haworth Document Delivery Center. Call 1-800-3-HAWORTH (1-800-342-9678) between 9:00 - 5:00 (EST) and ask for DOCUMENT DELIVERY CENTER.

© 1993 by The Haworth Press, Inc. All rights reserved.

meet their academic responsibilities despite the profound psychological and physical changes associated with teenage pregnancy and parenthood. For many students, however, the demands of pregnancy and parenting are overwhelming. The routines, regulations, and facilities of most high schools are not well suited to the needs of pregnant and parenting students and special supports and services are rarely provided (Hayes, 1987).

As a result, approximately half of all students who become mothers drop out of high school (Card & Wise, 1978; Mott & Marsiglio, 1985). An adolescent mother who drops out and does not go back to school increases her risk for multiple pregnancies and welfare dependence (Baldwin & Cain, 1980; Furstenberg, 1976; Scott-Jones & Turner, 1990).

Given these risks, as well as federal policies mandating that childbearing students have equal access to educational resources,[1] schools have begun to pay special attention to the educational needs of pregnant and parenting teenagers. Although some school systems offer relevant coursework and special services within the regular school context, many have developed alternative academic settings for pregnant students. These alternative schools, which are physically and administratively separate from regular schools, typically offer smaller classes, a less stigmatizing environment, and specialized assistance to young women (Zellman, 1982). Prenatal and postpartum health care, career and psychological counselling, job skills training, and parent education are among the services often provided at the schools. Some programs also include child care facilities which function as parenting education laboratories. In addition, because many students were at academic risk prior to their pregnancy, supplemental academic services are also provided (Osofsky & Osofsky, 1978; Seitz, Apfel, & Rosenbaum, 1991).

Many communities have at least one such school, and major cities often have several. Chicago, for example, has three alternative schools for pregnant students, each serving different districts in the city. These specialized settings appear to contribute favorably to students' postpartum academic adjustment. Indeed, alternative schools often incorporate many of the components that have been shown to be effective in forestalling or preventing academic failure and drop out. These include fewer students per teacher, the presence of supportive staff to monitor and encourage students, and relatively small and consistent peer groupings (Felner, Ginter, & Primavera, 1982; Seitz et al., 1991).

Seitz et al. (1991) provide preliminary support for the efficacy of alternative schools, particularly among academically at-risk students. Students who were doing poorly in school prior to their pregnancy, were very responsive to an intervention at an alternative school. With sufficient time in the program, they were as likely as the better students to achieve postpartum educational success. Similarly, in their longitudinal study of teenage pregnancy, Furstenberg, Brooks-Gunn, and Morgan (1987) found that women who attended an alternative school when they were pregnant were more likely than controls to be economically independent 17 years later.

POSTPARTUM TRANSITIONS

Despite these benefits, most alternative schools provide support only for the duration of the pregnancy, at which point students are required to return to their regular public high schools (Hayes, 1987). Zellman (1982) points out that, historically, programs for pregnant teenagers ended at the time of delivery because most of the teens put their infants up for adoption. Given that young mothers are now far less likely to give up their infants, rapid postpartum transition may no longer be appropriate and may actually increase students' vulnerability to academic adjustment problems (Zellman, 1982).

The dual demands of parenthood and school transition can be overwhelming to the young mother. Moreover, this transition occurs in the absence of the specialized services that were readily available at the alternative schools. There are typically no attempts by alternative school staff to provide follow-up support and the regular school staff often mistakenly believe that the alternative school has fully prepared the students for the transition after delivery (Zellman, 1982). As such, little effort is made by either the alternative or regular school staff to monitor the new mother's return to her regular school. Not surprisingly, the school performance of many postpartum students suffers as they negotiate their new roles. A negative trajectory that begins with multiple conflicting demands can easily progress toward poor school attendance, underachievement, and eventual school drop out.

Some alternative schools recognize this heightened vulnerability during the postpartum transition and attempt to make provisions. Regular high schools sometimes provide a liaison person who attempts to facilitate readjustment. This person meets with the student and her parents to help plan the return schedule (Seitz et al., 1991). In most cases, however, special services are terminated soon after the transition. Clearly, there is a need for continuous support and assistance to students making postpartum transitions from their alternative schools to their regular schools.

Programs aimed at building long-term, one-on-one relationships between students and volunteer support persons, or mentors, appear to provide this important link. Mentor relationships can be initiated while the student is still pregnant, providing a needed bridge between the alternative and regular school settings. In addition, because mentor programs do not depend on extensive resources and are a natural extension of helping relationships, they may represent a cost-effective and culturally-sensitive approach to prevention and intervention with this population. In the following sections, a general overview of the literature on mentoring will be provided, followed by a description of a mentoring program for pregnant and parenting students.

MENTORING

The term mentoring is generally used to describe a relationship between two unrelated individuals–an older, more experienced mentor and a younger protegee. The mentor typically provides ongoing guidance, instruction, and encouragement aimed at developing the competence and character of the protegee. Over the course of the relationship, the mentor and protegee develop a special bond of mutual commitment, respect, and loyalty (Freedman, 1992).

Williams and Kornblum (1985) provide evidence for the importance of natural mentoring relationships in the lives of inner-city youth. They found that youth generally fall into two categories: those who will make it despite their disadvantages and those who will end up on the streets, either on welfare, or in jail. They suggest that most urban youth are in the middle; depending on the influences to which they are exposed, they could become successful or they could engage in a life of crime or unemployment. The authors conclude that one of the key differences between successful and unsuccessful youth from lower-income, urban communities is that the successful ones have mentors. More recently, Rhodes, Ebert, and Fischer (1992) found natural mentors to be an important stress buffering resource in the social networks of young mothers.

Given their apparent benefits, there has been growing interest in replicating these natural helping relationships through assigned mentoring programs. Hundreds of mentoring programs, essentially modelled after the Big Brothers-Big Sisters prototype, have emerged in the past few years (Freedman, 1992). These programs include a wide range of youth (e.g., pregnant teenagers, disabled youth, African-American males, youth at risk for high school drop out) and volunteer mentors (e.g., community members, executives, the elderly, teachers, peer leaders).

In the following sections a program that pairs pregnant students at an alternative school with volunteer mentors will be described. The mentors provide ongoing support to the students during the transition from the protected environment of the alternative school to the regular schools and communities. Within this context, the mentors provide individualized training that is designed to encourage self-sufficiency and skills.

PROGRAM DESCRIPTION

The parent mentoring program is currently being implemented in an urban alternative school for pregnant students. The communities in the school's catchment area rank among the highest in its state for adolescent pregnancy and infant mortality. Transition to the school is voluntary, as pregnant students have the option of continuing in their regular public schools. Although the school administrators prefer to accept new students at the beginning of the fall or spring semesters, they will accept pregnant students into the school up to four weeks before the end of a semester. Young women are typically referred to the school by teachers, counselors, or peers at their public high schools. In addition, the school recruits students through community agencies and family services. Typically the students attend the school for the duration of the semester or school year in which they deliver.

Thirty full-time teachers are employed and approximately 250 students attend the school. There is considerable flux in enrollment as new students matriculate and postpartum students make the transition back to their schools. Many of the students have a history of poor school performance and attendance that persists throughout their pregnancy. For example, during the first semester of the 1991-92 school year, 41.5% of the students failed two or more courses and the average attendance rate was only 54.8%. Approximately 84% of the students are considered to come from low income homes. A full 96.5% of the students are African-American, while 3.5% are Hispanic. In addition to the basic educational curriculum and small classes, the school provides a range of support services (e.g., Women, Infants, and Children (WIC) Nutritional Program, prenatal health care, counselling, parent training).

Volunteers are recruited to the parent mentor program through an intensive community outreach. Public service announcements, presentations at agencies, and networking with community agencies, churches, block clubs, and schools are among the strategies that are used to attract volunteers. The mentors are then paired with pregnant students in one-on-one relationships. In addition to providing ongoing informal support, mentors are trained to provide information about available resources and systematic cognitive-behavioral training. This training is based largely on Kanfer's self-management model, which seeks to help students in their current circumstances and to develop the skills they need to work toward the goals they ultimately want to achieve (Kanfer & Goldstein, 1986; Kanfer & Hagerman, 1978; Kanfer & Schefft, 1988). Through this training, the mentors assist the young women in clarifying their values and long- and short-term goals. The mentors assist the protegees in developing a plan for coping with the transition from the alternative school to the regular school and for eventually moving toward their career and educational goals.

SELF-MANAGEMENT STRATEGY

There are three components to the self-management strategy: self-monitoring, self-evaluation, and self-reinforcement (Kanfer, Rhodes, Englund, & Lennhoff, in press). Self-monitoring includes monitoring some unwanted behaviors and noticing the conditions under which they are most likely to occur. The student might record the time that a certain behavior occurred, what happened immediately prior to and following it, and how she felt before, during, and after it happened. By recording the circumstances and feelings surrounding the behavior, the young woman can become more aware of the factors sustaining it. For example, if she wants to complete her homework assignments, but has trouble concentrating on them, she may discover through self-monitoring that she tends to daydream and procrastinate when she feels anxious about the material. After discovering such a pattern, she and her mentor could discuss some alternative anxiety-reducing activities. She may be able to gradually increase her concentration by getting extra tutoring on difficult subjects.

Self-evaluation and self-reinforcement are used after a pattern of unwanted behavior is noticed and the student has attempted to change it. Self-evaluation refers to closely monitoring one's attempts to modify a behavior and making careful note of the progress one is making. The mentor can be an important figure in this technique, helping her partner to notice and appreciate the positive changes she is making. Self-reinforcement refers to rewarding oneself for progress one has made. The reward may be a few words of praise or a small treat that the student chooses for herself.

Beyond these self-management strategies, the young women are introduced to specific problem-solving rules that are intended to assist them throughout the transition. These rules are designed to help the mentors and students decide how to approach problems or difficult situations that arise throughout the pregnancy, school transition, and parenthood. The rules are presented as a way of thinking about one's life that promotes hope, as well as movement toward goals and change. The young women are encouraged to look for the things about their lives that they can positively influence and to work toward changing them. They are encouraged to take things one small step at a time and to keep an open mind with regard to the future. The mentors also teach their protegees a variety of skills, including stress management, problem solving, and strategies for dealing with intense emotions.

Finally, the mentors are provided with a guidebook which cites information and resources that students may need, particularly after their transition from the alternative school. With the assistance of the guidebook, the mentors are able to give their students information and direct them to places where they can receive needed information and services. The program is set up in such a way as to encourage mentors to integrate the information from the guidebook with their understanding of the self-management techniques and the other skills they teach. For example, if a mentor looked under "parenting" in the guidebook, in addition to information about parenting skills and listings for further information and self-help programs, she would find a suggestion to refer back to the self-management model to help her student deal with immediate problems.

Overall, the self-management strategy is useful because it teaches the students some of the skills they will need during the postpartum transition as their external supports become less available. The active participation by the student in setting her own goals increases her motivation and autonomy in working toward these goals. As she works hard and begins to see positive change, she becomes more enthusiastic about her future plans. With the support of her mentor she can notice the progress that she is making, thereby increasing her self-esteem and sense of independence.

CONCLUSION

Students making the postpartum transition from alternative schools to regular schools face extraordinary challenges. They are typically required to return to their regular public high schools soon after delivery with few, if any, specialized supports or services. The adjustment to parenthood and to the academic and social climate of their regular school can be overwhelming. As a result, the academic performance of many postpartum students often suffers and may eventually lead to high school drop out.

Mentoring programs, which are initiated while students are still pregnant, may provide an important bridge between the alternative and regular school settings. The parent mentoring program described above incorporates self-management strategies to encourage independence and goal attainment. The mentor relationships may ease the stress associated with the postpartum school transition and ultimately forestall or prevent some of the academic and social problems typically associated with adolescent pregnancy and parenthood (Rhodes & Englund, in press).

Of course, this is an individual solution to what is clearly a much broader social problem. By advocating this program, a message may be sent to both the young women and others that adolescent pregnancy, postpartum dropout, and the surrounding circumstances are problems of individuals rather than society. Clearly, the problem needs to be addressed at additional levels. School systems need to take more responsibility for coordinating ongoing services both during and after the pregnancy and health and child care services should be made more readily available to all young women. Finally, comprehensive efforts should be taken to prevent unwanted school-age pregnancy and to provide access to alternative means for young women to achieve adult status. Nonetheless, such system level solutions are not, at this time, forthcoming and the school-aged mothers are in immediate need of assistance. Mentoring programs draw on the strength and compassion of community residents to offer immediate, sustained support to pregnant and parenting students.

NOTES

1. Title IX of the Education Amendments (1972) prohibits discrimination in education on the basis of pregnancy, childbearing, or marital status. As a result, all public school systems must allow students to remain in school throughout pregnancy and to return following the birth of their child.

REFERENCES

Baldwin, W., & Cain, V.S. (1980). The children of teenage parents. *Family planning perspectives, 12*, 34-43.
Card, J.J., & Wise, L.L. (1978). Teenage mothers and teenage fathers: The impact of early childbearing on the parents' personal and professional lives. *Family Planning Perspectives, 10*, 199-205.
Felner, R.D., Ginter, M., & Primavera, J. (1982). Primary prevention during

school transitions: Social support and environmental structure. *American Journal of Community Psychology, 10*, 277-290.
Freedman, M. (1992). *The kindness of strangers: Reflections on mentoring.* Philadelphia, PA: Public Private Ventures.
Furstenberg, F.F., Brooks-Gunn, J., & Morgan, S.P. (1987). *Adolescent mothers in later life.* New York: Cambridge University Press.
Hamilton, S.F. (1990). *Apprenticeship for adulthood.* New York: Free Press.
Hayes, C.D. (Ed.). (1987). *Risking the future: Adolescent sexuality, pregnancy, and childbearing, 1,* Washington, DC: Academy Press.
Kanfer, F.H., & Goldstein, A.P. (Eds.). (1986). *Helping people change: A textbook of methods* (3rd. ed.). New York: Pergamon.
Kanfer, F.H., & Hagerman, S.M. (1978). A model of self-regulation. In F. Halisch & J. Kuhl (Eds.), *Motivation, intentions, and volition* (pp. 87-125). New York: Springer Verlag.
Kanfer, F.H., & Schefft, B.K. (1988). *Guiding the process of therapeutic change.* Champaign, IL: Research Press.
Kanfer, F.H., Rhodes, J.E., Englund, S., & Lennhoff, C. (In press). *Working with pregnant and parenting adolescents: A guidebook for mentors.* Washington, DC: Child Welfare League.
Mott, F.L., & Marsiglio, W. (1985). Early childbearing and completion of high school. *Family planning perspectives, 17*, 234-237.
Osofsky, J.D., & Osofsky, J.D. (1978). Teenage pregnancy: Psychosocial considerations. *Clinical Obstetrics and Gynecology, 21*, 1161-1173.
Rhodes, J.E., Ebert, L., & Fischer, K. (1992). Natural mentors: An overlooked resource in the social networks of African-American adolescent mothers. *American Journal of Community Psychology, 20*, 445-462.
Rhodes, J.E., & Englund, S. (in press). School-based, behavioral interventions for promoting social competence. In D. Glenwick & L.A. Jason (Eds.), *Promoting health and mental health: Behavioral approaches to prevention.* NY: Springer-Verlag.
Ruch-Ross, H.S., Jones, E.D., & Musick, J.S. (1992). Comparing outcomes in a statewide program for adolescent mothers with outcomes in a national sample. *Family Planning Perspectives, 24*, 66-96.
Scott-Jones, D., & Turner, S. (1990). The impact of adolescent childbearing on educational attainment and income of black females. *Youth and Society, 22*, 35-53.
Seitz, V., Apfel, N.H., & Rosenbaum, L.K. (1991). Effects of an intervention program for pregnant adolescents: Educational outcomes at two years postpartum. *American Journal of Community Psychology, 19*, 911-930.
Williams, T.M., & Kornblum, W. (1985). *Growing up poor.* Lexington, MA: Lexington Books.
Zellman, G.L. (1982). Public school programs for adolescent pregnancy and parenthood: An assessment. *Family Planning Perspectives, 14*, 15-22.

Transition Tasks and Resources: An Ecological Approach to Life After High School

Charles Barone

Yale University

Edison J. Trickett
Kathleen D. Schmid
Peter E. Leone

University of Maryland, College Park

SUMMARY. This paper examines the transition of twelfth grade students graduating from high school. The authors followed two groups, one drawn from mainstream educational programs, and the other from special education programs for students with learning disabilities or behavioral disorders. Participants were followed from

---

This research was made possible by U.S. Department of Education Grant G008730225. Work by Charles Barone was supported, in part, by the NIMH-funded Prevention Research Training Program at Yale University (MH18920-0351). The services of the University of Maryland Computer Science Center are gratefully acknowledged. Special thanks are also extended to members of the Community Based Research Team who assisted in measurement development, data collection, and coding. Correspondence should be addressed to Charles Barone, Department of Psychology, Yale University, Box 11A Yale Station, New Haven, CT 06520.

[Haworth co-indexing entry note]: "Transition Tasks and Resources: An Ecological Approach to Life After High School." Barone, Charles et al. Co-published simultaneously in *Prevention in Human Services* (The Haworth Press, Inc.) Vol. 10, No. 2, 1993, pp. 179-204; and: *Prevention and School Transitions* (ed: Leonard A. Jason, Karen E. Danner, and Karen S. Kurasaki) The Haworth Press, Inc., 1993, pp. 179-204. Multiple copies of this article/chapter may be purchased from The Haworth Document Delivery Center. Call 1-800-3-HAWORTH (1-800-342-9678) between 9:00 - 5:00 (EST) and ask for DOCUMENT DELIVERY CENTER.

© 1993 by The Haworth Press, Inc. All rights reserved.

the last semester of their senior year until six months following their graduation from high school. The study is presented through an ecological perspective that emphasizes the relationships between individuals and their social contexts. Attention is paid to both education- and employment-related transition outcomes, and to the processes involved in negotiating the transition, both generally and with regard to seeking employment. Results indicate that while most of the participants in both groups were engaged in some type of meaningful activity following the transition, the special education group showed higher risk for disengagement. Respondents reported relying on informal resources (e.g., family, friends, and other adults) more than they did on formal resources (e.g., schools, governmental agencies) in seeking help with the transition generally and in obtaining employment. Further, participants reported significant changes in the composition of their social networks over the six months following the transition. These results are used as a framework within which to discuss potential preventive interventions aimed at promoting successful adjustment following the transition.

As prevention research has evolved, psychologists have developed an interest in naturally occurring transitions and life events as foci for the study of various aspects of human behavior and adjustment. Many early studies focused on the cumulative stress of multiple life events (see Dohrenwend & Dohrenwend, 1978; Holmes & Rahe, 1967; Rabkin & Struening, 1976). Over time, such interests have become more differentiated, with researchers increasingly focused on the more specific aspects of singular, discrete life events. Some have been interested in how individuals cope with unexpected or traumatic life events, such as death of a parent (Primavera, Farber, and Felner, 1982). Others have been interested in examining adjustment following predictable, planned, or scheduled changes such as entering a new school (e.g., Barone, Aguirre-Deandreis, & Trickett, 1991; Elias et al., 1986). The latter hold dual interest in that such transitions represent important developmental crossroads and/or opportunities for growth and advancement, as well as potentially stressful or threatening disruptions (Bronfenbrenner, 1979; Felner, Farber, & Primavera, 1983; Parkes, 1971). Further, their predictability provides a distinctive opportunity for planned preventive interventions.

The present paper examines one example of the latter type of transition, that of adolescents graduating from high school and moving into the outside world. The study uses an ecological model of transition to illustrate and inform the challenges posed by the transition and the changes it brings about in adolescents' lives. In particular, the study contrasts the experiences of two groups of graduating adolescents: those receiving special education services while in high school and those not receiving such services. These two groups of students were initially assessed during May of their senior year and were followed for six months after graduation. Because of prior research showing special education graduates to be at greater risk for unemployment and disengagement (Edgar, Levine, Levine, & Dubey, 1988; Neel, Meadows, Levine, & Edgar, 1988), special consideration is given to this group.

This introduction is presented in two parts. First, we review aspects of an ecological model relevant to the adolescent transition out of high school. Here, special attention is given to the role of personal and social resources available to adolescents at this time. Second, we review prior studies of this transition for both special education and non-special education populations to provide a context for the present study.

ECOLOGICAL CONSIDERATIONS IN ADOLESCENT TRANSITIONS

The transition from high school is one example of what Bronfenbrenner (1979) has termed an ecological transition, involving a "change in role, setting, or both" (p. 26). Such a description emphasizes the relationships between the individual and his or her environment as key aspects of the transition. Others have advanced similar perspectives (e.g., Parkes, 1971; Pearlin, Menaghan, Lieberman, & Mullen, 1981). For example, Felner et al. (1983) emphasized the dynamic qualities of social relationships in highlighting the shifting constellations of interpersonal relationships that follow transitions.

A number of specific role and setting changes may be anticipated as part of the adolescent transition from high school. Some are best viewed as defining moments in ongoing processes begun before the actual transition which unfold over an extended period of time (Felner et al., 1983). For example, the gradual developmental shift in role status from "minor" or "dependent" to "adult" is highlighted as young people make decisions about education and careers and assume greater financial responsibility and increased independence.

Shifts in settings may also present unique challenges. Unlike transitions between elementary, middle, and secondary schools, adolescents departing high school face environments that do not necessarily parallel the ones they have left behind. Such setting changes are particularly pronounced for the majority of special education students who are more likely to enter the world of work than pursue post-secondary education (Edgar et al., 1988). Social relationships and social supports, often developed over the course of years in a structured setting, now must be maintained on a more individualized basis, and new relationships are formed as young people enter new settings. Contact may cease completely with teachers and other school personnel who have served salient roles, especially for special education students (Barone, Schmid, Leone, & Trickett, 1990).

Given these varied shifts in ecology, both across and between the two groups of students, the current project adopted an ecological "person-in-context" perspective in characterizing the transition from high school. Emphasis is placed on the transactions between the individual and the local context as influential in understanding both the transition process and adjustment-related outcomes. Within this framework, individuals and environments each bring resources to bear on this ecological transition (Kelly, 1987; Kelly, 1968; Trickett, Kelly, & Todd, 1972). Individuals, for example, bring various personal resources such as academic and coping skills, while environments provide both informal and formal resources of relevance to the task. The social networks of adolescents represent one such informal resource, while formal programs, classes, and guidance counselors represent examples of school-based resources. Both individual and environmental resources are assessed in the present study.

Further, the present study focuses on descriptive data on the post-transition status of adolescents, the strategies they report using to cope with the transition, including use of social resources, and the changes they report occurring in their social network. The emphasis on description stems from the importance of understanding the processes of transition. How adolescents use their social environment—both formal and informal—is relevant not only because of its relative absence in the current transition literature, but because of its potential in targeting preventive interventions. Further, description of these person-environment transactions concertizes the meaning of an ecological approach to the study of transitions.

OUTCOME STUDIES

While several major studies have examined the post-secondary school status of mainstream and/or special education students (Edgar et al., 1988; Fardig, Algozzine, Schwartz, Hensel, & Westling, 1985; Hasazi, Gordon, & Roe, 1985; Horn, O'Donnell, & Vitulano, 1983; Mithaug, Horiuchi, & Fanning, 1985; Sitlington, Frank, & Carson, 1992), they have focused far more on outcomes than on the processes used by adolescents in making the post-high school transition. Also, perhaps because most emanated from the field of special education, emphasis focused on indices of independent living, such as finding and holding a job.

Overall these studies find that, in the short-term (six months to two years), the majority of youth who have exited high school are either employed or enrolled in some type of higher education. Students not identified as requiring special education in high school are more likely to be employed and/or be enrolled in some type of postsecondary education program than those with mild disabilities. Among the latter group, those identified as learning disabled or behaviorally disordered show relatively similar employment and educational outcomes, with mildly retarded persons faring more poorly.

In the most recent study to include both mainstream and special education samples, Edgar et al. (1988) found that six months following graduation, 50% of non-special education students were enrolled in college or training school; at 2 years the figure was 32%. The comparable figures for mildly disabled (learning disabled and behaviorally disordered) students were 25% and 18% respectively. About 75-80% of mainstream students were employed at both six months and two year follow-ups, while the comparable figures for learning disabled and behaviorally disordered students were 57-68% at six months and 59-78% at two years following graduation. In identifying students functioning least adaptively, Edgar et al. (1988) cite figures for disengagement, i.e., those students neither enrolled in school nor employed. At both six months and two years following high school, 8% of non-special education students were disengaged, compared to 24% at six months and 18% at two years for learning disabled students, and 28% at sixth months and 32% at two years for behaviorally disordered students. Thus special education students were 3-4 times more likely to be involved in neither employment nor post-secondary education.

Most outcome studies with both mainstream and special education samples that have examined use of personal and social resources have done so only in relation to employment. These studies consistently find that adolescents most often secure employment through informal means, either as the result of their own efforts, or through their informal network of family members and friends (Hasazi et al., 1985; Mithaug et al., 1985; Sitlington et al., 1992). Formal resources, such as employment agencies and vocational development programs, are cited by only a small percentage of youth as having assisted them in actually obtaining employment.

None of the previous studies has focused on adolescent use of social resources more generally in adapting to the post-secondary transition. Further, none has studied formally the actual changes that occur in students' social networks that may influence the availability of network resources in the transition process. Thus, one purpose of the present study is to provide data on the use of social resources both with regard to seeking employment and with regard to general social support available during the transition. Additionally, we examine specific changes in the composition of adolescents' social networks following the transition from high school. Analysis of these changes illustrates key transformations in the social environments of adolescents, and in turn provides a useful context within which to discuss the implications of the data for preventive interventions.

METHODS

Research Participants

The research participants were 234 high school graduates surveyed both in the Spring of their senior year (Time 1) and at a six-month follow-up (Time 2). One-hundred seventy-five were enrolled in mainstream education programs, and 59 were enrolled in special education programs for students with learning disabilities and/or behavioral and emotional problems. The sample represents 55.3% (53.4% of the mainstream sample, 62.1% of the special education sample) of those surveyed at Time 1. Of those mainstream students surveyed at Time 2, 14.9% had disconnected phones and could not be reached by mail, 4.6% refused a second interview, 2.4% were in the military and could not be contacted, 1.8% were still in school (repeating 12 grade), and 22.9% could not be reached for other reasons. For special education students the reasons were: 18.9% disconnected phones, 2.1% refused, 10.5% still in school, 6.4% other.[1]

Demographic data (Time 1) indicate that the average age of the two samples was comparable (mainstream 18.4 years, special education 18.6 years). The mainstream sample was 55.4% female, the special education sample 41.4% female, a statistically non-significant difference. The mainstream sample is 69.9% Black, 23% White, and 7.1% other race/ethnicity; the special education sample was 61.1% Black, 35.2% White, and 3.7% other race/ethnicity ($X^2 = 12.4, p < .01$). Father's education for mainstream and special education groups, respectively, was: 61.5/69.8% high school graduates or less, 5.0/4.7% vocational or business school, 12.1/9.3% some college, 21.4/16.3% college or graduate/professional degree. For mothers, comparable educational data indicate: 56.6/71.1% high school or less, 6.8/2.2% vocational or business school, 16.1/15.6% some college, and 20.5/11.1% college or graduate/professional degree. While the parent education levels of the mainstream and special education samples differ slightly, they are not statistically significant. In summary, the two samples differ only in their racial/ethnic composition, with the special education sample containing a greater proportion of Whites and a lower proportion of Blacks and students of other races. The data also suggest a trend such that the special education sample is slightly older, includes a higher proportion of females, and has slightly lower parent education levels.

Procedure

Students were recruited through their homeroom and English classes by research assistants who explained the study and distributed consent forms. Interested students age eighteen or older provided their own written consent, while written parental consent was obtained for students under eighteen years of age. Time 1 data were gathered in person from students during the school day, while Time 2 interviews (post-transition), conducted 6 months following graduation, were done either through interview (49.1%) or by phone (50.9%).

Teacher ratings of classroom behavior (see below) were also obtained for each student from English teachers within a few weeks of the Time 1 (pre-transition) interview.[2] Grade point average, attendance, and achievement test scores were gathered from school records.

Measures

Analysis of Social Support in School Transitions (ASSIST). The ASSIST is an interview-format measure in which the administrator asks the participant to name people in his or her life across three domains: non-family adults, family, and peers. Participants are instructed to nominate members in each group as appropriate, and to name only those persons who are important to them in some way, to discourage overinclusion. The interviewer then asks the participant to indicate which members provide each of four respective support functions (emotional support, cognitive guidance, companionship, and caring), and to rate the helpfulness and stressfulness of their relationship with each network member. Prior studies have supported the distinctiveness of the three reference groups (Schmid et al., 1988) and have shown that the ASSIST has adequate test-retest reliability (see Schmid, Barone, & Trickett, 1992). In this study, we focus on the overall composition of the social network to provide information on the relative importance of different network subgroups.

In addition to giving the ASSIST at Time 1, we asked students at Time 2 whether or not they received support from Time 1 network members related to the transition from high school. We also developed a follow-up questionnaire that assessed the amount of network change between Time 1 and Time 2 due to the departure of previous network members and the addition of new ones. Care was taken to distinguish actual departures and additions from inadvertent omissions and spurious additions by reviewing participants' Time 1 responses with them.

Child and Adolescent Profile (CAAP). The CAAP (Ellsworth & Ellsworth, 1979) consists of teacher ratings of five aspects of classroom behavior and school performance. Three scales assess the presence of negative classroom behaviors (aggression, withdrawal, dependency) and two scales assess the occurrence of positive behaviors (peer relations and classroom productivity). The instrument has been used widely to assess the behavioral adjustment of students and demonstrates adequate test-retest reliability.

Interview Questions. The post-transition (Time 2) status of participants was assessed through several interview questions. We asked students at Time 2 where they lived, who paid their expenses, if they were working, and if they were enrolled in post-secondary education. Follow-up questions differed as a function of student status. For those working, information was gathered on wages, hours worked, and benefits, while those enrolled in postsecondary education were asked about the type of school (e.g., college or training school).

To assess the personal strategies and social resources used in negotiating the transition from high school, we asked participants about the types of strategies they used to adapt to the transition generally, with particular emphasis on how they attempted to secure employment. At the general level, in addition to asking about transition support from network members nominated during the administration of the ASSIST, we asked whether or not students had also talked with a teacher or guidance counselor, or taken a school course related to the transition. We further asked students about their use (yes/no) of nine specific job-seeking strategies. These included students' individual efforts (self-search, want-ads), use of social network (friends, family, acquaintances) and use of formal resources (vocational rehabilitation services, employment agencies, state unemployment office, school services). Students were then asked about which of these means actually resulted in their finding jobs.

RESULTS

Results are presented in four subsections. First, we present data on the pre-transition status of the two groups of adolescents. Second, we present descriptive data on the post-transition status of the sample in terms of employment, educational status, and living situation. The third and fourth sections describe the processes used by these adolescents to cope with the high school transition. Specifically, section three examines the use of formal and informal resources in the transition more generally as well as their role in securing post-high school employment. Finally, we examine reported changes in the social networks of adolescents to elucidate the socio-environmental changes that occurred as a result of the transition. Within each section, we also report data on differences related to sex and race (Black vs. White).[3]

Pre-Transition Status

Data on the pre-transition status of the two groups is presented to portray some of the individual differences they bring to the post-high school transition. Both school performance-related data and teacher ratings of student classroom behavior are found in Table 1. Predictably, the mainstream group scored significantly higher on both the reading and math scores of the California Achievement Test, though no differences were apparent in grades or absenteeism. Teacher ratings on the CAAP showed significant differences on the Aggression and Dependency subscales, with special education students rated more highly in each case. Taken together, these data suggest the school-related difficulties of special education students in both academic and behavioral aspects of classroom performance.

Analyses of race and sex differences yielded several significant differences. With respect to academic indicators, mainstream females

Table 1

Pre-transition Status of High School Seniors

Variable	Mainstream (n=175)	Special Education (n=59)	t
Grade Point Average	2.67	2.42	N.S.
Attendance (Mean Days per Full Year)	20.9	27.8	N.S
CAT Achievement Test Scores			
Reading	52.9	13.8	9.65***
Math	51.6	19.0	8.19***
Teacher Ratings			
Learning Productivity	10.9	10.8	N.S.
Peer Relations	12.6	11.8	N.S.
Aggression	4.7	5.6	3.15**
Dependency	5.5	7.0	3.85***
Withdrawal	5.8	6.5	N.S.

* p < .05 ** p < .01 ***p < .001

had higher GPA's (2.84 vs. 2.44, $t = 3.2$, $p < .01$) and CAT reading scores (58.4 vs. 47.0, $t = 2.63$, $p < .01$) than did mainstream males. Further, they were rated higher than mainstream males on learning productivity (11.9 vs. 9.6, $t = 4.27$, $p < .001$). While no sex differences occurred for the special education sample on academic indicators, females in special education were rated higher by teachers on learning productivity (12.56 vs. 9.65, $t = 4.27$, $p < .001$) and lower on dependency (5.9 vs. 7.7, $t = 3.46$, $p < .001$) and withdrawal (5.6 vs. 7.0, $t = 2.46$, $p < .05$).

Because of the small numbers in other groups, only Black/White race differences were examined. The only differences occurred in the mainstream sample, where Whites had higher CAT math subtest scores (59.7 vs. 48.2, $t = 2.34$, $p < .05$) and were rated as less aggressive by their teachers (4.1 vs. 4.9, $t = 2.56$, $p < .05$).

Post-Transition Status

Data for the 6-month post-high school status of mainstream and special education students are presented in Table 2. Significant differences were found between the post-high school activities of the two samples, with mainstream students much more likely to be in college, either while working at the same time or not ($X^2 = 41.5, p < .001$). Special education students are more likely to be exclusively working, while not being enrolled in college or training school, than their mainstream counterparts. Of those former mainstream students enrolled in post-secondary education, 86.2% are attending college, while 13.8% are attending training school; for former special education students, the percentage is 50% and 50% respectively. Finally, former special education students are much more likely than mainstream students to be disengaged, neither working nor attending college or training school (23.7% vs. 4.1%).

Additional analyses indicate that former mainstream students, on average, had worked at their job for 10.4 months (30% held jobs secured in high school), worked 32.5 hours per week, and made $6.06 per hour. Thirty-eight percent of those working had health insurance. Students formerly enrolled in special education programs, on average, had held their jobs for 9.8 months (35% held jobs secured in high school), worked 37.5 hours per week, and made $5.62 per hour. Thirty-four percent had health insurance. The only significant difference between the two group was in hours worked per week ($t(179) = 2.62, p < .01$).

With respect to living arrangements, 75% of the former mainstream students lived with their family of origin; 11.6% lived with other family members; 8.7% lived on a college campus; and 4.1% lived on their own, with the remaining .6% (n = 1) reporting other

Table 2

Post-Transition Status at Six Months Following Graduation

Status	Mainstream ($n=175$)	Special Education ($n=59$)
Working	43.4%	64.4%
Attending College or Training School	19.4	8.5
Both Working and Attending College or Training School	33.1	3.4
Unengaged	4.1	23.7

unspecified living arrangements. Of the special education sample, 77.2% were living at home with their family of origin; 8.8% were living with other family members; 8.8% moved away to attend school; 3.5% lived on their own; and 1.8% resided on a military base. A chi-square test indicated no statistically significant differences. When asked who paid most of their living expenses, 34.5% of mainstream students said they did, 62.6% said their parents did, and 2.9% reported other unspecified means. Twenty-two percent of special education students reported paying for their own expenses, 69.5% said their parents did, 5.1% said social services, and 3.4% reported other unspecified means. These group differences were significant ($X^2 = 11.2, p < .01$), although these results should be interpreted with caution due to small cell sizes.

No race differences emerged on these post-transition variables. Males and females in the mainstream sample differed in their post-transition status ($X^2 = 13.6, p = <.01$). Mainstream females were more likely to be disengaged than males (7.2% vs. 0%), less likely to be only in college (33.0% vs. 56.4%), and more likely to be both attending college and working (39.2% vs. 25.6%). Further, they reported working fewer hours per week (37.1 vs. 28.9, $t = 4.36, p < .001$) and receiving less pay ($5.72 vs. $6.54 per hour, $t = 2.49, p < .05$).

Use of Formal and Informal Resources in the Transition

Data on the use of resources in making the transition from high school include two main emphases: results for general network help, and more specific results related to job-seeking strategies.

A. Network Help with the Transition

Table 3 presents data on help received from school-based resources. While both groups are equally likely to have talked with a teacher about the transition, mainstream students are more likely to have spoken to a guidance counselor ($X^2 = 3.95, p < .05$), while special education students are more likely to have taken a course related to post-high school planning ($X^2 = 5.49, p < .01$). Table 4 presents data on the use of social network resources in coping with

Table 3

Transition Help Received from School-Based Resources

Activity	Mainstream (n=175)		Special Education (n=59)	
	Yes	No	Yes	No
Talked to a Teacher About the Transition	48.2%	51.8%	52.6%	47.4%
Talked to a Guidance Counselor About the Transition	50.6	49.4	35.6	64.4
Took a Course Related to the Transition	16.7	83.3	31.0	69.0

Table 4

Transition Help Received from Social Network Members

	Number of People Who Provided Help with the Transition					
	Mainstream			Special Education		
Reference Group	None	One	Two or More	None	One	Two or More
Family Members	23.4	18.9	57.7	38.9	11.9	55.2
Peers	48.5	23.4	28.1	61.0	23.7	15.3
Non-Family Adults	53.7	26.9	19.4	61.0	20.3	18.7

the transition. Here, a large proportion of participants report having received some sort of help from family members. Friends and non-family adults were used relatively less frequently than family. Non-significant trends suggest that special education students reported receiving slightly less support across all three reference groups, in that they are more likely to report receiving help from *no* members within each particular reference group, and less likely to report receiving help from two or more peers.

No sex or race differences emerged in the use of social network resources for the mainstream group. For special education graduates, males reported receiving more help from friends than did females

(1.25 vs. .4, $t = 2.43$, $p < .05$), and Blacks from special education programs were more likely to have spoken to a counselor than Whites from those programs (51.5% vs. 21.1%, $X^2 = 4.65$, $p < .05$).

B. Use of Formal and Informal Resources in the Job Search

In addition to data on the use of resources more generally in the transition, the specific role of formal and informal resources in adolescents' job seeking strategies was also explored. Table 5 presents data on the percentage of participants who reported using one or more of 9 possible formal and informal job-seeking strategies; the table also includes percentages (for the same 9 strategies) of participants who reported a particular method to have *actually helped them in getting a job*. The most frequently employed strate-

Table 5

Strategies Used in Searching for a Job and How Jobs Were Actually Obtained

	Mainstream		Special Education	
Job Search Strategy	Strategy Used	How Job Obtained	Strategy Used	How Job Obtained
Self-search	46.1%	32.8%	39.0%	21.7%
Close Friends	46.1	20.4	42.4	23.9
Family	39.0	19.7	42.4	26.1
Weak Ties (acquaintances of self or other network members)	29.8	8.8	28.8	10.9
Want-ads	19.1	6.6	25.4	8.7
School services	18.4	13.9	16.9	10.9
Employment Agency	4.3	1.5	6.8	0.0
Unemployment Office	2.1	.7	3.4	0.0
Vocational Rehabilitation Services	.7	1.5	5.1	0.0

Note: All data are in percentages. Percentages total greater than 100 given that respondents could check multiple categories. Questions on strategies used to find a job were asked at Time 1 and all participants responded. Smaller sample sizes for how job obtained (Mainstream $n = 134$, Special Education $n = 46$) reflect inclusion of only those students who actually found jobs at some point prior to or in the six months following graduation.

gies involved (a) individuals searching for employment on their own, either through self-searches (e.g., door-to-door) or use of wants-ads, and (b) searches through family, friends, and acquaintances. Formal resources were utilized much less frequently, with school services cited as the most frequently used formal resource. Results were generally similar with regard to obtaining jobs, with differences appearing a bit more sharply between use of informal means and formal services. Thus, the data show convincingly that informal rather than formal structures are used most frequently and are perceived as most helpful in seeking and finding employment.

Network Change During the Transition

A final source of data on the resources relevant to adolescent transitions from high school comes from changes in their social network during this time. Table 6 shows the size of participants' social networks (by reference group) at Time 1 and Time 2, and includes the number of members who left and were added to the network during the six months following graduation. The data indicate a substantial change in the overall composition of the network over the six-month period for both groups.[4] Particularly notable are the changes in the peer and non-family adult networks, which show a greater degree of turnover than does that part of the network composed of family members. T-tests reveal no between group differences on these variables. However, repeated measures t-tests indicate that for mainstream students, the decrease in the size of each network subgroup was significant (Family: $t = 3.29, p < .001$;

Table 6

Social Network Changes Occurring Between Graduation and Six Month Follow-up

Group	Mainstream				Special Education			
	Size Time 1	No. Left	No. Added	Size Time 2	Size Time 1	No. Left	No. Added	Size Time 2
Family	4.46	1.15	.62	3.84	5.23	.83	.88	4.90
Peers	3.73	1.87	1.33	3.17	3.70	2.5	1.37	2.93
Non-Family Adults	2.72	1.96	1.06	1.91	2.67	1.62	.7	1.76

Peers: $t = 3.84, p < .001$; Adult: $t = 5.52, p < .001$). For special education students, differences were significant for decreases in the size of their peer ($t = 2.68, p < .01$) and adult ($t = 3.28, p < .01$) network subgroups.

For the mainstream group, no sex or race differences were found. For the special education group, Blacks reported a larger family network at Time 1 (6.46 vs. 3.72, $t = 3.42, p < .001$), and a larger turnover in their family network both with regard to the departure of important family members (2.27 vs. 1.33, $t = 2.03, p < .05$) and the addition of newly important family members (2.24 vs. .72, $t = 2.32$, $p < .05$).

DISCUSSION

The intent of the present study was to provide descriptive data on two different samples of adolescents making the transition from high school to the world beyond. Emphasis was placed not only on their post-transition status six months after graduation, but on the processes they used in coping with the transition and in seeking of employment. These data not only provide descriptively useful information on mainstream and special education adolescents but also suggest areas for preventive interventions.

Data related to employment status, enrollment in post-secondary education, and living arrangements six months after graduation indicate that most youth in both samples were engaged in meaningful activity; that is, some form of post-secondary education and/or employment. However, mainstream and special education students showed significant differences in their level and type of engagement. Students from mainstream educational programs were much more likely to be enrolled in post-secondary education, while youth graduating from special education programs were much more likely to be disengaged, i.e., neither enrolled in post-secondary education nor employed. These data, plus high school data on the differences in achievement tests and teacher ratings of classroom behavior, suggest that particular attention be paid to the transition tasks of special education youth. Most youth in both categories, including those enrolled in post-high secondary education, live at home with their parents or relatives, and rely on their parents and family members for financial support.

A major emphasis in this paper was an examination of the processes used by these adolescents in coping with this transition. Emphasis was placed on the use of social network resources in coping with the transition in general as well as the use of formal and informal resources in seeking employment. Further, we highlighted the degree of change that occurs in adolescents networks following their graduation from high school.

With respect to the transition in general, data indicate that most youths' social networks provided help during the transition, with family members being cited most frequently, followed by non-family adults and friends. Approximately 50% of each group spoke with teachers, though guidance counselors played a larger role for mainstream youth as a school resource, probably in relation to planning for post-secondary education. Employment for the large majority of youths was secured through informal means, either on their own or through family and close friends in their social network. Relatively few students secured employment through utilization of formal resources, with the most frequently cited formal resource being students' high schools.

Data on social network change suggest some of the post-transition adjustment challenges students encountered, as well as some of the difficulties they faced in attempting to obtain help from others in coping with the transition. The social networks of both groups showed considerable change in the six months following high school, becoming slightly smaller, with over half of their members actually departing, and others being incorporated. Thus, the data suggest considerable discontinuity in social relationships, as well as a potential threat to the availability of stable social resources to guide adolescents through this transitional period.

While space prevents a thorough discussion of race and gender differences, some findings are particularly notable. For example, despite higher school performance as indicated by school archive data, females earned less than their male counterparts. While this may reflect their increased likelihood of both working and attending school, it may also reflect enduring gender biases in the workplace. Thus, females may require a special focus in prevention efforts to assist them in meeting the unique challenges they face in the job market and in work settings.

In the following section, these descriptive data will be used as a foundation to discuss potential preventive interventions that may be useful in facilitating successful adjustment following adolescents' departure from high school. The ecological model of Bronfenbrenner (1979) will frame this discussion and provide a link between the data presented here and intervention-related issues.

Implications for Preventive Interventions

Bronfenbrenner (1979) emphasizes that transitions occur in a context of concentric and interdependent social environments, and that adaptation is shaped by the transaction between the person and the settings with, and within which, he or she interacts. Using this framework, Bronfenbrenner (1979) advances several hypotheses about factors which are likely to facilitate adjustment to an ecological transition. These involve efforts to (a) assist the individual to acquire the requisite knowledge and skills for successful adjustment, (b) provide appropriate knowledge, training, and support to those persons in a position to act as resources, and (c) promote continuity across settings, especially with regard to interaction between persons in the setting being exited and that being entered. We will review each of these points in succession, using the data from the present study to inform the discussion.

At the individual level, Bronfenbrenner (1979) asserts that "development is enhanced to the extent that, prior to entry into a new setting... the person... is provided with information, advice, and experience relevant to the impending transition" (p. 225). Given the degree to which individuals in the present study relied on their own initiative to secure employment, and the relatively large number of individuals who did not access their network for help with the transition in general, interventions intended to provide such help seem important as a prelude to leaving high school. Such interventions might take many forms. One approach is to teach general skills for dealing with the stressors and challenges which accompany transitions. For example, Jason and Burrows (1983) describe a successful program for high school seniors that provided training in problem-focused coping strategies (relaxation, cognitive restructuring, and problem solving). The authors hypothesize that such skills would generalize to success in coping with the transition from high school. The potential effectiveness of this approach is supported by other successful programs which teach broad-based coping skills to students undergoing other types of school transitions (e.g., Elias et al., 1986).

As Bronfenbrenner (1979) emphasizes, such programs will likely be maximally useful when they are linked directly to the tasks faced by those making the transition. In addition to the types of formal programs usually implemented by schools such as vocational training classes, school-sponsored job placement, or college preparation seminars (see Hasazi et al., 1985; Sitlington et al., 1992) data from other studies (Mithaug et al., 1985) suggest that following the transition, a majority of special education students desired additional training in understanding their own abilities, job search and job application skills, and getting along with others. The present data highlight the need for training in social skills, especially those pertaining to accessing formal and informal social resources. Many students relied heavily on informal resources and did not access formal resources. In addition, the degree of turnover in students' networks may have attenuated their potential usefulness in helping with the transition. Thus, orientation to available resources and instruction in how to access and fully utilize formal services may be a beneficial intervention. (see Azrin & Besalele, 1980; and Quintiliani & Furry-Irish, 1983, cited in Hasazi et al., 1983).

A second approach suggested by the present study is to bolster the ability of individuals important in the lives of adolescents to act as resources through informal or unstructured means, such as providing advice, emotional support, and practical help. Here, we wish to maximize the potential of others to be of help, and ensure they have the skills and resources to facilitate students' post-transition adjustment.

One important resource, especially for students from special education programs, is teachers and other school personnel. In addition to formal role functions, many teachers also act as "informal" resources for students. Prior research by our team suggests that adolescents often include adults in formal service roles (e.g., teachers, coaches) in their social networks, and that these persons are important and helpful sources of emotional and practical support, especially for students enrolled in special education programs (Barone et al., 1990; Barone et al., 1989). Similarly, reports from teachers indicate that they spend a substantial amount of time providing informal help to students (Schmid et al., 1990). School support of such efforts is crucial. Schmid et al. (1990), for example, found that provision of informal support by teachers occurring outside the domain of regular classroom instruction was correlated with feelings of personal accomplishment and uncorrelated with stress and burnout. However, perceived adequacy of school resources supportive of such interactions was related to both perceived stress and burnout. Thus, systems and school building-level support is necessary to facilitate the efforts of teachers and other key school personnel to act as informal helping resources.

Family members, especially parents, also represent a possible focus of preventive efforts. The present data clearly suggest that family members play an important role in providing both general support related to the transition and specific support related to securing employment and living expenses. Thus, it would seem important in preventive interventions to maximize the ability of family members to provide broad-based support and to supplement their efforts to help their children to secure employment by providing relevant information on job availability and job training.

Formal resources played a less significant role in this transition. The data indicate that school resources were used more frequently and resulted in the actual obtainment of jobs, while other formal resources, such as employment agencies or vocational rehabilitation, played a marginal role. On the positive side, the data suggest the potential effectiveness of school-based resources in helping students find jobs and adjust to the transition. However, the data also suggest that other formal services are not offered, are not publicized, or are not seen as potentially helpful. Thus, there is significant room for improvement in the role that public services play in assisting students after they leave public education.

A final consideration with regard to the development of preventive interventions relates to promoting continuity across the transition period. While transitions inherently, and often desirably, result in change, some degree of connection across settings may promote successful adjustment. Bronfenbrenner (1979) asserts that positive development is enhanced if "the transition into the new setting is not made alone, that is if he [she] enters the new setting in the company of one or more persons with whom he [she] has participated in prior settings" (p. 211).

This thesis has a number of potential applications to the post-secondary transition. As noted, prior research indicates that many adolescents, especially those enrolled in special education programs, rely on non-family adults, such as teachers, coaches, and guidance counselors for emotional support and advice and guidance. At the same time, the present data indicate that the post-secondary transition brings about significant turnover in the network of non-family adults. Many of these changes assumedly involve cessation of contact with important figures at school. Thus, one potential preventive intervention involves follow-up by school personnel who have established rapport and trust with adolescents, and who could be made available on a scheduled or as-needed basis (Edgar, 1990).

Peers represent another potentially useful and perhaps underused source of support. A great degree of turnover takes place in adolescents' peer networks, and at the same time adolescents report relying significantly on their friends for both general and specific support. One potential preventive intervention is to foster adolescent peer support groups comparable to peer counseling and peer advocacy groups that have been successful in promoting adjustment among high school and junior high school students (e.g., Bowman & Myricks, 1985). Such groups could be started in high school, with school-based guidance and supervision, and planned carefully such that students would maintain contact themselves following graduation to provide each other with general emotional support, as well as practical support such as transportation and tips on employment, training, and educational opportunities.

Several cautions should be advanced in interpreting the results of the present study. First, the present sample included only those adolescents who actually graduated high school and may not be representative of those who leave high school by other means (e.g., drop-out or "age-out"). Second, there were slight differences between the original and follow-up samples[3] and thus the present sample may not be wholly representative of those interviewed at

Time 1. Third, the current study represents a short-term follow-up; adjustment may differ for these young adults over the long-term. Fourth, the small size of the special education sample precluded the use of multivariate statistics that may have uncovered other relationships among the variables studied here.

In summary, the present results highlight the adjustment challenges faced by adolescents graduating from high school, and their use of social resources in meeting the challenges of the transition. They suggest that while many youth are engaged in meaningful activity following high school, there exists a significant at-risk group, especially among those formerly enrolled in special education programs for learning disabilities and behavioral disorders. The social network analyses presented here emphasize the importance of informal resources in relation to both general and problem-specific support, and the changes that take place in social relationships over the short-term following departure from high school. The data proved useful descriptively in contextualizing the processes involved in the transition, and heuristically in suggesting directions for prevention programs. Future study of the high school transition would be enriched by more detailed accounts of the person-environment interactions taking place during this period, and of analysis of longitudinal data over longer periods of time.

NOTES

1. Attrition analyses suggest that the mainstream follow-up sample contains a higher proportion of females than those not available to participate, and that the special education follow-up sample reports slightly higher parental education status than those who were not followed-up. No other differences were found on any of the other demographic variables.

2. English teachers were chosen given that this was the only class in which all high school seniors were enrolled.

3. These analyses were performed only for simple main effects within each group (mainstream and special education) due to the prohibitively small sample sizes that would have resulted for analyses of two-way interaction effects in the special education group, or for analyses of three-way interaction effects between these groups (education status × gender × race/ethnicity). Thus, these findings may mask two- and three-way interaction effects and should be interpreted with appropriate caution.

4. It should be restated that all changes from Time 1 to Time 2 were reviewed with the participant by the interviewer to gauge why members were added or de-

leted. Thus, these figures represent actual changes in network membership as reported by participants, rather than deletions or additions for other reasons (e.g., forgetting). These changes are much larger than those found in reliability studies for shorter time periods. For comparison, see Schmid, Barone, and Trickett (1992).

REFERENCES

Barone, C., Aguirre-Deandreis, A.I., & Trickett, E.J. (1991). Means-end problem solving skills, life stress, and social support as mediators of adjustment in the normative transition to high school. *American Journal of Community Psychology, 19,* 205-215.

Barone, C., Schmid, K.D., Leone, P.E., & Trickett, E.J. (1990). Social networks of students in special education programs: Contrasts with non-special education students and correlates of school adjustment. In R.B. Rutherford, Jr. & S.A. DiGangi (Eds.), *Severe Behavior Disorders of Children and Youth* (Vol. 13, pp. 23-37). Reston, VA: Council for Children with Behavioral Disorders.

Barone, C., Schmid, K.D., Bendure, C.O., Shidla, M.C., Nordling, W., Leone, P.E., and Trickett, E.J. (1989). Development of a measure to assess life stress in special education and mainstream students: The Survey of Adolescent Events. In R.B. Rutherford, Jr. & S.A. DiGangi (Eds.), *Severe Behavior Disorders of Children and Youth* (Vol. 12, pp. 54-71). Reston, VA: Council for Children with Behavioral Disorders.

Bowman, R.P., & Myrick, R.D. (1985). Students as helpers: An untapped resource. *Social Work in Education, 7,* 124-133.

Bronfenbrenner, U. (1979). *The ecology of human development.* Cambridge, MA: Harvard.

Dohrenwend, B.S., & Dohrenwend, B.P. (1978). Some issues in research on stressful life events. *Journal of Nervous and Mental Disease, 166,* 7-15.

Edgar, E. (1990). Quality of life for persons with disabilities: A Time to change how we view the world. In R.B. Rutherford, Jr. & S.A. DiGangi (Eds.), *Severe Behavior Disorders of Children and Youth* (Vol. 13, pp. 1-10). Reston, VA: Council for Children with Behavioral Disorders.

Edgar, E., Levine, P., Levine, R., & Dubey, M. (1988). *Washington State follow-along studies, 1983-1987: Final report.* Seattle: University of Washington, Experimental Education Unit, Child Development and Mental Retardation Center.

Elias, M.J., Gara, M., Ubriaco, M., Rothbaum, P.A., Clabby, J.F., & Schuyler, T. (1986). Impact of a preventive social problem solving intervention on children's coping with middle-school stressors. *American Journal of Community Psychology, 14,* 259-275.

Ellsworth, R., & Ellsworth, S. (1979). *Child and Adolescent Adjustment Profile.* Palo Alto: Consulting Psychologists Press.

Fardig, D.B., Algozzine, R.F., Schwartz, S.E., Hensel, J.W., & Westling, D.L.

(1985). Postsecondary vocational adjustment of rural, mildly handicapped students. *Exceptional Children, 52,* 115-121.

Felner, R.D., Farber, S.S., & Primavera, J. (1983). Transitions and stressful life events. In R.D. Felner, L.A. Jason, J.N. Moritsugu, & S.S. Farber (Eds.), *Preventive Psychology: Theory, research, and practice* (pp. 199-215). New York: Pergamon.

Hasazi, S., Gordon, L., & Roe, C. (1985). Factors associated with the employment status of handicapped youth exiting high school from 1979-1983. *Exceptional Children, 51,* 455-469.

Holmes, T.H., & Rahe, R.H. (1967). The social readjustment rating scale. *Journal of Psychosomatic Research, 11,* 213-218.

Horn, W., O'Donnell, J., & Vitulano, A. (1983). Long-term follow-up studies of learning disabled persons. *Journal of Learning Disabilities, 16,* 542-555.

Jason, L.A., & Burrows, B. (1983). Transition training for high school seniors. *Cognitive Therapy and Research, 7,* 79-91.

Kelly, J.G. (1987). An ecological paradigm: Defining mental health consultation as a preventive service. In J.G. Kelly & R.E. Hess (Eds.), *The ecology of prevention: Illustrative mental health consultation.* New York: The Haworth Press, Inc.

Kelly, J.G. (1968). Toward an ecological conception of preventive interventions. In J.W. Carter, Jr. (Ed.), *Research contributions from psychology to community mental health.* New York: Behavioral Publications.

Mithaug, D.E., Horiuchi, C.N., & Fanning, P.N. (1985). A report on the Colorado statewide follow-up survey of special education students. *Exceptional Children, 51,* 397-404.

Neel, R., Meadows, N., Levine, P., & Edgar, E. (1988). What happens after special education?: A statewide follow-up study of secondary students who have behavioral disorders. *Behavioral Disorders, 13,* 209-216.

Parkes, C.M. (1971). Psycho-social transactions: A field for study. *Social Science and Medicine, 5,* 101-115.

Pearlin, L.I., Menaghan, E.G., Lieberman, M.A., & Mullen, J.T. (1981). The stress process. *Journal of Health and Social Behavior, 22,* 337-356.

Primavera, J., Farber, S.S., & Felner, R.D. (1982, August). *Parental death and adolescents: Factors mediating adaptation.* Paper presented at the 90th meeting of the American Psychological Association, Washington, D.C.

Rabkin, J.G. & Struening, E.L. (1976). Life events, stress, and illness. *Science, 194,* 1013-1020.

Schmid, K.D., Barone, C., & Trickett, E.J. (1992). Reliability and stability in the assessment of adolescent social networks: Results from a measure development study. Manuscript submitted for publication.

Schmid, K.D., Bendure, C., Barone, C., Walter, M., Leone, P.E., & Trickett, E.J. (1988). *Development and validation of a social support interview for adolescents: The analysis of social support in school transitions (ASSIST).* Paper presented at the meeting of the American Psychological Association, Atlanta, GA.

Schmid, K.D., Schatz, C.J., Walter, M.B., Shidla, M.C., Leone, P.E., & Trickett, E.J. (1990). Providing help: Characteristics and correlates of stress, burnout, and accomplishment across three groups of teachers. In R.B. Rutherford, Jr. & S.A. DiGangi (Eds.), *Severe Behavior Disorders of Children and Youth* (Vol. 13, pp. 115-127). Reston, VA: Council for Children with Behavioral Disorders.

Sitlington, P.L., Frank, A.R., & Carson, R. (1992). Adult adjustment among high school graduates with mild disabilities. *Exceptional Children, 59,* 221-233.

Trickett, E.J., Kelly, J.G., & Todd, D.M. (1972). The social environment of the high school: Guidelines for individual change and organizational development. In S. Golann & C. Eisdorfer (Eds.), *Handbook of Community Mental Health,* New York: Appleton Century Crofts.

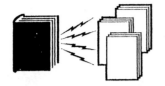

Haworth
DOCUMENT DELIVERY
SERVICE

and Local Photocopying Royalty Payment Form

This new service provides (a) a single-article order form for any article from a Haworth journal and (b) a convenient royalty payment form for local photocopying (not applicable to photocopies intended for resale).

- *Time Saving:* No running around from library to library to find a specific article.
- *Cost Effective:* All costs are kept down to a minimum.
- *Fast Delivery:* Choose from several options, including same-day FAX.
- *No Copyright Hassles:* You will be supplied by the original publisher.
- *Easy Payment:* Choose from several easy payment methods.

Open Accounts Welcome for ...
- Library Interlibrary Loan Departments
- Library Network/Consortia Wishing to Provide Single-Article Services
- Indexing/Abstracting Services with Single Article Provision Services
- Document Provision Brokers and Freelance Information Service Providers

MAIL or FAX THIS ENTIRE ORDER FORM TO:

Attn: **Marianne Arnold**
Haworth Document Delivery Service
The Haworth Press, Inc.
10 Alice Street
Binghamton, NY 13904-1580

or FAX: (607) 722-1424
or CALL: 1-800-3-HAWORTH
(1-800-342-9678; 9am-5pm EST)

PLEASE SEND ME PHOTOCOPIES OF THE FOLLOWING SINGLE ARTICLES:
1) Journal Title: _____
   Vol/Issue/Year: _____ Starting & Ending Pages: _____
   Article Title: _____

2) Journal Title: _____
   Vol/Issue/Year: _____ Starting & Ending Pages: _____
   Article Title: _____

3) Journal Title: _____
   Vol/Issue/Year: _____ Starting & Ending Pages: _____
   Article Title: _____

4) Journal Title: _____
   Vol/Issue/Year: _____ Starting & Ending Pages: _____
   Article Title: _____

(See other side for Costs and Payment Information)

COSTS: Please figure your cost to order quality copies of an article.
1. Set-up charge per article: $8.00
   ($8.00 × number of separate articles) _____
2. Photocopying charge for each article:
   1-10 pages: $1.00 _____
   11-19 pages: $3.00 _____
   20-29 pages: $5.00 _____
   30+ pages: $2.00/10 pages _____
3. Flexicover (optional): $2.00/article _____
4. Postage & Handling: US: $1.00 for the first article/
   $.50 each additional article _____
   Federal Express: $25.00 _____
   Outside US: $2.00 for first article/
   $.50 each additional article _____
5. Same-day FAX service: $.35 per page _____
6. Local Photocopying Royalty Payment: should you wish to copy the article yourself. Not intended for photocopies made for resale. $1.50 per article per copy
   (i.e. 10 articles × $1.50 each = $15.00) _____

GRAND TOTAL: _____

METHOD OF PAYMENT: (please check one)

❏ Check enclosed ❏ Please ship and bill. PO # _____
(sorry we can ship and bill to bookstores only! All others must pre-pay)

❏ Charge to my credit card: ❏ Visa;   ❏ MasterCard;   ❏ American Express;

Account Number: _____ Expiration date: _____

Signature: X_____ Name: _____
Institution: _____ Address: _____
City: _____ State: _____ Zip: _____
Phone Number: _____ FAX Number: _____

MAIL or *FAX* THIS ENTIRE ORDER FORM TO:

Attn: **Marianne Arnold**
Haworth Document Delivery Service
The Haworth Press, Inc.
10 Alice Street
Binghamton, NY 13904-1580

or **FAX:** (607) 722-1424
or **CALL:** 1-800-3-HAWORTH
(1-800-342-9678; 9am-5pm EST)